Coding with JavaScript

FOR DUMMIES®

A Wiley Brand

by Chris Minnick and Eva Holland

FOR DUMMIES®

A Wiley Brand

Coding with JavaScript For Dummies®

Published by: **John Wiley & Sons, Inc.,** 111 River Street, Hoboken, NJ 07030-5774, www.wiley.com

Copyright © 2015 by John Wiley & Sons, Inc., Hoboken, New Jersey

Media and software compilation copyright © 2015 by John Wiley & Sons, Inc. All rights reserved.

Published simultaneously in Canada

For general information on our other products and services, please contact our Customer Care Department within the U.S. at 877-762-2974, outside the U.S. at 317-572-3993, or fax 317-572-4002. For technical support, please visit www.wiley.com/techsupport.

Wiley publishes in a variety of print and electronic formats and by print-on-demand. Some material included with standard print versions of this book may not be included in e-books or in print-on-demand. If this book refers to media such as a CD or DVD that is not included in the version you purchased, you may download this material at http://booksupport.wiley.com. For more information about Wiley products, visit www.wiley.com.

Library of Congress Control Number: 2015938674

ISBN: 978-1-119-05607-2

ISBN 978-1-119-05607-2 (pbk); ISBN 978-1-119-05605-8 (ePDF); ISBN 978-1-119-05606-5 (ePub)

Manufactured in the United States of America

10 9 8 7 6 5 4 3 2 1

Contents at a Glance

Table of Contents

Introduction

JavaScript is hot! What started as a quick-and-dirty language created for one of the first web browsers has turned into the world's most popular programming language. Demand for JavaScript programmers is at an all-time high and only continues to grow.

This book is your key to becoming proficient in the core concepts of JavaScript. Whether your goal is to land a high-paying job as a programmer or to make your own personal website more interactive, you can be confident that the content and techniques presented in this book are fully up to date with the most current JavaScript standards and best practices.

Coupled with engaging and interactive online exercises, each chapter contains complete examples of real code that you can try and test in your own web browser at home.

Just as the only way to Carnegie Hall is to practice, practice, practice, the only way to become a better programmer is to code, code, code!

About This Book

This book is a friendly and approachable guide to getting started with writing JavaScript code. As programming languages go, JavaScript is fairly easy to pick up and start using. Because it's so accessible, many people who started as web page authors have found themselves in the position of being responsible for maintaining, modifying, and writing JavaScript code. If that describes you, this book will quickly and easily bring you up to speed.

Whether you know a little JavaScript or you've never seen it, this book shows you how to write JavaScript the right way.

Topics covered in this book include the following:

- ✔ Understanding the basic structures of JavaScript programs
- ✔ Integrating JavaScript with HTML5 and CSS3
- ✔ Structuring your programs with functions
- ✔ Working with JavaScript Objects

✔ Using advanced JavaScript techniques, such as AJAX, callbacks, and closures

✔ Getting started with jQuery

Learning JavaScript isn't only about learning the syntax of the language. It's also about accessing the tools and community that has been built around the language. Professional JavaScript programmers have greatly refined the tools and techniques used to write JavaScript over the language's long and exciting history. Throughout the book, we mention important best practices and tools for testing, documenting, and writing better code faster!

To make this book easier to read, keep in mind the following:

✔ As a convention for this book, all JavaScript code and all HTML and CSS markup appears in monospaced type like this:

```
document.write("Hi!");
```

✔ The margins on a book page don't have the same room as your monitor likely does. Therefore, long lines of HTML, CSS, and JavaScript may break across multiple lines. Remember that your computer sees such lines as single lines of HTML, CSS, or JavaScript. We indicate that everything should be on one line by breaking it at a punctuation character or space and then indenting any overage, like so:

```
document.getElementById("anElementInTheDocument").
        addEventListener("click",doSomething,false);
```

✔ HTML and CSS don't care very much about whether you use uppercase or lowercase letters or a combination of the two, but JavaScript cares a lot! In order to make sure that you get the correct results from the code examples in the book, always stick to the same capitalizations that we use.

Foolish Assumptions

We have a policy at our company, WatzThis?, to never assume (but, frankly, Eva is better at following the policy than Chris is). If you were ever 12 years old, you've probably heard the saying about what happens when you assume. If you don't know, email us.

You don't need to be a programming ninja or a hacker to understand programming. You don't need to understand how the guts of your computer work. You don't even need to know how to count in binary.

However, we do need to make a couple of assumptions about you. We assume that you can turn your computer on, that you know how to use a mouse and a keyboard, and that you have a working Internet connection and web browser. If you already know something about how to make web pages (it doesn't take much!), you have a jump start on the material.

The other things you need to know to write and run JavaScript code are details we cover in this book. And the one thing you'll find to be true is that programming requires attention to details.

Icons Used In This Book

Here's a list of the icons we use in this book to flag text and information that's especially noteworthy:

This icon highlights helpful tips that show you easy ways or shortcuts that will save you time or effort.

Whenever you see this icon, pay special attention. You won't want to forget the information you're about to read.

Be careful — very careful. This icon warns you of pitfalls to avoid.

This icon highlights the great exercises you can find on the website. If you're interested in trying your hand at JavaScript, go online and visit www.dummies.com/go/codingwithjavascript.

This icon highlights technical details that you may or may not find interesting. Feel free to skip this information, but if you're the techie type, you might enjoy reading it.

Beyond the Book

Here's where you can find the online content for this book:

- ✔ **Exercises:** You can find all the exercises online by going to www.dummies.com/go/codingwithjavascript to access the exercises at Codeacademy.

- ✔ **Examples:** You can find all the examples in the chapters at www.dummies.com/go/codingwithjavascript. Here you will find a directory labeled by chapter. Within the chapter, you will find each example labeled by its listing number

- ✔ **Cheat Sheet:** You can find lists of useful information at www.dummies.com/cheatsheet/codingwithjavascript.

- ✔ **Extras:** You can even find additional articles related to each part of the book. You can access this extra content at www.dummies.com/extras/codingwithjavascript.

- ✔ **Updates:** From time to time, we will need to make updates to a book. Code and specifications are constantly changing, so the commands and syntax that work today may not work tomorrow. You can find this information at www.dummies.com/extras/codingwithjavascript.

Where to Go from Here

Coding with JavaScript is fun, and once you get a little knowledge under your belt, the world of interactive web applications is your oyster! So buckle up! We hope you enjoy the book and our occasional pearls of wisdom.

Part I
Getting Started with JavaScript

getting started
with

coding with
JavaScript

In this part . . .

- ✏ Find out how to write your first JavaScript program.
- ✏ Get the inside scoop on how to work with variables and arrays.
- ✏ Discover how to work with operators, expressions, and statements.
- ✏ Use loops and branches in your JavaScript coding.
- ✏ Visit `http://www.dummies.com` for great Dummies content online.

Chapter 1

The World's Most Misunderstood Programming Language

"People understand me so poorly that they don't even understand my complaint about them not understanding me."

— Søren Kierkegaard

*J*avaScript hasn't always been as highly regarded as it is today. Some people have called it the best and worst programming language in the world. Over the last few years, there have been a great number of improvements made to the way programmers write JavaScript and to JavaScript interpreters. These improvements have made JavaScript a much better language today than it's been in the past.

In this chapter, you discover what JavaScript is and a little bit of the history of the language. You also find out what JavaScript does and why you need to know it.

Don't forget to visit the website to check out the online exercises relevant to this chapter!

What Is JavaScript?

Back in the very early days of the web, browsers were simple readers for web pages (see Figure 1-1). They had virtually no capabilities themselves, except for the ability to display text in various sized fonts. As soon as Microsoft released its Internet Explorer browser, the browser wars were on, and the features started flying! One browser introduced the ability to display images, then another introduced the capability to have different fonts, and then blinking text, moving text, and all sorts of other wacky capabilities were introduced!

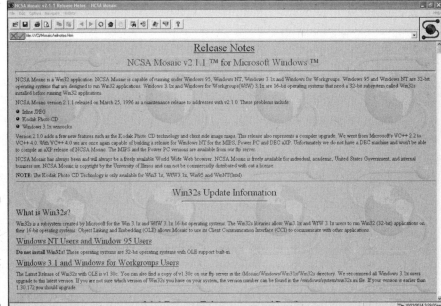

Figure 1-1:
The first
web brow-
sers weren't
much to
look at.

It wasn't long before someone got the idea that browsers could actually do useful things themselves, rather than just acting as fancy document display programs.

The Eich-man cometh

JavaScript got its start back in 1995 at Netscape. The creator of JavaScript, Brandon Eich, wrote JavaScript in record time (some say in as few as ten days!) by borrowing many of the best features from various other programming languages. The rush to market also created some interesting quirks (or, less politely described, mistakes) in the design of the language. The result is a sort of Esperanto-like language that looks deceptively familiar to people who are experienced with other programming languages.

Mocha-licious

The original name of JavaScript was Mocha. It was renamed LiveScript with the first beta deployment of Netscape Navigator and was then changed to JavaScript when it was built into the Netscape 2 browser in 1995. Microsoft very quickly reverse-engineered JavaScript and introduced an exact clone of it in Internet Explorer, calling it Jscript in order to get around trademark issues.

Netscape submitted JavaScript to the standards organization known as Ecma International, and it was adopted and standardized as EMCAScript in 1997.

Brandon Eich, the creator of JavaScript, famously commented about the name of the standardized language; stating that ECMAScript was an "unwanted trade name that sounds like a skin disease."

Not only is ECMAScript an unappealing name for a programming language, the name given to the language by Netscape and which most people refer to it as, is rather unfortunate as well. If you already know how to program in Java or if you learn how to at some point, it's a very good idea to keep in mind that the two languages may have some similarities, but they are, in fact, quite different animals.

We need more effects!

When JavaScript debuted, it quickly became very popular as a way to make web pages more dynamic. So-called Dynamic HTML (DHTML) was an early result of JavaScript being built into web browsers, and it enabled all sorts of fun effects, like the falling snowflake effect (see Figure 1-2), pop-up windows, and curling web page corners, but also more useful things like drop-down menus and form validation.

JavaScript grows up

Now entering its third decade, JavaScript has become the world's most widely used programming language and virtually every personal computer in the world has at least one browser on it that can run JavaScript code.

JavaScript is flexible enough that it can be used and learned by nonprogrammers, but powerful enough that it can (and is) used by professional programmers to enable functionality on nearly every website on the Internet today, ranging from single-page sites to gigantic sites like Google, Amazon, Facebook, and many, many others!

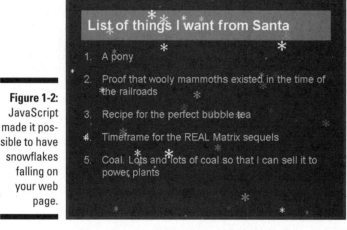

Figure 1-2: JavaScript made it possible to have snowflakes falling on your web page.

Dynamic scripting language

JavaScript is often described as a *dynamic scripting language*. In order to understand what this means, we need to first define a couple of terms and provide some context.

Common misconceptions about JavaScript

Over the years, JavaScript has had some pretty nasty things said about it. While sometimes rumors are interesting, they aren't always true. The following list explains some common misconceptions about JavaScript:

- **Myth:** JavaScript is not a real programming language. **Reality:** JavaScript is often used for trivial tasks in web browsers, but that doesn't make it any less of a programming language. In fact, JavaScript has many advanced features that have raised the bar for programming languages and are now being imitated in languages such as PHP, C++, and even Java.

- **Myth:** JavaScript is related to Java. **Reality:** Nope. The name JavaScript was invented purely as a marketing strategy because Java was incredibly popular at the time JavaScript came out.

- **Myth:** JavaScript is new. **Reality:** JavaScript has been around for over 20 years! Some of the professional JavaScript programmers we know weren't even born when JavaScript was created.

- **Myth:** JavaScript is buggy and runs differently in different browsers. **Reality:** While this used to be true in some cases, browser makers decided to support the standardized version of JavaScript long ago. Every browser will run JavaScript the same today.

Computer programs are sets of instructions that cause computers to do things. Every computer programming language has a set of instructions and a certain way that humans must write those instructions. The computer can't understand these instructions directly. In order for a computer to understand a programming language, it needs to go through a conversion process that translates human-readable (and writable) instructions into machine language. Depending on when this translation takes place, programming languages can be roughly divided into two types: compiled and interpreted (see Figure 1-3).

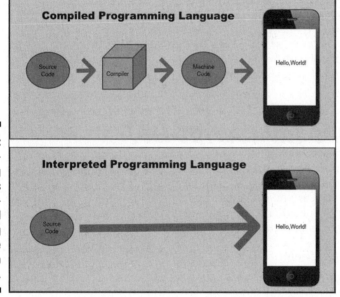

Figure 1-3: Programming languages are classified according to when the compilation takes place.

Compiled programming languages

Compiled programming languages are languages in which a programmer must write the code and then run it through a special program called a *compiler* that interprets the given code and then converts it into machine language. The computer can then execute the compiled program.

Examples of compiled languages include C, C++. Fortran, Java, Objective-C, and COBOL.

Interpreted programming languages

Interpreted languages are technically still compiled by the computer into machine language, but the compiling takes place by the user's web browser right as the program is being run. Programmers who write interpreted languages don't need to go through the step of compiling their code prior to handing it off to the computer to run.

The benefit of programming in an interpreted language is that it's easy to make changes to the program at any time. The downside, however, is that compiling code as it's being run creates another step in the process and can slow down the performance of programs.

Partially because of this performance factor, interpreted languages have gotten a reputation for being less than serious programming languages. However, because of better just-in-time compilers and faster computer processors, this perception is rapidly changing. JavaScript is having a big impact in this regard.

Examples of interpreted programming languages include PHP, Perl, Haskell, Ruby and of course, JavaScript

What Does JavaScript Do?

If you use the web, you're making use of JavaScript all the time. The list of things that can be enabled with JavaScript is extensive and ranges from simple notices you get when you forget to fill out a required field on a form to complex applications, such as Google Docs or Facebook. Here's a short list of the most common uses for JavaScript on the web:

- ✔ Nifty effects
- ✔ Input validation
- ✔ Rollover effects
- ✔ Drop-down/fly-out menus
- ✔ Drag and drop features
- ✔ Infinitely scrolling web pages
- ✔ Autocomplete
- ✔ Progress bars
- ✔ Tabs within web pages
- ✔ Sortable lists
- ✔ Magic Zoom (see Figure 1-4)

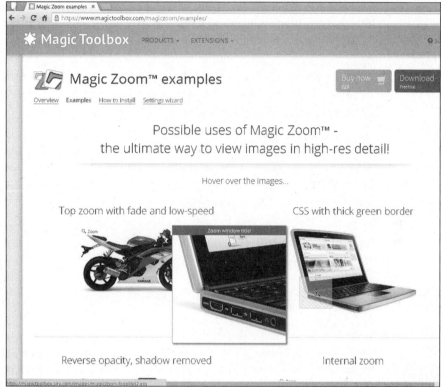

Figure 1-4:
So-called
Magic Zoom
effects are
enabled
using
JavaScript.

Why JavaScript?

JavaScript has become the standard for creating dynamic user interfaces for the web. Pretty much any time you visit a web page with animation, live data, a button that changes when you hover over it, or a drop-down menu, JavaScript is at work. Because of its power and ability to run in any web browser, JavaScript coding is the most popular and necessary skill for a modern web developer to have.

JavaScript is easy to learn

Keep in mind that programming languages were created in order to give people a simple way to talk to computers and tell them what to do. Compared with machine language, the language that the computer's CPU speaks, every programming language is easy and understandable. To give you a sample of what sort of instructions your computer is actually obeying, here is a machine language program to write out `"Hello World"`.

```
b8    21 0a 00 00
a3    0c 10 00 06
b8    6f 72 6c 64
a3    08 10 00 06
b8    6f 2c 20 57
a3    04 10 00 06
b8    48 65 6c 6c
a3    00 10 00 06
b9    00 10 00 06
ba    10 00 00 00
bb    01 00 00 00
b8    04 00 00 00
cd    80
b8    01 00 00 00
cd    80
```

Now look at one way you can accomplish this simple task with JavaScript:

```
alert("Hello World");
```

Much easier, yes?

Once you learn the basic rules of the road (called the *syntax*), such as when to use parentheses and when to use curly brackets ({}), JavaScript actually resembles plain old English.

The first step in learning any language, including programming languages, is to get over your fear of getting started. JavaScript makes this easy. There are thousands of sample bits of JavaScript code on the web that anyone can just pick up and start messing around with. You already have all the tools you need (see Chapter 2), and it's easy to start small with JavaScript and gradually build up to making great and wonderful things.

Where is JavaScript? JavaScript is everywhere!

Although JavaScript was originally designed to be used in web browsers, it has found a home in many other places. Today, JavaScript runs on smartphones and tablets, on web servers, in desktop applications, and in all sorts of portable devices.

JavaScript in the web browser

The most common place to find JavaScript, and what it was originally designed to do, is running in web browsers. When JavaScript runs in this way, it's called *client-side JavaScript*.

Client-side JavaScript adds interactivity to web pages. It accomplishes this in several ways:

- ✔ By controlling the browser itself or making use of functionality of the browser
- ✔ By manipulating the structure and content of web pages
- ✔ By manipulating the styles (such as fonts and layout) of web pages
- ✔ By accessing data from other sources

In order to understand how JavaScript is able to manipulate the structure and style of web pages, you need to know a little bit about HTML5 and CSS3.

HTML5

Hypertext Markup Language (HTML) is the language used to structure web pages. It works by marking up content (text and images) to give web browsers information about the content, such as what is a heading, what is a paragraph, where an image goes, and so on. Listing 1-1 shows a simple HTML document. Figure 1-5 shows how a web browser displays this document.

Listing 1-1: A Simple HTML Document

```
<!DOCTYPE html>
<html>
<head>
 <title>Hello, HTML!</title>
</head>
<body>
 <h1>This is HTML</h1>
 <p id="introduction">This simple document was written
          with Hypertext Markup Language.</p>
</body>
</html>
```

Here is everything you need to know about HTML right now in order to move forward with learning JavaScript:

- ✔ In HTML, the characters surrounded by angle brackets are called *tags*.
- ✔ The *ending tag* (which comes after the content being marked up) has a slash after the first angle bracket. For example `</p>` is an ending tag.

- ✔ A group of two tags (beginning and ending), plus the content in between them, is called an *element.*

- ✔ Elements are generally organized in a hierarchal way (with elements nested within elements).

- ✔ Elements may contain name/value pairs, called *attributes.* If an element has attributes, they go in the beginning tag. *Name/value pairs* assign values, in quotes, to names (which aren't in quotes) by putting an equals sign between them. For example, in the following tag, `width` and `height` are both attributes of the `div` element:

```
<div width="100" height="100"></div>
```

- ✔ Some elements don't have content and therefore don't need an ending tag. For example, the `img` tag, which simply inserts an image into a web page, looks like this:

```
<img src="myimage.jpg" width="320" height="200"
        alt="Here is a picture of my dog.">
```

Figure 1-5:
Web browsers use HTML to render web pages.

All the data necessary to show the image is included in the beginning tag using attributes, so the `img` tag doesn't require an ending tag.

When you write a web page with HTML, you can include JavaScript code directly in that document, or you can reference JavaScript code file (which end in `.js`) from the HTML document. Either way, your viewer's web browser will download the JavaScript code and run it when a user accesses a web page containing that JavaScript.

Client-side JavaScript runs inside of your users' web browsers.

CSS3

Cascading Style Sheets (CSS) is the language used to add formatting and different layouts to web pages. The word *style,* when used in CSS, refers to many aspects of how the HTML document is presented to the user, including

- Typefaces (or font faces)
- Type size
- Colors
- Arrangement of elements in the browser window
- Sizes of elements
- Borders
- Backgrounds
- Creation of rounded corners on element borders

Like JavaScript, CSS can be either placed directly into an HTML document, or it can be linked to from the HTML document. Once it's downloaded, it immediately does its thing and formats the document according to your specifications.

Style sheets in CSS are made up of CSS rules, which contain properties and values that should be applied to an element or a group of elements. Here's an example of a CSS rule:

```
p{font-size: 14px; font-color: black; font-family: Arial,
       sans-serif}
```

This rule, reading from left to right, specifies that all p elements (which indicate paragraphs in HTML) should be displayed in text that is 14px large, black, and using the Arial font. If Arial isn't available on the user's computer, it should be displayed in some sans serif typeface.

The part of the CSS rule that's outside of the curly brackets is called the *selector.* It selects the elements that the properties within the curly brackets apply to.

Throughout this book, you find out how to use JavaScript with HTML and CSS. We provide just enough information here to be able to show you how HTML and CSS work. If you need to learn more, you can find some excellent books about them. One that we highly recommend is *Beginning HTML5 and CSS3 For Dummies* by Ed Tittel and Chris Minnick (Wiley).

JavaScript is powerful!

JavaScript running in a web browser used to be slow, and JavaScript got a bad reputation early on among programmers. Today, JavaScript code runs 80 percent as fast as compiled code. And, it keeps getting faster all the time. What this means is that today's JavaScript is much more powerful than the JavaScript of just a few years ago. And, it's many times more powerful than the JavaScript that was first introduced in 1995.

JavaScript is in demand

JavaScript is not only the most widely known programming language, it's also one of the most in-demand skills in the job market. It's projected that the job market for JavaScript programmers will increase by 22 percent between 2010 and 2020. Exciting things are happening with JavaScript, and there has never been a better time than right now to learn it.

Chapter 2

Writing Your First JavaScript Program

. . . .

In This Chapter

▶ Arranging your development environment

▶ Getting to know JavaScript code

▶ Understanding a simple JavaScript program

▶ Understanding the value of commenting your code

. . . .

"The secret of getting ahead is getting started."

— Mark Twain

Simple JavaScript programming isn't difficult to understand. In this chapter, you go through the process of setting up your computer for writing JavaScript. You also write your first JavaScript program and get to know the basic syntax behind everything you'll do with JavaScript in your future as a programmer.

Don't forget to visit the website to check out the online exercises relevant to this chapter!

Setting Up Your Development Environment

It's important to have all of your tools set up and in place before beginning to write your first JavaScript program. We walk you through the process of downloading and installing our favorite JavaScript development tools, which are, coincidentally, the ones we use in this book. If you have similar tools that you prefer, please feel free to use those. However, we recommend that you still read this section of the book in order to learn why we've chosen these tools and to make your own decisions about whether to use them.

After you install each of the tools, we share some tips and tricks with you for how to get the most out of each of them.

Downloading and installing Chrome

The web browser that we prefer to use when working with JavaScript is Google Chrome. If you prefer to use a different web browser day to day, that's fine, of course. All browsers will run JavaScript very fast and correctly. However, some of the instructions in this book will be specific to Google Chrome, so we recommend that you at least go through the process of installing it on your computer in this chapter. We chose to use Google Chrome in this book because it offers excellent tools for making JavaScript programmers' jobs easier and because it's currently the most widely used web browser on the Internet. (Yes, it's even more popular than Internet Explorer.)

If you don't have Chrome installed, follow these steps to install it:

1. **Go to `www.google.com/chrome`.**

   Figure 2-1 shows you what Google Chrome looks like.

2. **Hover over the Download tab and choose the appropriate version for your computer.**

3. **Open the downloaded file and follow the instructions to install Chrome.**

Now you have a supercharged JavaScript engine!

Google Chrome uses Google's V8 JavaScript engine to parse, compile, and run JavaScript code. Depending on whose benchmarking test you believe, Chrome is either the fastest way to run JavaScript in a browser, or it's one of the fastest. The major browser makers are constantly competing to outdo each other. It doesn't matter too much who is actually the fastest at any one time; the competition has increased the speed of every browser's JavaScript engine by leaps and bounds in recent years.

If you want to see actual comparisons of how different browsers do in JavaScript performance tests, you can do so at `http://arewefastyet.com` (see figure). This site, which is maintained by Mozilla, creator of the Firefox browser, automatically checks and graphs JavaScript performance of the most popular browsers and is updated multiple times every day.

Figure 2-1:
Installing
Chrome
is easy on
either Mac
or Windows.

Downloading and installing a code editor

A *source code editor,* commonly referred to as code editor, is a text editor
with added functionality that helps you write and edit programming code.
The one we use is Sublime Text.

There are many code editors to choose from, so if you already have a favorite that you like to use and that you're comfortable with, please use it! A
programmer's code editor is a very personal choice, and many people will
find that they just feel more comfortable with a specific one. If you find that
Sublime Text just doesn't fit your style, Table 2-1 lists some other options.

Table 2-1	Examples of Other Code Editors	
Name	*Location*	*Compatible with . . .*
Coda	http://panic.com/coda	Mac only
Aptana	www.aptana.com	Mac or Windows
Komodo Edit	www.activestate.com/komodo-edit/downloads	Mac or Windows

(continued)

Table 2-1 *(continued)*

Name	Location	Compatible with ...
Dreamweaver	`http://adobe.com/products/dreamweaver.html`	Mac or Windows
Eclipse	`www.eclipse.org`	Mac or Windows
Notepad++	`http://notepad-plus-plus.org`	Windows only
TextMate	`http://macromates.com`	Mac only
BBEdit	`www.barebones.com/products/bbedit`	Mac only
EMacs	`www.gnu.org/software/emacs`	Mac or Windows
TextPad	`www.textpad.com`	Windows only
vim	`www.vim.org`	Mac or Windows
Netbeans	`https://netbeans.org`	Mac or Windows

We use Sublime Text (see Figure 2-2) for this book because it's popular among JavaScript programmers, and it provides a simple user interface along with a large number of plugins for handling more advanced programming tasks as you gain more programming experience.

To install Sublime Text, follow these steps:

1. **Go to `http://sublimetext.com` and choose the appropriate version for your operating system.**

2. **Open the downloaded file and follow the instructions for installing Sublime Text.**

Getting started with Sublime Text

When you first open Sublime Text, you see a simple blank page with a cursor on it (see Figure 2-3).

If you've used Sublime Text, you may see a sidebar on the left, as shown in Figure 2-4. This sidebar shows your open files and the files in your project, if you've created one. The sidebar is useful, and we recommend that you have it open.

To open the sidebar, click View ➪ Sidebar ➪ Show Sidebar.

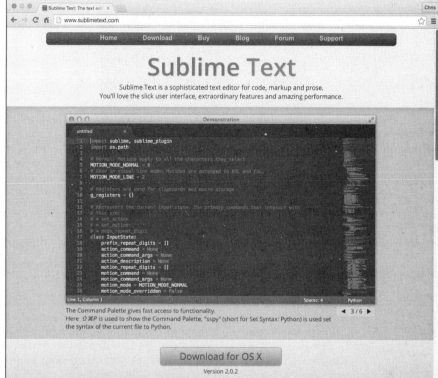

Figure 2-2:
Sublime Text is a seemingly simple-looking text editor with a lot of powerful features.

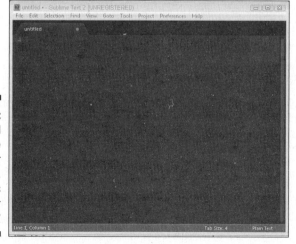

Figure 2-3:
The initial Sublime Text user interface. How's that for simplicity?

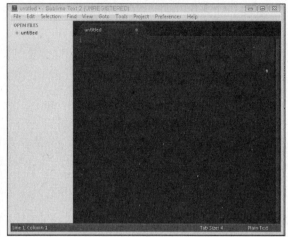

Figure 2-4:
Sublime
Text with
the sidebar
open.

To get started with your first Sublime Text project file, follow these steps:

1. **Choose File ⇨ Save As.**

   The Save dialog box appears, and your default save location is shown. If you're happy with storing your code in this folder (most likely the Documents folder [on OSX] or the My Documents folder [Windows]), then move on to Step 2. Otherwise, navigate to another location on your computer where you want to store your code files.

2. **Create a new folder and name the folder**

3. **In the Save As text area, give this first file a name and then click Save.**

   The new filename appears in the sidebar and the name on the open tab change to your selected name.

4. **Choose Project ⇨ Save Project As and save the Sublime Text project file inside the folder you created.**

   Sublime Text project files are where Sublime Text stores information about what files and folders are associated with a project. Creating a project folder allows you to keep all the different types of files in your program better organized.

5. **Choose Project ⇨ Add Folder to Project, select the folder you created in Step 1, and then click Open.**

   A new collapsible list appears in the sidebar called Folders, and your folder, along with the contents of it (including the project file and MyFirstProgram.html), will be listed underneath it, as shown in Figure 2-5.

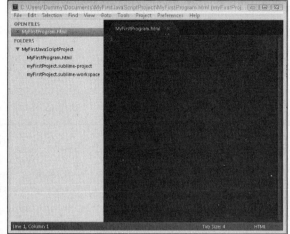

Figure 2-5:
Your first
Sublime
Text project
is ready
to go!

In order for you to keep all your files and folders organized, we provide some recommendations as to what you should name your files and folders. For example, you can name your new folder from Step 2 `MyFirstJavaScriptProject`. the file in Step 3 `MyFirstProgram`, and the project from Step 4 `myFirstProject`.

Choosing a syntax color scheme

Sublime Text syntax colors are based on the type of code that you're writing and the file extension. Input the following HTML and JavaScript code shown in Listing 2-1 into the file you've just created to see the default color scheme.

As you're about to find out, JavaScript is finicky. Make sure that you capitalize and spell everything exactly as it is in the listing, or your script may not work correctly or at all.

Listing 2-1: A Sample HTML File Containing JavaScript

```html
<!DOCTYPE html>
<html>
<head>
  <title>Hello, HTML!</title>
  <script>
    function countToTen() {
      var count = 0;
      while (count < 10) {
        count++;
        document.getElementById("theCount").innerHTML +=
          count + "<br>";
      }
    }
```

(continued)

Listing 2-1 *(continued)*

```
Code-Line Before Listing Code  </script>
</head>
<body onload="countToTen();">
  <h1>Let's Count to 10 with JavaScript!</h1>
  <p id="theCount"></p>
</body>
</html>
```

Figure 2-6 shows what the file looks like in Sublime Text for us.

If you don't like the color scheme that's currently selected, you can change it by choosing Preferences ⇨ Color Scheme and then selecting another color scheme.

Try out a few of the other color schemes and find one you like. The one we use for this book is called Monokai Bright.

If you'd like to try out the program you've just typed, follow these steps:

1. **Save the file by choosing File ⇨ Save.**

2. **Open your Chrome browser and press Ctrl + O.**

   An Open File window appears.

3. **Navigate to the file on your computer and select it.**

4. **Click the Open button.**

   The file will open in your browser.

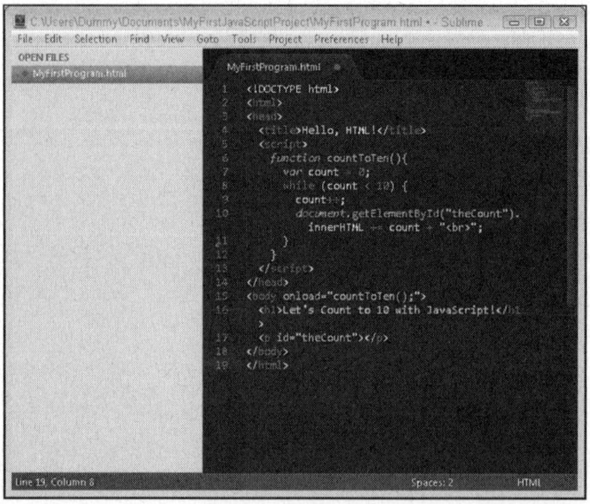

Figure 2-6:
Sublime
Text applies
colors to all
of the differ-
ent parts of
your code.

Your browser should look just like Figure 2-7. If it doesn't, very carefully check your code — you probably have a small typo somewhere. Don't forget to save your file after making any changes!

Figure 2-7:
Running
a simple
counting
program in
Chrome.

You can also save your file by pressing command + S (on the Mac) or Control + S (On Windows). Once you become proficient with them, keyboard shortcuts will save you a lot of time.

Some helpful Sublime Text shortcuts

Sublime Text looks like an ordinary text editor, but don't be fooled! A true mark of a master programmer is his or her ability to use keyboard shortcuts to crank out code and make edits as quickly as possible. Table 2-2 lists a few of the many keyboard shortcuts that Sublime Text provides. Practice these, and you'll quickly be able to impress your friends and colleagues with your super-elite skills.

Table 2-2	Commonly Used Sublime Text Editing Keyboard Shortcodes	
Mac	*Windows*	*Description*
Command+X	Ctrl+X	Delete line
Command+Return	Ctrl+Enter	Insert line after
Command+Shift+Return	Ctrl+Shift+Enter	Insert line before
Command+Control+Up Arrow	Ctrl+Shift+Up Arrow	Move line/Selection Up
Command+Control+Down Arrow	Ctrl+Shift+Down Arrow	Move line/Selection down

(continued)

Table 2-2 (continued)

Mac	Windows	Description
Command+L	Ctrl+L	Select line; repeat to select next lines
Command+D	Ctrl+D	Select word; repeat to select other occurrences
Control+M	Ctrl+M	Jump to closing parentheses; repeat to jump to opening parentheses
Control+Shift+M	Ctrl+Shift+M	Select all contents of current parentheses
Command+K+Command+K	Ctrl+k+k	Delete from cursor to end of line
Command+K+Delete	Ctrl+K+Delete	Delete from cursor to beginning of line
Command+]	Ctrl+]	Indent current line(s)
Command+[	Ctrl+[	Un-indent current line(s)
Command+Shift+D	Ctrl+Shift+D	Duplicate line(s)
Command+J	Ctrl+J	Join line below to the end of the current line
Command+/	Ctrl+/	Comment/un-comment current line
Command+Option+/	Ctrl+Shift+/	Block comment current selection
Command+Y	Ctrl+Y	Redo or repeat last keyboard shortcut command
Command+Shift+V	Ctrl+Shift+V	Paste and indent correctly
Control+Space	Ctrl+Space	Select next auto-complete selection
Control+U	Ctrl+U	Soft Undo; jumps to your last change before undoing change when repeated
Control+Shift+Up	Ctrl+Alt+Up	Column selection up
Control+Shift+Down	Ctrl+Alt+Down	Column selection down
Control+Shift+W	Alt+Shift+W	Wrap selection in html tag

Reading JavaScript Code

Before you get started with writing JavaScript programs, you need to be aware of a few rules of JavaScript:

✔ **JavaScript is case-sensitive.** We repeat this several times throughout the book, because it's an error that those who are new to JavaScript make quite frequently. To JavaScript, the words pants and Pants are completely different.

✔ **JavaScript doesn't care much about white space.** White space includes spaces, tabs, and line breaks — any character that doesn't have a visual representation. When you're writing JavaScript code, it doesn't matter if you use one space, two spaces, a tab, or even a line break (in most cases) within the code. JavaScript will ignore white space. The one exception is when you're writing out text that you want JavaScript to print to the screen. In this case, the white space you use will show up in the end result. The best practice, with regards to white space in your code, is to use enough space that your code is easy to read and to also be consistent with how you use this space.

✔ **Watch out for reserved words.** JavaScript has a list of words that have special meaning to the language. We list these words in Chapter 3. For now, just be aware that some words, such as function, while, break, and with have special meanings.

✔ JavaScript likes **semicolons:** JavaScript code is made up of statements. You can think of statements as similar to sentences. They are fundamental building blocks for JavaScript programs in the same way that sentences are the building blocks of paragraphs. In JavaScript, statements end with a semicolon.

If you don't use a semicolon at the end of a statement, JavaScript will put it there for you. This can lead to unexpected results, however, so it's considered a best practice to always end statements with a semicolon.

Running JavaScript in the Browser Window

Although it's seen in many different environments, the most common place to see JavaScript in the wild is running in web browsers. Controlling inputs and outputs, manipulating web pages, handling common browser events such as clicks and scrolls, and controlling the different features of web browsers is what JavaScript was born to do!

To run JavaScript in a web browser, you have three options, all of which will be shown in the following pages:

✔ Put it directly in an HTML event attribute

✔ Put it between an opening and closing script tag

✔ Put it in a separate document and include it in your HTML document

Many times, you'll use a combination of all three techniques within any one web page. However, knowing when to use each is important and is a skill that you'll learn with more practice.

Using JavaScript in an HTML event attribute

HTML has several special attributes that are designed for triggering JavaScript when something happens in the web browser or when the user does something. Here's an example of an HTML button with an event attribute that responds to mouse click events:

```
<button id="bigButton" onclick="alert('Hello
        World!');">Click Here</button>
```

In this case, when a user clicks on the button created by this HTML element, a popup will appear with the words "Hello World!".

HTML has over 70 different event attributes. Table 2-3 shows the most commonly used ones.

Table 2-3	Commonly Used HTML Event Attributes
Attribute	*Description*
onload	Runs the script after the pages finishes loading
onfocus	Runs the script when the element gets focus (such as when a text box is active)
onblur	Runs the script when the element loses focus (such as when the user clicks a new text box in a form)
onchange	Runs the script when the value of an element is changed

Attribute	Description
onselect	Runs the script when text has been submitted
onsubmit	Runs the script when a form has been submitted
onkeydown	Runs the script when a user is pressing a key
onkeypress	Runs the script when a user presses a key
onkeyup	Runs the script when a user releases a key
onclick	Runs the script when a user mouse clicks an element
ondrag	Runs the script when an element is dragged
ondrop	Runs the script when a dragged element is being dropped
onmouseover	Runs the script when a user moves a mouse pointer over an element

Although they're easy to use, using event attributes is actually considered a less-than-ideal practice by many JavaScript programmers. We demonstrate them in this book because they are so widely used and easy to learn. However, for now, just be aware that there is a better way to write JavaScript code that responds to events than to use event attributes. We cover this better method in Chapter 11.

Using JavaScript in a script element

The HTML script element allows you to embed JavaScript into an HTML document. Often script elements are placed within the head element, and, in fact, this placement was often stated as a requirement. Today, however, script elements are used within the head element as well as in the body of web pages.

The format of the script element is very simple:

```
<script>
  (insert your JavaScript here)
</script>
```

You saw an example of this type of script embedding in Listing 2-1. Listing 2-2 shows another example of an HTML document with a script tag containing JavaScript. In this case, however, we place the script element at the bottom of the body element.

Listing 2-2:   Embedding JavaScript within a Script Element

```
<!DOCTYPE html>
<html>
<head>
 <title>Hello, HTML!</title>
</head>
<body>
 <h1>Let's Count to 10 with JavaScript!</h1>
 <p id="theCount"></p>
 <script>
   var count = 0;
   while (count < 10) {
     count++;
     document.getElementById("theCount").innerHTML +=
          count + "<br>";
   }
 </script>
</body>
</html>
```

If you create a new file in Sublime Text, input Listing 2-2 into it, and then open it in a web browser, you'll notice that it does exactly the same thing as Listing 2-1.

Script placement and JavaScript execution

Web browsers normally load and execute scripts as they are loaded. A web page always gets read by the browser from the top down, just as you would read a page of text. Sometimes you'll want to wait until the browser is done loading the contents of the web page before the script runs. In Listing 2-1, we accomplished this by using the `onload` event attribute in the body element. Another common way to delay execution is to simply place the code to be executed at the end of the code as in Listing 2-2.

Limitations of JavaScript in <script> elements

While much more commonly used and more widely accepted than inline scripting (putting JavaScript into event attributes), embedding JavaScript into a script element has some serious limitations.

The biggest limitation is that scripts embedded in this way can be used only within the web page where they live. In other words, if you put your JavaScript into a script element, you need to copy and paste that script element exactly into every page where it exists. With some websites containing many hundreds of web pages, you can see how this can become a mainte-nance nightmare.

When to use JavaScript in <script> elements

This method of embedding JavaScript does have its uses. For bits of JavaScript that simply call other bits of JavaScript and that rarely (or preferably, never) change, it is acceptable and can even speed up the loading and display of your web pages by causing the web server to have to make fewer requests to the server.

Single page apps, which (as the name implies) contain only a single HTML page, are also great candidates for the use of this type of embedding because there will only ever be one place to update the script.

As a rule, however, you should seek to minimize the amount of JavaScript that you embed directly into an HTML document. The results will be easier maintenance and better organization of your code.

Including external JavaScript files

The third and most popular way to include JavaScript in HTML documents is by using the `src` attribute of the script element.

A script element with a `src` attribute works exactly like a script element with JavaScript between the tags, except that if you use the `src` attribute, the JavaScript is loaded into the HTML document from a separate file. Here's an example of a script element with a `src` attribute:

```
<script src="myScript.js"></script>
```

In this case, you would have a separate file, named `myScript.js`, that would reside in the same folder as your HTML document. The benefits of using external JavaScript files are that using them

- ✔ Keeps your HTML files neater and less cluttered
- ✔ Makes your life easier because you need to modify JavaScript in only one place when something changes or when you make a bug fix

Creating a .js file

Creating an external JavaScript file is similar to creating an HTML file or another other type of file. To replace the embedded JavaScript in Listing 2-1 with an external JavaScript file, follow these steps:

1. **In Sublime Text, choose File ⇨ New File.**

2. **Copy everything between** `<script>` **and** `</script>` **from** `MyFirstProgram.html` **and paste it into your new** `.js` **file.**

Notice that external JavaScript files don't contain `<script>` elements, just the JavaScript.

3. **Save your new file as** `countToTen.js` **in the same folder as** MyFirstProgram.html.

4. **In** `MyFirstProgram.html`, **modify your script element to add a** `src` **attribute, like this:**

```
<script src="countToTen.js"></script
```

Your copy of `MyFirstProgram.html` should now look like this:

```
<!DOCTYPE html>
<html>
<head>
 <title>Hello, HTML!</title>
 <script src="countToTen.js"></script>
</head>
<body onload="countToTen();">
 <h1>Let's Count to 10 with JavaScript!</h1>
 <p id="theCount"></p>
</body>
</html>
```

Your new file, `countToTen.js`, should look like this:

```
function countToTen(){
 var count = 0;
 while (count < 10) {
    count++;
    document.getElementById("theCount").innerHTML +=
          count + "<br>";
 }
}
```

After you've saved both files, you should see them inside your project in the Sublime Text sidebar, as shown in Figure 2-8.

Keeping your .js files organized

External JavaScript files can sometimes get to be very large. In many cases, it's a good idea to break them up into smaller files, organized by the type of functions they contain. For example, one JavaScript file may contain scripts related to the user login capabilities of your program, while another may contain scripts related to the blogging capabilities.

For small programs, however, it's usually sufficient to have just one file, and many people will name their single JavaScript file something generic, such as `app.js`, `main.js`, or `scripts.js`.

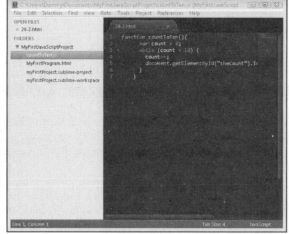

Figure 2-8:
Viewing
multiple
files in your
project
folder in
Sublime
Text.

JavaScript files don't need to be in the same folder as the HTML file that includes them. In fact, we recommend that you create a new folder specifically for storing your external JavaScript files. Most people we know call this something like js.

Follow these steps to create a js folder inside of your Sublime Text project and move your js file into it:

1. **Right-click on the name of your project in the Sublime Text sidebar.**

   A submenu appears.

2. **Choose New Folder from the submenu.**

   A Folder Name text area appears at the bottom of the Sublime Text window.

3. **Enter js into the folder name text field and press Enter.**

   A new folder called js appears in the sidebar.

4. **Open** countToTen.js **and choose File ⇨ Save As and save it in your new** js **folder.**

5. **Right-click on the version of** countToTen.js **that's outside of your folder and choose Delete File from the submenu.**

6. **Open up** MyFirstProgram.js **and change your script element to reflect the new location of your** js **file, like this:**

   ```
   <script src="js/countToTen.js"></script>
   ```

When you open `MyFirstProgram.html` in your browser (or simply click refresh), it should look exactly like it did before you moved the JavaScript file into its own folder.

Using the JavaScript Developer Console

Sometimes, it's helpful to be able to run JavaScript commands without creating an HTML page and including separate scripts or creating `<script>` blocks. For these times, you can use the Chrome browser's JavaScript Console (see Figure 2-9).

To access the JavaScript Console, find the Chrome menu in the upper-right corner of your browser. It looks like three horizontal lines. Click the Chrome menu and then find More Tools in the drop-down menu. Under More Tools, choose JavaScript Console from the drop-down menu.

And, yes, there is a faster way to open the JavaScript Console. Simply press Alt+Command+J (on Mac) or Control+Shift+J (on Windows).

Figure 2-9:
JavaScript
Console in
the Chrome
browser.

The JavaScript Console is perhaps the best friend of the JavaScript developer. Besides allowing you to test and run JavaScript code quickly and easily, it also is where errors in your code are reported, and it has features that will help you track down and solve problems with your code.

Once you've opened the JavaScript console, you can start inputting commands into it, which will run as soon as you press Enter. To try it out, open the JavaScript console and then type the following commands, pressing Enter after each one:

```
1080/33
40 + 2
40 * 34
100%3
34++
34--
```

Commenting your code

As you learn more JavaScript commands and start to write larger programs, it's often helpful to be able to leave yourself little reminders of what you were thinking or what certain things do. In programmer-speak, we call these tiny notes to ourselves (or to anyone else who may work with your code) *comments*. We call the process of writing these notes *commenting*.

The JavaScript engine completely ignores comments. They are there just for people. This is your time to explain things, clarify things, describe your thinking, or even leave reminders to yourself about things you want to do in the future.

It is always a good idea to comment your code. Even if you think that your code is pretty self-explanatory at the time that you write it, we guarantee that you won't think that eight months down the road when you need to modify it.

JavaScript gives you two ways to denote something as a comment:

- The single-line comment
- The multi-line comment

Single-line comments

Single-line comments start with //. Everything after these two slashes and up until the end of the line will be ignored by the JavaScript parser.

Single-line comments don't need to start at the beginning of a line. It's quite common to see a single-line comment used on the same line as a piece of code that is not commented, in order to explain what that line means. For example:

```
pizzas = pizza + 1; // add one more pizza
```

Multi-line comments

Multi-line comments start with /* and tell the JavaScript parser to ignore everything up to */. Multi-line comments are useful for more extensive documentation of code. For example:

```
/* The countToTen function does the following things:
  * Initializes a variable called count
  * Starts a loop by checking the value of count to make
          sure it's less than 10
  * Adds 1 to the value of count
  * Appends the the current value of count, followed by a
          line break, to the paragraph with id='theCount'
  * Starts the loop over
*/
```

Using comments to prevent code execution

Besides being useful for documenting code, comments are often useful for isolating pieces of code in order to find problems. For example, if we wanted to see what the countToTen function would do if we removed the line from the loop that increments the value of count, we could comment out that line using a single-line comment, like this:

```
function countToTen(){
 var count = 0;
 while (count < 10) {
   // count++;
   document.getElementById("theCount").innerHTML +=
         count + "<br>";
 }
}
```

When you run this program, the line count++; will no longer run, and the program will print out 0s forever (or until you close the browser window).

We call what we just created an *infinite loop*. If you do run a modified version of this program, it won't do any harm to your computer, but it will likely take your CPU for a wild ride of spinning in circles as fast as it can until you shut down the browser window in which you opened it in.

Chapter 3

Working with Variables

"Beauty is variable, ugliness is constant."

— Douglas Horton (1891 – 1968)

In this chapter, you discover how to create variables, fill them with values, use functions to find out what type of data is in your variables, convert between different data types, and manipulate the data in your variables.

Don't forget to visit the website to check out the online exercises relevant to this chapter!

Understanding Variables

Variables are representative names in a program. Just as *x* may stand for some as-yet-unknown value in algebra, or *x* may mark the spot where the treasure is buried on a pirate's map, variables are used in programming to represent something else.

You can think about variables as containers that contain data. You can give these containers names, and later you can recall and change the data in a variable by using its name.

Without variables, every computer program would have only one purpose. For example, the following one-line program doesn't use variables:

```
alert(3 + 7);
```

Its purpose is to add together the numbers 3 and 7 and to print out the result in a browser popup window.

The program isn't of much use, however (unless you happen to need to recall the sum of 3 and 7 on a regular basis). With variables, you can make a general purpose program that can add together any two numbers and print out the result, like the following example:

```
var firstNumber = 3;
var secondNumber = 7;
var total = Number(firstNumber) + Number(secondNumber);
alert (total);
```

Taken a step further, you can expand this program to ask the user for two numbers and then add them together, like the following example:

```
var firstNumber = prompt("Enter the first number");
var secondNumber = prompt("Enter the second number");
var total = Number(firstNumber) + Number(secondNumber);
alert (total);
```

Try out this program for yourself! (Chapter 2 shows how to use your code editor.) Follow these steps:

1. **Open your code editor and create a basic HTML template.**

2. **Between <body> and </body>, insert an opening <script> tag and a closing </script> tag.**

3. **Between the opening and closing script tags, enter the preceding example code.**

Your document should now look like this:

```
<html>
<head></head>
<body>
 <script>
 var firstNumber = prompt("Enter the first number");
 var secondNumber = prompt("Enter the second number");
 var total = Number(firstNumber) +
         Number(secondNumber);
 alert (total);
 </script>
</body>
</html>
```

4. **Save your new HTML document as addtwo.html.**

5. **Open your HTML document in your web browser.**

   You should be prompted for a first number, as shown in Figure 3-1.

6. **Enter the first number.**

   After you enter that number, you'll be prompted for a second number.

7. **Enter the second number.**

   After you give the program the second number, the result of adding the two numbers together will be displayed on the screen.

Figure 3-1:
A general-purpose program for adding two user submitted numbers.

Declaring Variables

Declaring a variable is the technical term that's used to describe the process of first creating a variable in a program. You may also hear it called *initialization.* Creating a variable, declaring a variable, and initializing a variable all refer to the same thing.

Variables in JavaScript can be created in one of two ways:

- ✔ **Using a var keyword:**

```
var myName;
```

- ✔ A variable created using a var keyword will have an initial value of undefined unless you give it a value when you create it, such as

```
var myName = "Chris";
```

When is equal not equal?

In English, it's common and correct to read statements containing "=" as "var myName equals Chris". However, this interpretation is not correct in programming.

Take, for example,

```
var myName = "Chris";
```

The character that looks like an equal sign between the variable name (myName) and the value ("Chris") in the preceding example may look exactly like an equal sign, and it's even produced using the key that is commonly called equal sign on the keyboard. However, in programming, the equal sign is actually called the *assignment operator*.

The difference between an assignment operator and an "equal to" is vital to understand:

✔ The assignment operator sets the thing to the left of it equal to the thing to the right of it, like this:

```
var myName = "Chris";
```

✔ "Equals" compares the value on the left to the value on the right and determines whether or not they are the same. Equals in JavaScript is written as ===.

✔ **Without a var keyword**

```
myName = "Chris";
```

When you create a variable without a var keyword, it becomes a global variable. (In order to understand what a global variable means, see the next section.)

Notice the quotes around the value on the right in the preceding examples. These quotes indicate that the value should be treated as text, rather than as a number, a JavaScript keyword, or another variable. See the section on data types later in this chapter for more information about how and when to use quotes.

Understanding Global and Local Scope

How and where you declare a variable determines how and where your program can make use of that variable. This concept is called variable scope. JavaScript has two types of scope:

✔ *Global variables* can be used anywhere inside of a program.

✔ *Local (function) variables* are variables that you create inside of a protected program within a program, called a *function*.

The tragic tale of the missing var

There is really never a reason to create a variable without using the `var` keyword, and doing so will cause you problems. If you leave out the `var` keyword, it just looks like you forgot it, so don't do it!

The following example shows the kind of problem and confusion that can happen from not using the `var` keyword. It also demonstrates the use of a more advanced programming tool, called a function, which we cover in much more detail in Chapter 7. In short, functions let you put smaller programs within your programs.

In this first example, the programmer wants to have a variable called `movie` that is global, and a separate variable with the same name that is only valid within the function called `showBadMovie`. This is a perfectly normal thing to do, and under normal circumstances, the `movie` variable inside the function wouldn't affect the global variable. However, if you forget to use the `var` keyword when declaring the movie variable inside the function, bad things happen.

```
var movie = "The Godfather";

function showGoodMovie () {
  alert (movie + " is a good
    movie!");
}

function showBadMovie () {
  movie = "Speed 2: Cruise
    Control";
  alert (movie + " is a bad
    movie!");
}
```

Notice that the `var` keyword is missing from before the movie variable in

`showBadMovie()`. JavaScript assumes that you want to override the global movie variable, rather than create a local function variable. The results are positively disastrous!

```
showGoodMovie(); // pops up
  "The Godfather is a good
  movie!"

showBadMovie(); // pops up
  "Speed 2: Cruise Control is
  a bad movie!"

/* Oh no! The global variable
  is now Speed 2: Cruise
  Control, not the good movie
  name anymore! */

showGoodMovie(); // pops up
  "Speed 2: Cruise Control is
  a good movie!"
```

In general, using local variables is preferable to using globals because limiting the scope of variables reduces the chance that you'll accidentally overwrite the value of a variable with another variable of the same name.

The use of globals can create problems in your program that can be difficult to track down and fix. We recommend that you never create variables without using the `var` keyword. If you do have a need for a global variable, it is possible to create them with the use of a `var` keyword, and we recommend that you do it that way.

Naming Variables

Variable names can start with the following characters:

- Upper- or lowercase letter
- An underscore (_)
- A dollar sign ($)

Although you can use an underscore or dollar sign to start a variable, it's best to begin with a letter. Unexpected characters can often cause your code to look confusing and difficult to read, especially if you are new to JavaScript coding.

After the first character, you can use any letter or number in your variable name, and it can be any length. JavaScript variables cannot contain spaces, mathematical operators, or punctuation (other than the underscore).

Always remember that JavaScript is case-sensitive. A variable named `myname` is not the same variable as `Myname` or `myName`.

Variable names are actually identifiers; the best thing you can do is to name a variable something precise and relevant. This naming convention may sometimes result in very long names, but as a rule, a longer name that accurately represents the variable is more useful than a shorter name that is vague.

Of course, there are limits to how long variable names can be without making your life more difficult. If you need to use 20 characters to accurately describe your variable, go for it. But, if you're creating variable names like `nameOfPersonWhoJustFilledOutTheFormOnMyWebsite`, you may want to see whether you can simplify your life (as well as that of anyone else who may need to work with your code) by shortening to something more like `personName`.

Guidelines for creating good variable names

Although JavaScript gives you a lot of freedom in how you name your variables, it's best to decide on some basic rules for yourself before you start programming. For example, do you start your variable names with a lowercase or uppercase letter? Do you use underscores between multiple words within a variable name, or do you use camelCase? As your code becomes more complex, the importance of correct naming becomes apparent.

Fortunately, you're not on your own when you're deciding on your style. There are some best practices that many professional JavaScript programmers agree upon and use when naming variables:

✔ Do not use names that are too short! Simple one letter names or nonsensical names are not a good option when naming variables.

✔ Use multiword names to be as precise as possible.

✔ In multiword names, always put adjectives to the left, as in `var greenPython;`.

Pick a style for multiple word names and be consistent. There are two ways to join words to create a name: camelCase and under_score. JavaScript is a flexible language, and you can use either method, although camelCase is generally the more commonly employed.

Some words cannot be used as variable names. Following is a list of reserved words that cannot be used as JavaScript variables, functions, methods, loop labels, or object names.

abstract	else	instanceof	switch
boolean	enum	int	synchronized
break	export	interface	this
byte	extends	long	throw
case	false	native	throws
catch	final	new	transient
char	finally	null	true
class	float	package	try
const	for	private	typeof
continue	function	protected	var
debugger	goto	public	void
default	if	return	volatile
delete	implements	short	while
do	import	static	with
double	in	super	

Creating Constants Using the const Keyword

Occasionally, your program may have a need for variables that can't be changed. In these cases, you can declare your variable using the const keyword. For example:

```
const heightOfTheEmpireStateBuilding = 1454;
const speedOfLight = 299792458;
const numberOfProblems = 99;
const meanNumberofBooksReadIn2014 = 12;
```

Constants abide by the same rules as other variables, but once you create a constant, its value cannot be changed during its lifetime (which lasts as long as the script is running).

Working with Data Types

A variable's data type is the kind of data the variable can hold and what operations can be done with the value of the variable. The number 10, used in a sentence, is different than the number 10 used in an equation, for example. Data types are the way JavaScript distinguishes between values that are meant to be words and values that are meant to be treated as mathematical expressions.

If you think about all the types of data that you work with on a daily basis — pie charts, recipes, short stories, newspaper articles, and so on — you'll see just how much potential there is for things to get very complicated when it comes to data. The generous creators of JavaScript decided to make things very simple for you. It has just five basic data types.

Furthermore, JavaScript is what's called a loosely typed language. What *loosely typed* means is that you don't even need to tell JavaScript, or even know, whether a variable you're creating will hold a word, a paragraph, a number, or a different type of data.

Loosely typed doesn't mean that JavaScript doesn't distinguish between words and numbers. JavaScript just is friendly about it and handles the work of figuring out what type of data you store in your variables largely behind the scenes.

JavaScript recognizes five basic, or primitive, types of data.

The C++ programming language has at least 12 different data types!

Number data type

Numbers in JavaScript are stored as 64-bit, floating point values. What this means, in English, is that numbers can range from 5e-324 (that's -5 followed by 324 zeros) to 1.7976931348623157e+308 (move the decimal 308 spots to the right to see this giant number). Any number may have decimal points or not. Unlike most programming languages, JavaScript doesn't have separate data types for integers (positive or negative numbers without a fractional part) and floating points (decimals).

Just how big is the biggest number JavaScript can use? Here it is, written out without scientific notation:

17976931348623157000000000000000000000000000000000000000000000000000
00000000000000000000000000000000000000000000000000000000000000000000
00000000000000000000000000000000000000000000000000000000000000000000
00000000000000000000000000000000000000000000000000000000000000000000
000000000000000000000000000000000000000

When you declare a number variable, you compile it from all of the following elements:

- ✔ The `var` keyword
- ✔ The name you want to give your variable
- ✔ The assignment operator
- ✔ A number (or even an equation that resolves to a number
- ✔ A semicolon

Here are some examples of valid number variables declarations:

```
var numberOfDucks = 4;
```

```
var populationOfSpain = 47200000;
```

```
var howManyTacos = 8;
```

Number functions

JavaScript includes a built-in `Number` function for converting values to numbers. To use the `Number` function, simply put the value (or a variable holding the value) that you want to convert to a number between the parentheses after the `Number` function.

The `Number` function produces four kinds of output:

✔ Numbers that are formatted as text strings are converted to numbers that can be used for calculations, like this:

```
Number("42") // returns the number 42
```

✔ Text strings that can't be converted to numbers return the value `NaN`, like this:

```
Number("eggs") // returns NaN
```

✔ The Boolean value `true` returns the number 1, like this:

```
Number(true) // returns 1
```

✔ The Boolean value `false` returns the number 0, like this:

```
Number(false) // returns 0
```

parseInt ( ) function

To JavaScript, all numbers are actually floating point numbers. However, you can use the `parseInt()` function to tell JavaScript to consider only the non-fractional part of the number (the integer), discarding everything after the decimal point.

```
parseInt(100.33); // returns 100
```

parseFloat ( ); function

You can use `parseFloat()` to specifically tell JavaScript to treat a number as a float. Or, you can even use it to convert a string to a number. For example:

```
parseFloat("10"); // returns 10
parseFloat(100.00); //returns 100.00
parseFloat("10"); //returns 10
```

Examples

Now you can play around with some numbers and number functions. Try entering the following expressions into the JavaScript console in your Chrome browser to see what results they produce.

You can open the JavaScript console in Chrome by pressing Command+Option+J (Mac) or Ctrl+Shift+J (Windows).

```
1 + 1
3 * 3
parseFloat("839");
parseInt("33.333333");
12 + "12"
"12" + 12
"12" * 2
```

Number variables must be declared without quotation marks. "10" is not the same as 10. The former is a string (which is covered in the next section), and if you accidentally declare a number variable inside of quotes, you'll get unexpected results.

If you're following along, you may have noticed some odd behaviors with the previous examples. For example, when you add "12" (a string) to 12 (a number), the result is "1212" (a string). But, when you multiply "12" (a string) by 2 (a number) the result is 24 (a number). This is a case where JavaScript is really using its head!

In the first example, when you add, JavaScript guesses that, because one of the values in the addition equation is a string, you meant for both of them to be. So, it converts the number to a string and treats the plus symbol as a *concatenation operator.*

In the second example, when you multiply, one of the values in the operation is a number, and there's no way to multiply strings together. JavaScript converts the string to a number and then proceeds with the multiplication. But, what happens when you try to multiple two strings together?

```
"sassafras" * "orange"
```

The result is NaN (not a number). There's just no way to convert sassafras or orange into a number, so JavaScript throws up its hands.

String data type

Strings can be made up of any characters:

- Letter
- Number
- Punctuation (such as commas and periods)
- Special characters that can be written using a backslash followed by character

Some characters, such as quotes, have special meaning in JavaScript or require a special combination of characters, such as a tab or new line, to represent inside of a string. We call these *special characters*. Table 3-1 lists the special characters that you can use inside JavaScript strings.

Table 3-1	JavaScript Special Characters
Code	*Outputs*
\'	single quote
\"	double quote
\\	backslash
\n	new line
\r	carriage return
\t	tab
\b	backspace
\f	form feed

You create a string variable by enclosing it in single or double quotes, like this:

```
var myString = "Hi, I'm a string.";
```

It doesn't actually matter whether you use single or double quotes, as long as the beginning and ending quotes surrounding the string match up.

If you surround your string with single quotes, you can actually use double quotes within that string without a problem. The same goes for if you surround your strings with double quotes; you can use single quotes within the string without a problem.

However, if you create a string and surround it with one type of quote, you can't use that type of quote inside the string, or the JavaScript parser will think you mean to end the string and will generate an error.

Escaping quotes

The solution to the problem of not being able to include quotes inside of a string surrounded with that type of quotes is to preface the quotes with a \. Adding a backslash before a quote is called *escaping* the quotes.

String functions

JavaScript includes many helpful functions for working with and converting strings.

Here's a list of the most frequently used built-in string functions:

- charAt() produces the character at a specified position. Note that the counting of characters starts with 0:

```
var watzThisString = 'JavaScript is Fun!';
console.log (watzThisString.charAt(3));
// returns a
```

- concat() combines one or more strings and returns the incorporated string:

```
var watzThisString = 'JavaScript is Fun!';
console.log (watzThisString.concat(' We love
    JavaScript!'));
// returns JavaScript is Fun! We love JavaScript!
```

- indexOf() searches and returns the position of the first occurrence of the searched character or substring within the string:

```
var watzThisString = 'JavaScript is Fun!';
console.log (watzThisString.indexOf('Fun');
// returns 14
```

- split() splits strings into an array of substrings:

```
var watzThisString = 'JavaScript is Fun!';
console.log (watzThisString.split('F'));
// returns ["JavaScript is ", "un!"]
```

- substr() extracts a portion of a string beginning at "start" through a specified length:

```
var watzThisString = 'JavaScript is Fun!';
console.log (watzThisString.substr(2,5));
// returns vaScr
```

- substring() extracts the characters within a string between two specified positions:

```
var watzThisString = 'JavaScript is Fun!';
console.log (watzThisString.substring(2,5));
// returns Vas
```

✔ `toLowerCase()` produces the string with all of its characters converted to lowercase:

```
var watzThisString = 'JavaScript is Fun!';
console.log (watzThisString.toLowerCase());
// returns javascript is fun!
```

✔ `toUpperCase()` produces the string with all of its characters converted to uppercase:

```
var watzThisString = 'JavaScript is Fun!';
console.log (watzThisString.toUpperCase());
// returns JAVASCRIPT IS FUN!
```

Boolean data type

Boolean variables store one of two possible values: either true or false.

The term *Boolean* is named after George Boole (1815–1864), who created an algebraic system of logic. Because it's named after a person, you generally write it with an initial capital letter.

Boolean variables are often used for storing the results of comparisons. You can find out the Boolean value of a comparison or convert any value in JavaScript into a Boolean value by using the `Boolean()` function. For example:

```
var isItGreater = Boolean (3 > 20);
alert (isItGreater); // returns false

var areTheySame = Boolean ("tiger" === "Tiger");
alert (areTheySame); // returns false
```

The result of converting a value in JavaScript into a Boolean value using the `Boolean()` function depends on the value:

✔ In JavaScript, the following values always evaluate to a Boolean `false` value:

- `NaN`
- undefined
- `0` (numeric value zero)
- `-0`
- `""` (empty string)
- `false`

✔ Anything that is not one of the preceding values evaluates to a Boolean `true`. For example:

- 74
- "Eva"
- "10"
- "NaN"

The number character `"0"` is not the same as the numeric value `0` (zero). While `0` will always result in a Boolean value of `false`, the string `"0"` will always result in a Boolean `true`.

Boolean values are primarily used with conditional expressions. The following program creates a Boolean variable and then test its value using an `if/then` statement (which you can find out about in Chapter 5).

```
var b = true;
if (b == true) {
  alert ("It is true!");
  } else {
  alert ("It is false.");
  }
```

Boolean values are written without quotes around them, like this:

```
var myVar = true
```

On the other hand, `var myVar = "true"` creates a string variable.

NaN data type

NaN stands for Not a Number. It's the result that you get when you try to do math with a string, or when a calculation fails or can't be done. For example, it's impossible to calculate the square root of a negative number. Trying to do so will result in NaN.

A more common occurrence that will produce NaN is an attempt to perform mathematical operations using strings that can't be converted to numbers.

undefined data type

Even if you create a variable in JavaScript and don't specifically give it a value, it still has a default value. This value is `"undefined"`.

Chapter 4

Understanding Arrays

"I am large. I contain multitudes."

— Walt Whitman

A rrays are a fundamental part of any programming language. In this chapter, you discover what they are, how to use them, and what makes JavaScript arrays distinct from arrays in other programming languages. You work with arrays to create lists, order lists, and add and remove items from lists.

Don't forget to visit the website to check out the online exercises relevant to this chapter!

Making a List

The earlier chapters in this book involve working with variables that are standalone pieces of data, such as: `var myName = "Chris"`, `var firstNumber = "3"`, and `var how ManyTacos = 8`. There are often times in programming (and in life) where you want to store related data under a single name. For example, consider the following types of lists:

- A list of your favorite artists
- A program that selects and displays a different quote from a list of quotes each time its run
- A holiday card mailing list
- A list of your top music albums of the year
- A list of all your family and friends' birthdays
- A shopping list
- A to-do list
- A list of New Year's resolutions

Using single-value variables (see Chapter 3), you would need to create and keep track of multiple variables in order to accomplish any of these tasks. Here is an example of a list created using single-value variables:

```
var artist1 = "Alphonse Mucha";
var artist2 = "Chiara Bautista";
var artist3 = "Claude Monet";
var artist4 = "Sandro Botticelli";
var artist5 = "Andy Warhol";
var artist6 = "Wassily Kadinski";
var artist7 = "Vincent Van Gough";
var artist8 = "Paul Klee";
var artist9 = "William Blake";
var artist10 = "Egon Schiele";
var artist11 = "Salvador Dali";
var artist12 = "Paul Cezanne";
var artist13 = "Diego Rivera";
var artist14 = "Pablo Picasso";
```

This approach could work in the short term, but you'd quickly run into difficulties. For example, what if you wanted to sort the list alphabetically and move artists into the correct variable names based on their position in the alphabetical sort? You'd need to first move Mucha out of the artist1 variable (maybe into a temporary holding variable) and then move Bautista into the artist1 variable. The artist2 spot would then be free for Blake, but don't forget that Mucha is still in that temporary slot! Blake's removal from artist9 frees that up for you to move someone else into the temporary variable, and so on. Creating a list in this way quickly becomes complicated and confusing.

Fortunately, JavaScript (and every other programming language we know of) supports the creation of variables containing multiple values, called *arrays*.

Arrays are a way to store groups of related data inside of a single variable. With arrays, you can create lists containing any mix of string values, numbers, Boolean values, objects, functions, any other type of data, and even other arrays!

Array Fundamentals

An array consists of array elements. Array elements are made up of the array name and then an index number that is contained in square brackets. The individual value within an array is called an *array element.* Arrays use numbers (called the *index numbers*) to access those elements. The following example illustrates how arrays use index numbers to access elements:

```
myArray[0] = "yellow balloon";
myArray[1] = "red balloon";
myArray[2] = "blue balloon";
myArray[3] = "pink balloon";
```

In this example, the element with the index number of 0 has a value of "yellow balloon". The element with an index number 3 has a value of "pink balloon". Just as with any variable, you can give an array any name that complies with the rules of naming JavaScript variables. By assigning index numbers in arrays, JavaScript gives you the ability to make a single variable name hold a nearly unlimited list of values.

Just so you don't get too carried away, there actually is a limit to the number of elements that you can have in an array, although you're very unlikely to ever reach it. The limit is 4,294,967,295 elements.

In addition to naming requirements (which are the same for any type of variable, as described in chapter 3), arrays have a couple of other rules and special properties that you need to be familiar with:

- Arrays are zero-indexed
- Arrays can store any type of data

Arrays are zero indexed

JavaScript doesn't have fingers or toes. As such, it doesn't need to abide by our crazy human rules about starting counting at 1. The first element in a JavaScript array always has an index number of 0 (see Figure 4-1).

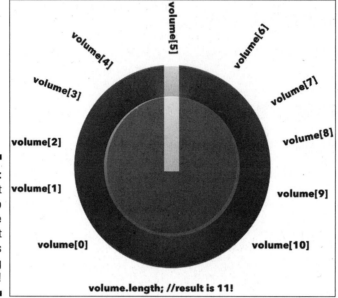

What this means for you is that myArray[3] is actually the fourth element in the array.

Zero-based numbering is a frequent cause of bugs and confusion for those new to programming, but once you get used to it, it will become quite natural. You may even discover that there are benefits to it, such as the ability to turn your guitar amp up to the 11th level.

Arrays can store any type of data

Each element in an array can store any of the data types (see Chapter 3), as well as other arrays. Array elements can also contain functions and JavaScript objects (see Chapters 7 and 8).

While you can store any type of data in an array, you can also store elements that contain different types of data, together, within one array, as shown in Listing 4-1.

Listing 4-1: Storing Different Types of Data in an Array

```
item[0] = "apple";
item[1] = 4+8;
item[2] = 3;
item[3] = item[2] * item[1];
```

Creating Arrays

JavaScript provides in two different ways for you to create new arrays:

- ✔ new keyword
- ✔ Array literal notation

Using the new keyword method

The `new` keyword method uses `new Array()` to create an array and add values to it.

```
var catNames = new Array("Larry", "Fuzzball",
        "Mr. Furly");
```

You may see this method used in your career as a programmer, and it's a perfectly acceptable way to create an array.

Many JavaScript experts recommend against using this method, however. The biggest problem with using the `new` keyword is what happens when you forget to include it. Forgetting to use the `new` keyword can dramatically change the way your program operates.

Array literal

A much simpler and safer way to create arrays is to use what is called the array literal method of notation. This is what it looks like:

```
var dogNames =["Shaggy", "Tennesee", "Dr. Spock"];
```

That's all there is to it. The use of square brackets and no special keywords means that you're less likely to accidentally leave something out. The array literal method also uses less characters than the `new` keyword method — and when you're trying to keep your JavaScript as tidy as possible, every little bit helps!

Populating Arrays

You can add values to an array when it is first created, or you can simply create an array and then add elements to it at a later time. Adding elements to an array works exactly the same as creating or modifying a variable, except that you specify the index number of the element that you want to create or modify. Listing 4-2, shows an example of creating an empty array and then adding elements to it.

Listing 4-2:   Populating an Empty Array

```
var peopleList =[];
peopleList[0]  = "Chris Minnick";
peopleList[1]  = "Eva Holland";
peopleList[2]  = "Abraham Lincoln";
```

You don't always need to add elements sequentially. It is perfectly legal in JavaScript to create a new element out of sequence. For example, in the preceding array, from Listing 4-2, you could add the following:

```
peopleList[99]  = "Tina Turner";
```

Creating an array out of sequence like this effectively creates blank elements for all of the indexes in between `peopleList[2]` and `peopleList[99]`.

So, if you check the length property of the `peopleList` array after adding an element with an index of 99, something interesting happens:

```
peopleList.length // returns 100
```

Even though you've only created four elements, JavaScript will say that the length of an array is 100 because the length is based on the highest numbered index, rather than on how many elements you've actually created.

Understanding Multidimensional Arrays

Not only can you store arrays inside of arrays, you can even put arrays inside of arrays inside of arrays. This can go on and on.

An array that contains an array is called a *multidimensional array*. To write a multidimensional array, you simply add more sets of square brackets to a variable name. For example:

```
var listOfLists[0][0];
```

Multidimensional arrays can be difficult to visualize when you first start working with them. Figure 4-2 shows a pictorial representation of a multidimensional array.

You can also visualize multidimensional arrays as hierarchal lists or outlines. For example:

Top Albums by Genre

1. Country

  1.1 Johnny Cash:Live at Folsom Prison

  1.2 Patsy Cline:Sentimentally Yours

  1.3 Hank Williams:I'm Blue Inside

2. Rock

  2.1 T-Rex:Slider

  2.2 Nirvana:Nevermind

  2.3 Lou Reed:Transformer

3. Punk

   3.1 Flipper:Generic

   3.2 The Dead Milkmen:Big Lizard in my Backyard

   3.3 Patti Smith:Easter

Here is a code that would create an array based on Figure 4-2:

```
var bestAlbumsByGenre = []
bestAlbumsByGenre[0] = "Country";
bestAlbumsByGenre[0][0] = "Johnny Cash:Live at Folsom
        Prison"
bestAlbumsByGenre[0][1] = "Patsy Cline:Sentimentally
        Yours";
bestAlbumsByGenre[0][2] = "Hank Williams:I'm Blue Inside";
bestAlbumsByGenre[1] = "Rock";
bestAlbumsByGenre[1][0] = "T-Rex:Slider";
bestAlbumsByGenre[1][1] = "Nirvana:Nevermind";
bestAlbumsByGenre[1][2] = "Lou Reed:Tranformer";
bestAlbumsByGenre[2] = "Punk";
bestAlbumsByGenre[2][0] = "Flipper:Generic";
bestAlbumsByGenre[2][1] = "The Dead Milkmen:Big Lizard in
        my Backyard";
bestAlbumsByGenre[2][2] = "Patti Smith:Easter";
```

Accessing Array Elements

You can access the elements of arrays in the same way that you set them, using square brackets and the index number. For example, to access the third element in any array called myArray, you would use the following:

```
myArray[2];
```

To access elements in a multidimensional array, just add more square brackets to get to the element you want:

```
bestAlbumsByGenre[0][1]; // returns "Patsy_
        Cline:Sentimentally Yours";
```

To test out setting and accessing the elements of an array, follow these steps:

1. **Open your Chrome browser and the open the JavaScript console.**

   You can open your JavaScript Console using the Chrome menu or by pressing Command + Option + J on Mac or Ctrl + Shift + J in Windows.

2. **In the console, type the following statement, followed by the Return or Enter key, to create an array called** `lengthsOfString`:

```
var lengthsOfString = [2,4,1.5,80];
```

3. **Type the array name followed by the index number in square brackets to retrieve the value of each array element.**

   For example:

```
lengthsOfString[0];
lengthsOfString[3];
lengthsOfString[2];
```

4. **Enter an index number that doesn't exist in the array.**

   For example:

```
lengthsOfString[4];
```

   Notice that the value of this array element is undefined.

5. **Type the following command to create a new variable to hold the total length of string that you have:**

```
var totalLength = lengthsOfString[0] +
        lengthsOfString[1] + lengthsOfString[2] +
        lengthsOfString[3];
```

6. **Finally, get the value of** `totalLength` **with this command:**

```
totalLength;
```

Looping through arrays

As you can imagine, working with multiple values of arrays by typing the array name and the index number can get tiring for your fingers after a while. Fortunately, there are easier ways to work with all of the elements in an array. The most common method is to use a programming construct called a *loop*. (We cover loops in much more detail in Chapter 6.)

It's also possible to work with multiple elements in an array by using JavaScript's built-in array functions.

Array properties

You can access certain data about an array by accessing array properties. The way to access array properties in JavaScript is by using *dot notation*. To use dot notation, you type the name of the array, followed by a period, followed by the property you want to access. (You can find out much more about properties in Chapter 8.) Table 4-1 lists all of the properties of JavaScript arrays.

Table 4-1	JavaScript's Array Properties
Property	**Return Value**
prototype	Allows the addition of properties and methods to an Array object
constructor	A reference to the function that created the Array object's prototype
length	Either returns or sets the number of elements in an array

The most commonly used array property is length. You have already seen the length property in action. Its purpose is to provide the number of elements in an array, whether defined or undefined. For example:

```
var myArray = [];
myArray[2000];
myArray.length; // returns 2001
```

You can also use the length property to truncate an array:

```
myArray.length;// returns 2001
myArray.length = 10;
myArray.length; // returns 10
```

Array methods

JavaScript array methods (also known as array functions) provide handy ways to manipulate and work with arrays. Table 4-2 shows a list of all the array methods along with descriptions of what they do or the values they produce.

Using array methods

The syntax for using array methods differs depending on the particular method you are trying to use. You do, however, access the functionality of every array method the same way that you access array properties: by using dot notation.

Table 4-2	JavaScript Array Methods
Method	***Return Value***
`concat()`	A new array made up of the current array, joined with other array(s) and/or value(s)
`every()`	`true` if every element in the given array satisfies the provided testing function
`filter()`	A new array with all of the elements of a current array that test true by the given function
`forEach()`	Completes the function once for each element in the array
`indexOf()`	The first occurrence of the specified value within the array. Returns `-1` if the value is not found
`join()`	Joins all the elements of an array into a string
`lastIndexOf()`	The last occurrence of the specified value within the array. Returns `-1` if value is not found
`map()`	A new array with the result of a provided function on every element in the array
`pop()`	Removes the last element in an array
`push()`	Adds new items to the end of an array
`reduce()`	Reduces two values of an array to a single value by applying a function to them (from left to right)
`reduceRight()`	Reduces two values of an array to a single value by applying a function to them simultaneously (from right to left)
`reverse()`	Reverses the order of elements in an array
`shift()`	Removes the first element from an array and returns that element, resulting in a change in length of an array
`slice()`	Selects a portion of an array and returns it as a new array
`some()`	Returns `true` if one or more elements satisfy the provided testing function
`sort()`	Returns an array after the elements in an array are sorted (default sort order is alphabetical and ascending)
`splice()`	Returns a new array comprised of elements that were added or removed from a given array
`toString()`	Converts an array to a string
`unShift()`	Returns a new array with a new length by the addition of one or more elements

For a complete reference to JavaScript array methods, with examples, visit https://docs.webplatform.org/wiki/javascript/Array#Methods.

Listing 4-3 shows some examples of the most commonly used JavaScript methods.

Listing 4-3:   Commonly Used JavaScript Array Methods in Action

```
<html>
<head>
  <title>common array methods</title>
</head>
<body>
  <script>
    var animals = ["tiger" , "bear"];
    var fruit = ["cantaloupe" , "orange"];
    var dishes = ["plate" , "bowl" , "cup"];

    var fruitsAndAnimals = fruit.concat(animals);
    document.write (fruitsAndAnimals + "<br>");

    var whereIsTheTiger = animals.indexof("tiger";
    document.write ("The tiger has and index number of: "
            + whereIsTheTiger + "<br>");
  </script>
</body>
</html>
```

Figure 4-3 shows the result of Listing 4-3 when run in a browser.

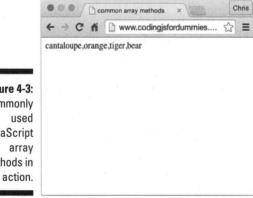

Figure 4-3:
Commonly
used
JavaScript
array
methods in
action.

Chapter 5

Working with Operators, Expressions, and Statements

In This Chapter

▶ Reading and coding JavaScript expressions

▶ Changing values with assignment operators

▶ Thinking logically with comparison operators

▶ Doing the math with arithmetic operators

▶ Getting wise to bitwise operators

▶ Putting it together with string operators

"Hello Operator. Can you give me number 9?"

— The White Stripes

*J*avaScript operators, expressions, and statements are the basic building blocks of programs. They help you manipulate and change values, perform math, compare two or more values, and much, much more.

In this chapter, you discover how operators, expressions, and statements do their work and how you can best use them to your advantage.

Don't forget to visit the website to check out the online exercises relevant to this chapter!

Express Yourself

An *expression* is a piece of code that resolves to a value. Expressions can either assign a value to a variable, or they can simply have a value. For example, both of the following are examples of valid expressions:

```
1 + 1
```

```
a = 1;
```

Expressions can be short and simple, as illustrated in these examples, or they can be quite complicated.

The pieces of data (1 or a in these examples) in an expression are called *operands*.

Hello, Operator

The engines that make expressions do their work are called *operators*. They operate on data to produce different results. The = and + in the preceding expressions are examples of operators.

Operator precedence

A single expression often will contain several operators. Consider the following example:

```
a + 1 + 2 * 3 / 4;
```

Depending on the order in which you perform the different calculations, the final value of a could be any one of the following:

```
a = 1.75
```

```
a = 2.5
```

```
a = 2.25
```

In fact, the actual result of this expression will be 2.5. But how do you know this? Depending on the person doing the math, the division could be done first (3 / 4), the addition could be done first (1 + 2), or the multiplication could be done first (2 * 3).

Clearly, there must be a better way to figure out the answer, and there is! This is where *operator precedence* comes in. Operator precedence is the order in which operators in an expression are evaluated.

Operators are divided into groups of different levels of precedence, numbered from 0 to 19, as shown in Table 5-1.

Table 5-1		**Operator Precedence**		
Operator	*Use*	*Operator Associativity*	*Precedence*	*Sample Use*
(..)	grouping	n/a	0 — highest precedence	(1 + 3)
.. . ..	operator property access	left to right	1	myCar.color
[..]	array access	left to right	1	thingsToDo[4]
new . . .()	creates an object (with arguments list)	n/a	1	new Car ("red")
function . . .()	function call	left to right	2	function add Numbers (1,2)
new . . .	create an object (without a list)	right to left	2	new Car
. . .++	postfix increment	n/a	3	number++
. . .--	postfix decrement	n/a	3	number--
! . . .	logical not	right to left	4	!myVal
~ . . .	bitwise not	right to left	4	~myVal
- . . .	negation	right to left	4	-aNumber
++ . . .	prefix increment	right to left	4	++aNumber
-- . . .	prefix decrement	right to left	4	--aNumber
typeof . . .	typeof	right to left	4	typeof myVar
void . . .	void	right to left	4	void(0)
delete . . .	delete	right to left	4	delete object. property
. . . * . . .	multiplication	left to right	5	result = 3 * 7
. . . / . . .	division	left to right	5	result = 3 / 7
. . . % . . .	remainder	left to right	5	result = 7 % 3
. . . + . . .	addition	left to right	6	result = 3 + 7

(continued)

Table 5-1 *(continued)*

Operator	Use	Operator Associativity	Precedence	Sample Use
. . . - . . .	subtraction	left to right	6	result = 3 - 7
. . . << . . .	bitwise left shift	left to right	7	result = 3 << 7
. . . >> . . .	bitwise right shift	left to right	7	result = 3 >> 7
. . . >>> . . .	bitwise unsigned right shift	left to right	7	result = 3 >>> 7
. . . < . . .	less than	left to right	8	a < b
. . . <= . . .	less than or equal to	left to right	8	a <= b
. . . > . . .	greater than	left to right	8	a > b
. . . >= . . .	greater than or equal to	left to right	8	a >= b
. . . in . . .	in	left to right	8	value in values
. . . instanceof . . .	instanceof	left to right	8	myCar instanceof car
. . . == . . .	equality	left to right	9	3 == "3" // true
. . . != . . .	inequality	left to right	9	3 != "3" // false
. . . === . . .	strict equality	left to right	9	3 === "3" // false
. . . !== . . .	strict inequality	left to right	9	3 !== "3" // true
. . . & . . .	bitwise and	left to right	10	result = a & b
. . . ^ . . .	bitwise xor	left to right	11	result = a ^ b
. . . | . . .	bitwise or	left to right	12	result = a | b
. . . && . . .	logical and	left to right	13	a && b
. . . || . . .	logical or	left to right	14	a || b
. . . ? . . . : . . .	conditional	right to left	15	a ? 3 : 7
. . . = . . .	assignment	right to left	16	a = 3
. . . += . . .	assignment	right to left	16	a += 3
. . . -= . . .	assignment	right to left	16	a -= 3
. . . *= . . .	assignment	right to left	16	a *= 3
. . . /= . . .	assignment	right to left	16	a /= 3

Operator	Use	Operator Associativity	Precedence	Sample Use
... %= ...	assignment	right to left	16	a %= 3
... <<= ...	assignment	right to left	16	a <<= 3
... >>= ...	assignment	right to left	16	a >>= 3
... >>>= ...	assignment	right to left	16	a >>>= 3
... &= ...	assignment	right to left	16	a &= 3
... ^= ...	assignment	right to left	16	a ^= 3
... |= ...	assignment	right to left	16	a |= 3
yield ...	yield	right to left	17	yield [expression]
... , ...	comma / sequence	left to right	18	a + b, c + d

The operator with the lowest number is said to have the highest precedence. This may seem confusing at first, but if you think of it in terms of the first person in a line (whoever is in spot 0, in this case) being the first person to get a delicious sandwich or cup of coffee, you'll have no problem keeping it straight.

When an expression contains two or more operators that have the same precedence, they are evaluated according to their *associativity*. Associativity determines whether the operators are evaluated from left to right or right to left.

Using parentheses

The operator with the highest precedence in an expression is parentheses. In most cases, you can ignore the rules of operator precedence simply by grouping operations into subexpressions using parentheses. For example, the previous multi-operator expression can be fully clarified in the following ways:

```
a = (1 + 2) * (3 / 4); // result: 2.25
a = (1 + (2 * 3)) / 4; // result: 1.75
a = ((1 + 2) *3) / 4; // result: 2.25
a = 1 + ((2 * 3) / 4); // result: 2.5
```

Parentheses in expressions force the JavaScript interpreter to evaluate the contents of the parentheses first, from the inner most parentheses to the outermost, before performing the operations outside of the parentheses.

Upon consulting Table 5-1, you'll see that the actual order of the precedence for the preceding expression is

```
a = 1 + ((2 * 3) / 4);
```

This statement makes the actual operator precedence explicit. Multiplication is done first, followed by division, followed by the addition.

Types of Operators

JavaScript has a number of types of operators. This section discusses the most commonly used types of operators.

Assignment operators

The *assignment operator* assigns the value of the operand on the right to the operand on the left:

```
a = 5;
```

After this expression runs, the variable a will have a value of 5. You can also chain assignment operators together in order to assign the same value to multiple variables, as in the following example:

```
a = b = c = 5;
```

Because the operator's associativity is right to left (see Table 5-1), 5 will first be assigned to c, then the value of c will be assigned to b, and then the value if b will be assigned to a. The result of this expression is that a, b, and c all have a value of 5.

What do you think the end value of a will be after these expressions are evaluated?

```
var b = 1;
```

```
var a = b += c = 5;
```

To find out, open up the JavaScript console in Chrome and type each line, followed by return or enter. The result of this statement is that a will be equal to 6.

You can find a complete list of the different assignment operators in in the "Combining operators" section, later in this chapter.

Comparison operators

Comparison operators test for equality or difference between operands and return a true or false value.

Table 5-2 shows a complete list of the JavaScript comparison operators.

Table 5-2	JavaScript Comparison Operators	
Operator	*Description*	*Example*
==	Equality	3 == "3" // true
!=	Inequality	3 != 3 // false
===	Strict equality	3 === "3" // false
!==	Strict inequality	3 !== "3" // true
>	Greater than	7 > 1 // true
>=	Greater than or equal to	7 >= 7 // true
<	Less than	7 < 10 // true
<=	Less than or equal to	2 <= 2 // true

Arithmetic operators

Arithmetic operators perform mathematical operations on operands and return the result. Table 5-3 shows a complete list of arithmetic operators.

Table 5-3	Arithmetic Operators	
Operator	*Description*	*Example*
+	Addition	a = 1 + 1
-	Subtraction	a = 10 - 1
*	Multiplication	a = 2 * 2
/	Division	a = 8 / 2
%	Modulus	a = 5 % 2
++	Increment	a = ++b
		a = b++
		a++
--	Decrement	a = --b
		a = b--
		a--

Listing 5-1 shows arithmetic operators at work.

Listing 5-1: Using Arithmetic Operators

```
<html>
<head>
  <title>arithmetic operators</title>
</head>
<body>
  <h1>Wild Birthday Game</h1>
  <p>
  <ul>
    <li>Enter the number 7</li>
    <li>Multiply by the month of your birth</li>
    <li>Subtract 1</li>
    <li>Multiply by 13</li>
    <li>Add the day of your birth</li>
    <li>Add 3</li>
    <li>Multiply by 11</li>
    <li>Subtract the month of your birth</li>
    <li>Subtract the day of your birth</li>
    <li>Divide by 10</li>
    <li>Add 11</li>
    <li>Divide by 100</li>
  </ul>
  </p>
  <script>
    var numberSeven = Number(prompt('Enter the number
          7'));
    var birthMonth = Number(prompt('Enter your birth
          month'));
    var calculation = numberSeven * birthMonth;
    calculation = calculation - 1;
    calculation = calculation * 13;
    var birthDay = Number(prompt('Enter the day of your
          birth'));
    calculation = calculation + birthDay;
    calculation = calculation + 3;
    calculation = calculation * 11
    calculation = calculation - birthMonth;
    calculation = calculation - birthDay;
    calculation = calculation / 10;
    calculation = calculation + 11;
    calculation = calculation / 100;

    document.write("Your birthday is " + calculation);
    </script>
</body>
</html>
```

The result of running Listing 5-1 in a browser is shown in Figure 5-1.

Figure 5-1:
The wild
arithmetic
game.

String operator

The *string operator* performs operations using two strings. When used with strings, the + operator becomes the concatenation operator. Its purpose is to join together strings. Note that when you're joining strings with the concatenation operator, no spaces are added. Thus, it's very common to see statements like the following, where strings containing nothing but a blank space are concatenated between other strings or spaces are added to the end or beginning of strings (before the quotation mark) in order to form a coherent sentence:

```
var greeting = "Hello, " + firstName + ". I'm" + " " +
               mood + " to see you.";
```

Bitwise operators

Bitwise operators treat operands as signed 32-bit binary representations of numbers in twos complement format. Here's what that means, starting with the term *binary*.

Binary numbers are strings of 1s or 0s, with the position of the digit determining the value of a 1 in that position. For example, here's how to write the number 1 as a 32-bit binary number:

00000000000000000000000000000001

The right most position has a value of 1. Each position to the left of this position has a value of twice the value of the number to its right. So, the following binary number is equal to 5:

00000000000000000000000000000101

Signed integers means that both negative and positive whole numbers can be represented in this form.

The term *twos complement* means that the opposite of any positive binary number is its negative (and vice versa, of course). So, to change the binary 5 to a binary -5, simply flip all the bits:

11111111111111111111111111111101

Bitwise operators convert numbers to these 32-bit binary numbers and then convert them back to what we would consider normal numbers after the operation has been done.

Bitwise operators are difficult to understand at first. They're not very commonly used in JavaScript, but we would be remiss if we didn't cover them.

Table 5-4 lists the JavaScript bitwise operators.

Table 5-4		JavaScript Bitwise Operators
Operator	*Usage*	*Description*
Bitwise AND	a & b	Returns a 1 in each bit position for which the corresponding bits of both operands are 1s
Bitwise OR	a | b	Returns a 1 in each bit position for which the corresponding bits of either or both operands are 1s
Bitwise XOR	a ^ b	Returns a 1 in each bit position for which the corresponding bits of either but not both operands are 1s
Bitwise NOT	~a	Inverts the bits of its operand
Left shift	a << b	Shifts a in binary representation b (<32) bits to the left shifting in zeros from the right
Sign-propagating right shift	a >> b	Shifts a in binary representation b (<32) bits to the right, discarding bits shifted off
Zero-fill right shift	a >>> b	Shifts a in binary representation b (<32) bits to the right, discarding bits shifted off, and shifting in zeros from the left

Figure 5-2 shows a demonstration of each of the bitwise operators in the Chrome JavaScript console.

Figure 5-2:
The
JavaScript
bitwise
operators.

Logical operators

Logical operators evaluate a logical expression for truthiness or falseness. There are three logical operators, shown in Table 5-5.

Table 5-5		Logical Operators
Operator	*Meaning*	*Description*
&&	And	Returns the first operand if it is `true`. Otherwise, it returns the second operand.
||	Or	Returns the first operand if it is `true`. Otherwise, it returns the second operand.
!	Not	Takes only one operand. Returns `false` if its operand can be converted to `true`. Otherwise, it returns `false`.

You can also use the OR operator to set a default value for variables. For example, in the following expression, the value of `myVar` will be set to the value of x unless x evaluates to a `false` value (for example, if x hasn't been defined). Otherwise, it will be set to the default value of 0.

```
var myVar = x||0;
```

Special operators

JavaScript's special operators are a hodge-podge of miscellaneous other symbols and words that perform other and important functions.

Conditional operator

The *conditional operator* (also known as the *ternary operator*) uses three operands. It evaluates a logical expression and then returns a value based on whether that expression is true or false. The conditional operator is the only operator that requires three operands. For example:

```
var isItBiggerThanTen = (value > 10) ? "greater than 10" :
        "not greater than 10";
```

Comma operator

The *comma operator* evaluates two operands and returns the value of the second one. It's most often used to perform multiple assignments or other operations within loops. It can also serve as a shorthand for initializing variables. For example:

```
var a = 10 , b = 0;
```

Because the comma has the lowest precedence of the operators, its operands are always evaluated separately.

delete operator

The delete operator removes a property from an object or an element from an array.

When you use the delete operator to remove an element from an array, the length of the array stays the same. The removed element will have a value of undefined.

```
var animals = ["dog","cat","bird","octopus"];
console.log (animals[3]); // returns "octopus"
delete animals[3];
console.log (animals[3]); // returns "undefined"
```

in operator

The in operator returns true if the specified value exists in an array or object.

```
var animals = ["dog","cat","bird","octopus"];
if (3 in animals) {
  console.log ("it's in there");
}
```

In this example, if the `animals` array has an element with the index of 3, the string `"it's in there"` will print out to the JavaScript console.

instanceof operator

The `instanceof` operator returns true if the object you specify is the type of object that has been specified.

```
var myString = new String();
if (myString instanceof String) {
  console.log("yup, it's a string!");
}
```

new operator

The `new` operator creates an instance of an object. As you can see in Chapter 8, JavaScript has several built-in object types, and you can also define your own. In the following example, `Date()` is a built-in JavaScript object, while `Pet()` and `Flower()` are examples of objects that a programmer could create to serve custom purposes within a program.

```
var today = new Date();
var bird = new Pet();
var daisy = new Flower();
```

this operator

The `this` operator refers to the current object. It's frequently used for retrieving properties within an object.

Chapter 8 covers the `this` operator in much more detail.

typeof operator

The `typeof` operator returns a string containing the type of the operand:

```
var businessName = "Harry's Watch Repair";
console.log typeof businessName; // returns "string"
```

void operator

The `void` operator causes an expression in the operand to be evaluated without returning a value. The place where you most often see void used is in HTML documents when a link is needed, but the creator of the link wants to override the default behavior of the link using JavaScript:

```
<a href="javascript:void(0);">This is a link, but it won't
        do anything</a>
```

Combining operators

You can combine assignment operators with the other operators as a short-hand method of assigning the result of an expression to a variable. For example, the following two examples have the same result:

```
a = a + 10;
```

```
a += 10;
```

Table 5-6 lists all the possible combinations of the assignment operators with other operators.

Table 5-6	Combining the Assignment Operators and Other Operators	
Name	*Shorthand*	*Standard Operator*
Assignment	x = y	x = y
Addition assignment	x += y	x = x + y
Subtraction assignment	x -= y	x = x - y
Multiplication assignment	x *= y	x = x * y
Division assignment	x /= y	x = x / y
Remainder assignment	x %= y	x = x % y
Left shift assignment	x <<= y	x = x << y
Right shift assignment	x >>= y	x = x >> y
Unassigned right shift assignment	x >>>= y	x = x <<< y
Bitwise AND assignment	x &= y	x = x & y
Bitwise XOR assignment	x ^= y	x = x ^ y
Bitwise OR assignment	x |= y	x = x	y

Chapter 6

Getting into the Flow with Loops and Branches

"It's not hard to make decisions when you know what your values are."

— Roy Disney

*I*n earlier chapters of this book, we generally talk about and demonstrate linear JavaScript code. However, more often than not, there comes a time (many times, actually) in a program where you need a choice to be made or where you need to alter the straight-ahead logic of a program to repeat statements multiple times with different values. In this chapter, we discuss looping and branching statements.

Don't forget to visit the website to check out the online exercises relevant to this chapter!

Branching Out

Looping and *branching statements* are called control statements because they control the order in which JavaScript programs are run. You can use *branching statements* to create different paths for the execution of JavaScript code, depending on conditional logic. *Loops* are the simplest way to group JavaScript statements together in a program.

The logic of a JavaScript program often comes to a point where a choice must be made which will make all the difference. Figure 6-1 demonstrates, using JavaScript, a real-world decision that can be solved using branching.

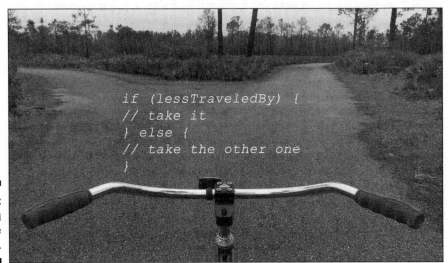

```
if (lessTraveledBy) {
// take it
} else {
// take the other one
}
```

Figure 6-1:
Branching
chooses the
path.

if . . . else

The `if` and `else` statements work together to evaluate a logical expression and run different statements based on the result. `if` statements can be, and often are, used by themselves. `else` statements must always be used in conjunction with an `if` statement.

The basic syntax for an `if` statement is

```
if (condition) {
...
}
```

The condition here is any expression that evaluates to a Boolean (true or false) value. If the result of the expression is `true`, the statements between the brackets will be executed. If it's `false`, they will just be skipped over.

The `else` statement comes in when you want to do something if the condition evaluates to `false`. For example:

```
var age = 19;
if (age < 21){
  document.write ("You are under the legal drinking age in
          the U.S.");
} else {
  document.write ("What'll it be?");
}
```

Many other programming languages have a combination keyword called the `elseif`, which can be used multiple times in an `if . . . else` statement until a `true` value occurs. JavaScript doesn't have an `elseif` keyword.

However, you can get the same functionality as an `elseif` keyword by using `if` and `else` together with a space between them. For example:

```
if (time < 12){
  document.write ("Good Morning!");
} else if (time < 17){
  document.write ("Good Afternoon!");
} else if (time < 20){
  document.write ("Good Evening!");
} else {
  document.write ("Good Night!");
}
```

Understanding if . . . else shorthand

You should be aware of a couple of shortcuts for using `if . . . else` statements. The first is to use a ternary operator in place of the `if . . . else`. This is somewhat more difficult to read than a standard `if . . . else`:

```
var whatToSay = (time < 12 ?
        "Good Morning" :
        "Hello");
```

In this case, the value of `whatToSay` is set to "Good Morning" if time is less than 12 and it's set to "Hello" if time is not less than 12.

Another shorthand methods for writing `if . . . else` statements uses the logical AND (`&&`) operator. Remember that the logical AND will only evaluate the second operand if the first evaluates to true. Programmers call this *short-circuiting* because it's not necessary for the second operand to be evaluated in a logical AND operation if the first operand results in a false value.

```
time < 12 && document.write
        ("Good Morning!");
```

In the preceding example, the `&&` statement first looks at whether times is less than 12. If it is, the string "Good Morning" will be written to the HTML document. If it isn't, nothing will be done because of the short-circuiting side effect of the `&&` operator.

This method is not commonly used, primarily because it's difficult to understand and confusing. However, you may come across something like this at times, and you'll need to understand how it works.

Notice the use of line breaks and spaces in the preceding examples. Many people have different styles for how to write if . . . else statements. You may also see them written with fewer line breaks or without space between the keywords and brackets. These will work, too. However, whenever possible, it is preferable to choose ease of reading over brevity.

Switch

The switch statement chooses between multiple statements to execute based on possible values of a single expression. Each of these values in a switch statement is called a case. In English, you may say, for example:

> "In the case that we are expecting six guests, order three pizzas. In the case that we are expecting 12 guests, order six pizzas. In the case that we're expecting more than 20 guests, freak out."

The syntax for the switch statement is

```
switch (expression) {
  case value1:
  // Statements
  break;
  case value2:
  // Statements
  break;
  case value3:
  // Statements
  break;
  default:
  // Statements
  break;
}
```

Notice the break statement after the statements associated with each case. The break statement tells the switch statement to stop and exit the switch statement. Without the break, the switch statement would continue and run the statements in the next clause, regardless of whether the expression meets the conditions of that case.

Forgetting a break statement within a switch can cause big problems, so be sure to always use it. Because a switch statement will run any statements within any case clause after a clause that evaluates to true, unpredictable results can occur when you forget a break statement. Problems caused by missing break statements are not easy to identify because they generally won't produce errors, but will frequently produce incorrect results.

If no match is found in any of the `case` clauses, the `switch` statement will look for a `default` clause and execute the statement it contains.

The exception to the rule that you should always use a `break` statement between `case` clauses is the `default` clause. As long as the `default` clause is the last statement in your switch (which, it should be), you can safely omit the break after it because the program will break out of the switch after the last statement anyway.

Listing 6-1 shows an example of how you might use a `switch` statement.

Listing 6-1:   Using a switch Statement to Personalize a Greeting

```
var languagePreference = "Spanish";
switch (languagePreference){
 case "English":
   console.log("Hello!");
   break;
 case "Spanish":
   console.log("Hola!");
   break;
 case "German":
   console.log("Guten Tag!");
   break;
 case "French":
   console.log("Bon Jour!");
   break;
 default:
   console.log("I'm Sorry, I don't Speak" +
          languagePreferance + "!");
}
```

Here We Go: Loop De Loop

Loops execute the same statement multiple times. JavaScript has several different types of loops:

- ✔ `for`
- ✔ `for . . . in`
- ✔ `do . . . while`
- ✔ `while`

for

The for statement creates a loop using three expressions:

- ✔ **Initialization:** The initial value of a variable, typically a counter.
- ✔ **Condition:** A Boolean expression to be evaluated with each iteration of the loop.
- ✔ **Final expression:** An expression to be evaluated after each loop iteration.

Although it's not required to use all three expressions in a for loop, all three of them are nearly always included. The for loop is usually used to run code a predetermined number of times.

The following is an example of a simple for loop:

```
for (var x = 1; x < 10; x++){
  console.log(x);
}
```

Broken down, this is how the preceding for loop example works:

1. **A new variable, in this case x, is initiated with the value of 1.**

2. **A test is performed to determine whether x is less than 10.**

   If it is, the statements inside the loop are executed (in this case, a con-sole.log statement).

3. If not, the value of x is incremented using the increment operator (++).

4. **The test is done again to determine whether x is less than 10.**

   If so, the statements inside the loop are executed.

5. **The test repeats, until the condition expression no longer evaluates to true.**

Figure 6-2 shows the result of running this for statement in the Chrome developer tools.

Looping through an array

You can use for loops to list the contents of an array by testing the value of the counter against the value of the length property of the array. Be sure to remember that JavaScript arrays are zero-indexed and that the value of any array.length will be one more than the highest index numbered element in the array. That is why we add -1 in Listing 6-2.

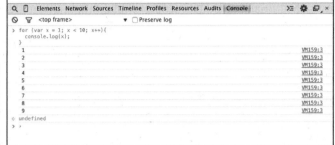

Figure 6-2:
A loop that
counts from
1 to 9.

Listing 6-2:   Listing the Contents of an Array with for Loop

```html
<html>
<head>
 <title>Different Area Codes</title>
</head>
<body>
 <script>
    var areaCodes = ["770", "404", "718", "202", "901",
          "305", "312", "313", "215", "803"];
    for (x=0; x < areaCodes.length - 1; x++){
      document.write("Different Area Code:" + areaCodes[x]
          + "<br>");
    }
 </script>
</body>
</html>
```

Figure 6-3 shows the output of running the program detailed in Listing 6-2.

Figure 6-3:
Output of
listing the
contents
of an array
with a `for`
loop.

Different Area Code:770
Different Area Code:404
Different Area Code:718
Different Area Code:202
Different Area Code:901
Different Area Code:305
Different Area Code:312
Different Area Code:313
Different Area Code:215

for . . . in

The `for . . . in` statements loop through the properties in an object. You can also use a `for . . . in` statement to loop through the values of an array.

The `for . . . in` loop has an interesting quirk. It doesn't care about the order of properties or elements that it's looping through. For this reason, and because using `for . . . in` loop is slower, you're much better off using a standard `for` loop to loop through array elements.

Objects are data containers that have properties (what they are) and methods (what they do). Web browsers have a set of built-in objects that programmers can use to control the function of the browser. The most basic of these is the `Document` object. The `write` method of the `Document` object, for example, tells your browser to insert a specified value into the HTML document.

The `Document` object also has properties that it uses to track and give programmers information about the current document. The `Document.images` collection, for example, contains all of the `img` tags in the current HTML document.

In Listing 6-3, the `for. . . in` loop is used to list all the properties of the `Document` object.

Listing 6-3:   Looping through the Document object with `for . . . in`

```html
<html>
<head>
 <title>document properties</title>
 <style>
   .columns {
   -webkit-column-count: 6; // Chrome, Safari, Opera
   -moz-column-count: 6; // Firefox
   column-count: 6;
   }
 </style>
</head>
<body>

 <div class="columns">

 <script>
   for (var prop in document){
     document.write (prop + "<br>");
 }
 </script>

 </div>

</body>
</html>
```

The results of running Listing 6-3 are shown in Figure 6-4.

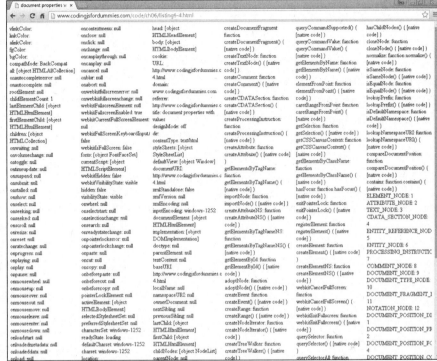

Figure 6-4:
A list of all the properties of a Document object using the `for...in` loop.

You can also use a `for...in` loop to output the values that are in the properties of the object, rather than just the property name. Listing 6-4 is a program that outputs the current values of each of the `Document` object's properties.

Listing 6-4:   Outputting the Property Names and Values of the Document Object with for...in

```html
<html>
<head>
 <title>document properties with values</title>
 <style>
  .columns{
  -webkit-column-count: 6; /* Chrome, Safari, Opera */
  -moz-column-count: 6; /* Firefox */
  column-count: 6;
  }
```

(continued)

Listing 6-4 *(continued)*

```
      </style>
   </head>
   <body>
    <div class="columns">
      <script>
        for (var prop in document){
          document.write (prop + ": " + document[prop] +
            "<br>");
        }
      </script>
    </div>
   </body>
</html>
```

Figure 6-5 shows the output of Listing 6-4. Notice that many of the values of properties are in square brackets ([ ]). The square brackets indicate that the value of the property has multiple elements, such as in the case of an array or object.

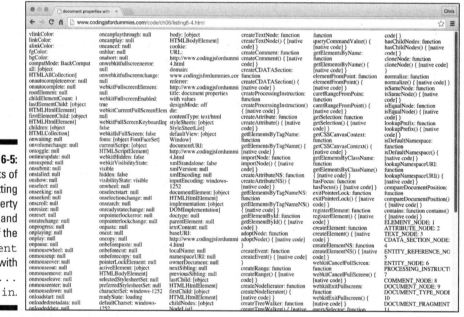

Figure 6-5: Results of outputting the property names and values of the Document object with for ... in.

while loops

The while statement creates a loop that runs as long as a condition evaluates to true. Listing 6-5 shows a webpage containing an example of the while loop.

Listing 6-5:   Using a while Loop

```html
<html>
<head>
 <title>Guess the Word</title>
</head>
<body>
 <script>
   var guessedWord = prompt("What word am I thinking
          of?");
   while (guessedWord != "sandwich") { // as long as the
          guessed word is not sandwich
    prompt("No. That's not it. Try again.");
                                                      }
     alert("Congratulations! That's exactly right!"); //
          do this after exiting the loop
 </script>
</body>
</html>
```

do...while

The do... while loop works in much the same way as the while loop, except that it puts the statements before the expression to test against. The effect is that the statements within a do . . . while loop will always execute as least once.

Listing 6-6 demonstrates the use of a do . . . while loop.

Listing 6-6:   Using a do...while Loop

```html
<html>
<head>
 <title>Let's Count</title>
</head>
<body>
 <script>
   var i = 0;
   do {
     i++;
     document.write(I + "<br>");
   } while (i<10);
 </script>
</body>
</html>
```

break and continue

You can use break and continue to interrupt the execution of a loop. The break statement was shown previously in this chapter in the context of a switch statement, where it serves to break out of the switch after a successful match.

In a loop, break does much the same thing. It causes the program to immediately exit the loop, no matter whether the conditions for the completion of the loop have been met.

For example, in Listing 6-7, the word-guessing game will progress just as it does in Listing 6-5, but the loop will immediately terminate if no value is entered.

Listing 6-7:   Using a break in a while Loop

```
<html>
<head>
 <title>Guess the Word</title>
</head>
<body>
 <script>
   var guessedWord = prompt("What word am I thinking
           of?");
   while (guessedWord != "sandwich") {
     if (guessedWord =="") {break;} // exit the loop
           right away if user doesn't enter a value
     prompt("No. That's not it. Try again.");
   }
   alert("Congratulations! That's exactly right!");
 </script>
</body>
</html>
```

The continue statement causes the current iteration of the loop to stop and tells the program to start up again with the next iteration of the loop, skipping the statements that come after the continue statement.

Listing 6-8 shows a program that counts from 1 to 20, but only prints out even numbers. Notice that the program determines whether a number is even by using the modulus operator to test whether the current value of the counter is divisible by two:

Listing 6-8:   Counting and Using continue to Display Even Numbers

```html
<html>
<head>
 <title>Count and show me even numbers</title>
</head>
<body>
 <script>
   for (var i = 0; i <= 20; i++){
     if (i%2 != 0){
       continue;
     }
     document.write (i + " is an even number.<br>");
   }
 </script>
</body>
</html>
```

When used in this way, continue can replace the functionality of an `else` statement.

Figure 6-6 shows the result of running Listing 6-8 in a browser.

Figure 6-6:
Counting
and using
continue to
display even
numbers.

The `break` and `continue` statements can be useful, but they can also be dangerous. Their small size and great power make them easy to overlook when reading through code. For this reason, some programmers consider using them inside of a loop to be a bad practice. For more information on why and the complexities of the issue, read this discussion:

```
http://programmers.stackexchange.com/questions/58237/are-
         break-and-continue-bad-programming-practices
```

Part II
Organizing Your JavaScript

```
Developer Tools - chrome-extension://laookkfknpbbblfpciffpaejjkokdgca/dashboard.html

🚫 ▽  <top frame> ▼  ☐ Preserve log
> function addZ(aString) {
    aString += "z";
    return aString;
  }
⟨ undefined
> addZ("I have JavaScript skill");
⟨ "I have JavaScript skillz"
>
```

Console Search Emulation Rendering

See the article "Underscore — A Utility Belt for JavaScript" at www.dummies.com/extras/codingwithjavascript.

In this part . . .

- ✔ Discover how to work with functions.
- ✔ Find out how to create and use objects.
- ✔ See the article "Underscore — A Utility Belt for JavaScript" at `www.dummies.com/extras/codingwith javascript`.

Chapter 7

Getting Functional

· ·

In This Chapter

▶ Writing functions

▶ Documenting functions

▶ Passing parameters

▶ Returning values

▶ Organizing programs with functions

· ·

"I write as a function. Without it I would fall ill and die. It's much a part of one as the liver or intestine, and just about as glamorous."

— Charles Bukowski

Functions help you reduce code repetition by turning frequently used bits of code into reusable parts. In this chapter, you write some functions and use them to make otherwise tedious tasks easy and fun!

Don't forget to visit the website to check out the online exercises relevant to this chapter!

Understanding the Function of Functions

Functions are mini programs within your programs. Functions serve to handle particular tasks within the main program that may be required multiple times by different parts of the program.

If you've read any of the preceding chapters, you've seen a few functions in action. The following example is a simple function that, when run, simply adds a z to the end of a string.

```
function addZ(astring) {
  aString += "z";
  return aString;
}
```

To try out this function, follow these steps:

1. **Open the JavaScript Console in Chrome.**

2. **Type in the function.**

   You can type it all on one line, or you can press Shift+Enter or Shift+Return after each line to create a line break without executing the code.

3. **Press Return or Enter after the final curly brace.**

   The console should write out `undefined`.

4. **Type the following command, followed by Return or Enter, to run the function:**

   ```
   addZ("I have JavaScript skill");
   ```

   The result of running this function is shown in Figure 7-1.

Functions are a fundamental part of JavaScript programming, and they have a lot of rules and special powers that you need to be aware of as a JavaScript coder. Don't worry if you aren't able to memorize each detail about functions. It will take some practice to understand some of the more abstract concepts, and you may even need to read this chapter again. Eventually, everything will become clear to you, so just stick with it!

Figure 7-1:
Running your first function in the JavaScript console.

Using Function Terminology

Programmers have a number of words that are important to understand when they talk about functions. We use these words extensively in this chapter and throughout this book. The following list is a quick summary of some of the lingo you'll run into when you're working with functions.

Define a function

When a function appears in JavaScript code, it doesn't run. It's simply created and made available for use at a later time. The creation of the function so that it can be used later on is called *defining* a function.

You only need to define a function once in a program or on a web page. If you accidentally define the same function more than once, however, JavaScript won't complain. It will simply use the most recently defined version of the function.

For example:

```
var myFunction = new Function() {
};
```

or

```
function myFunction(){
};
```

Function head

The *function head* is the part of the function definition that includes the function keyword, the function name, and the parentheses.

For example:

```
function myFunction()
```

Function body

The *function body* is made up of the statements between the curly braces of the function.

For example:

```
{
  // function body
}
```

Call a function

When you use a function, it's called *calling* the function. Calling a function causes the statements in the function body to be executed.

For example:

```
myFunction();
```

Defining parameters and passing arguments

Parameters are names that you give to pieces of data that are provided to a function when it's called. *Arguments* are the values you provide to functions. When a function is called with arguments (according to the specified parameters of the function), programmers refer to that as *passing* the arguments into the function.

The syntax for defining a parameter is as follows:

```
function myFunction(parameter) {
```

The syntax for calling a function with an argument is as follows:

```
myFunction(myArgument);
```

Return a value

In addition to being able to accept input from the outside world, functions can also send back values after they're finished running. When a function sends back something, it's called *returning a value*.

To return a value, use the return keyword. For example:

```
return myValue;
```

The Benefits of Using Functions

Listing 7-1 shows a program that adds numbers together. It works great and does exactly what it's supposed to do, using a `for ...... in` loop (see Chapter 6).

Listing 7-1: A Program for Adding Numbers Using the for . . . in Loop

```html
<html>
<head>
  <title>Get the total</title>
</head>
<body>
  <script>
    var myNumbers = [2,4,2,7];
    var total = 0;
    for (oneNumber in myNumbers){
      total = total + myNumbers[oneNumber];
    }
    document.write(total);
  </script>
</body>
</html>
```

If we had multiple sets of numbers to add together, however, we'd need to write a new loop statement specifically for each new array of numbers.

Listing 7-2 turns the program from Listing 7-1 into a function and then uses that function to find the sums of the elements in several different arrays.

Listing 7-2: A Function for Adding Numbers from an Array

```html
<html>
<head>
  <title>Get the sum</title>
</head>
<body>
  <script>
    /**
    *Adds elements in an array
    *@param {Array.<number>} numbersToAdd
    *@return {Number} sum
    */
    function addNumbers(numbersToAdd) {
      var sum = 0;
      for (oneNumber in numbersToAdd) {
        sum = sum + numbersToAdd[oneNumber];
```

(continued)

Listing 7-2 *(continued)*

```
    }
    return sum;
}

var myNumbers = [2,4,2,7];
var myNumbers2 = [3333,222,111];
var myNumbers3 = [777,555,777,555];
var sum1 = addNumbers(myNumbers);
var sum2 = addNumbers(myNumbers2);
var sum3 = addNumbers(myNumbers3);

document.write(sum1 + "<br>");
document.write(sum2 + "<br>");
document.write(sum3 + "<br>");

</script>
</body>
</html>
```

Documenting JavaScript with JSDoc

It's a good practice to always document your JavaScript code using a standard system. The most widely used JavaScript documentation system, and thus the de-facto standard, is JSDoc.

The JSDoc language is a simple markup language that can be inserted inside of JavaScript files. Currently in its third version, JSDoc is based on the JavaDoc system that's used for documenting code written in the Java programming language.

After you've annotated your JavaScript files with JSDoc, you can use a documentation generator, such as jsdoc-toolkit, to create HTML files documenting the code.

JSDoc markup goes inside of special block comment tags. The only difference between JSDoc markup and regular JavaScript block comments is that JSDoc markup starts with /** and ends with */, whereas normal block comments in JavaScript only require one asterisk after the beginning slash. The extra asterisk in JSDoc markup tags allows you to create normal block quotes without having them be a part of the generated documentation.

The figure shows some code from the open source Angular JS JavaScript framework that has been annotated using JSDoc.

Different parts and aspects of a program can be documented with JSDoc using JDDoc tags. Here are the most popular tags:

JSDoc Tag	Explanation
@author	Programmer's name
@constructor	Indicates that a function is a constructor
@deprecated	Indicates the method is deprecated
@exception	Describes an exception thrown by a method; Synonymous with @throws
@exports	Specifies a member that is exported by the module
@param	Describes a method parameter
@private	Indicates a member is private
@return	Describes a return value. Synonymous with @returns
@returns	Describes a return value. Synonymous with @return
@see	Records an association to another object
@this	Specifies the types of the object to which the keyword this refers within a function
@throws	Describes an exception thrown by a method
@version	Indicates the version number of a library

The block comment that precedes the function in Listing 7-2 follows the format specified by the JavaScript documenting system, JSDoc. By commenting your functions using this format, you not only make your programs much easier to read, you also can use these comments to automatically generate documentation for your programs. We cover function documentation in the sidebar "Documenting JavaScript with JSDoc." You can read more about JSDoc at `http://usejsdoc.org`.

Functions are a great time, work, and space saver. Writing a useful function may initially take longer than writing JavaScript code outside of functions, but in the long term, your programs will be better organized, and you'll save yourself a lot of headaches if you get into the habit of writing functions.

Writing Functions

A function declaration must be written in a specific order. A function declaration consists of the following items, in this order:

- Function keyword
- Name of the function
- Parentheses, which may contain one or more parameters
- Pair of curly brackets containing statements

Sometimes, a function's whole purpose will be to write a message to the screen in a web page. An example of a time when it's useful to have a function like this is for displaying the current date. The following example function writes out the current date to the browser window:

```
function getTheDate(){
  var rightNow = newDate();
  document.write(rightNow.toDateString());
}
```

Follow these steps to try out this function:

1. **Open the JavaScript Console in Chrome.**

2. **Type the function into the console.**

   Use Shift + Return (or Shift + Enter) after typing each line, in order to create a line break in the console without executing the code.

3. **After you enter the final }, press Return (or Enter) to run the code.**

   Notice that nothing happens, except that the word undefined appears in the console, letting you know that the function has been accepted, but that it didn't return a value.

4. **Call the function by typing the name of the function (getTheDate) followed by parentheses, followed by a semicolon:**

```
getTheDate();
```

   The function prints out the current date and time to the browser window, and then the console displays undefined because the function doesn't have a return value; its purpose is simply to print out the date to the browser window.

The default return value of functions is undefined, so technically, undefined is a return value.

Returning Values

In the example in the preceding section, we create a function that just prints a string to the browser window. After the single document.write statement executes, there are no more statements to run and so the program exits the function and continues with the next statement after the function call.

Most functions return a value (other than undefined) after their work is done. You can then use this value in the rest of the program. Listing 7-3 shows a function that returns a value. The return value of the function is then assigned to a variable and printed to the console.

Listing 7-3:   Returning a Value from a Function

```
function getHello(){
   return "Hello!";
}

var helloText = getHello();
console.log (helloText);
```

The return statement is generally the last statement in a function. When it executes, the function exits. You can use the return statement to send any type of literal value (such as "Hello!" or 3) outside of the function or to return the value of a variable, an expression, an array or object, or even another function! (See Listing 7-4)

Listing 7-4: Returning the Result of an Expression

```
function getCircumference(){
  var radius = 12;
  return 2 * Math.PI * radius;
}

console.log (getCircumference());
```

Passing and Using Arguments

In order for functions to be able to do the same thing with different input, they need a way for programmers to give them input. In Listing 7-2, earlier in this chapter, the parentheses after the name of a function in its declaration are used to specify parameters for the function.

The difference between parameters and arguments can be confusing at first. Here's how it works:

- ✔ Parameters are the names you specify in the function definition.
- ✔ Arguments are the values you pass to the function. They take on the names of the parameters when they are passed.

When you call a function, you include data (arguments) in the places where the function definition has parameters. Note that the arguments passed to the function must be listed in the same order as the parameters in the function definition.

In the following function, we define two parameters for the myTacos function:

```
function myTacos(meat,produce){
  ...
}
```

When you call this function, you include data (arguments) in the places where the function definition has parameters. Note that the arguments passed to the function must be listed in the same order as the parameters in the function definition:

```
myTacos("beef","onions");
```

The values passed to the function will become the values of the local variables inside of the function and will be given the names of the function's parameters.

Listing 7-5 expands the `myTacos` function to print out the values of the two arguments to the console. Passing an argument is like using a `var` statement inside of the function, except that the values can come from outside of the function.

Listing 7-5:   Referring to Arguments Inside a Function Using the Parameter Names

```
function myTacos(meat,produce){
   console.log(meat); // writes "beef"
   console.log(produce); // writes "onions"
}

myTacos("beef","onions");
```

You can specify up to 255 parameters in a function definition. However, it's highly unusual to need to write a function that takes anywhere near that many parameters! Just for the sake of keeping your code clean and understandable, if you find you need a lot of parameters, you should think about whether there's a better way to do it.

Passing arguments by value

If you use a variable with one of the primitive data types to pass your argument, the argument passes *by value*. What this means is the new variable created inside the function is totally separate from the variable used to pass the argument, and no matter what happens after the value gets into the function, the variable outside of the function won't change.

Primitive data types in JavaScript are `string`, `number`, `Boolean`, `undefined`, and `null`.

In Listing 7-6, you see that several variables are created, given values, and then passed into a function. In this case, the parameters of the function have the same names as the variables used to pass the arguments. Even though the values of the variables inside the function get changed, the values of the original variables remain the same.

Listing 7-6:   Demonstration of Arguments Passed by Value

```html
<html>
<head>
  <title>Arguments Passed By Value</title>
</head>
<body>
  <script>
    /**
    * Increments two numbers
    * @param {number} number1
    * @param {number} number2
    */
    function addToMyNumbers(number1,number2){
      number1++;
      number2++;
      console.log("number 1: " + number1);
      console.log("number 2: " + number2);
    }

    var number1 = 3;
    var number2 = 12;

    addToMyNumbers(number1,number2); // pass the arguments

    console.log("original number1: " + number1);
    console.log("original number2: " + number2);
  </script>
</body>
</html>
```

Figure 7-2 shows the output of this program in the JavaScript console.

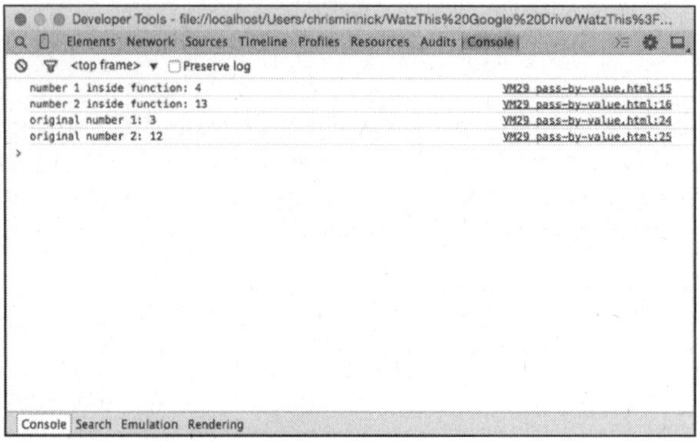

Figure 7-2:
Variables
outside of
a function
aren't
affected by
what
happens
inside the
function.

Passing arguments by reference

Whereas JavaScript primitive variables (strings, numbers, Boolean, undefined, and null) are passed to functions by value, JavaScript objects are passed *by reference*. What this means is that if you pass an object as an argument to a function, any changes to that object within the function will also change the value outside of the function. The implications and uses of passing by reference are beyond the scope of this chapter but are covered in Chapter 8.

Calling a function without all the arguments

You don't need to always call a function with the same number of parameters as are listed in the function definition. If a function definition contains three parameters, but you call it with only two, the third parameter will create a variable with a value of `undefined` in the function.

Setting default parameter values

If you want arguments to default to something other than `undefined`, you can set default values. The most widely supported and generally accepted way to do this is to test the arguments inside of the function value and set default values if the data type of the argument is `undefined`.

For example, in Listing 7-7, the function takes one parameter. Inside the function, a test is done to check whether the argument is `undefined`. If so, it will be set to a default value.

Listing 7-7:   Setting Default Argument Values

```
function welcome(yourName){
  if (typeof yourName === 'undefined'){
    yourName = "friend";
  }
}
```

In the next version of JavaScript, called ECMAScript 6, you will be able to set default values for parameters inside the function head, as shown in Listing 7-8.

Listing 7-8:   Setting Default Arguments in the Function Head

```
function welcome(yourName = "friend") {
  document.write("Hello," + yourName);
}
```

EMCAScript 6 isn't yet supported in every browser as of the publication date of this book, so this method of setting default argument values may not work for all the users of your program. For this reason, it's still best to use the more compatible method of setting defaults, as shown in Listing 7-7.

Calling a function with more argument than parameters

If you call a function with more arguments than the number of parameters, local variables won't be created for the additional arguments because the function has no way of knowing what to call them.

There is a neat trick that you can use to retrieve the values of arguments that are passed to a function but don't have a matching parameter: the `Argument-` object.

Getting into arguments with the arguments object

When you don't know how many arguments will be passed into a function, you can use the argument object, which is built-in to functions by JavaScript, to retrieve all the arguments and make use of them.

The `Arguments` object contains an array of all the arguments passed to a function. By looping through the array (using the `for` loop or the `for . . . in` loop — see Chapter 6), you can make use of every argument, even if the number of arguments may change each time the function is called.

Listing 7-9 demonstrates the use of the `Arguments` object to present a welcome message to someone with two middle names as well as someone with one middle name.

Listing 7-9:   Using the Arguments Object to Define a Function That Can Add an Arbitrary Number of Numbers

```
<html>
<head>
  <title>Welcome Message</title>
</head>
<body>
  <script>
```

```
/**
*Flexible Welcome Message
*/
function flexibleWelcome(){
  var welcome = "Welcome,";
  for (i = 0; I < arguments.length; i++) {
    welcome = welcome + arguments[i] + "";
  }
  return welcome;
  }
document.write(flexibleWelcome("Christopher" ,
      "James" , "Phoenix" , "Minnick") + "<br>");
document. write(flexibleWelcome("Eva" , "Ann" ,
      "Holland") + "<br>");

  </script>
</body>
</html>
```

Function Scope

Variables created inside a function by passing arguments or using the var keyword are only available within that function. Programmers call this feature of JavaScript *function scope.* Variables created inside of a function are destroyed when the function exits.

However, if you create a variable inside a function without using the var keyword, that variable becomes a global variable and can be changed and accessed anywhere in your program.

Accidentally creating a global variable is the source of a large number of JavaScript bugs and errors, and it's recommended that you always properly scope variables and never create a global variable unless it's absolutely necessary.

Anonymous Function

The function name part of the function head isn't required, and you can create functions without names. This may seem like an odd thing to do because a function with no name is like a dog with no name; you have no way to call it! However, anonymous functions can be assigned to variables when they are created, which gives you the same capabilities as using a name within the function head:

```
var doTheThing = function(thingToDo) {
  document.write("I will do this thing: " + thingToDo);
}
```

Knowing the differences between anonymous and named functions

There are a couple important, and sometimes useful, differences between creating a named function and assigning an anonymous function to a variable. The first is that an anonymous function assigned to a variable only exists and can only be called after the program executes the assignment. Named functions can be accessed anywhere in a program.

The second difference between named functions and anonymous functions assigned to variables is that you can change the value of a variable and assign a different function to it at any point. That makes anonymous functions assigned to variables more flexible than named functions.

Self-executing anonymous functions

Another use for anonymous functions is as *self-executing functions*. A self-executing anonymous function is a function that executes as soon as it's created.

To turn a normal anonymous function into a self-executing function, you simply wrap the anonymous function in parentheses and add a set of parentheses and a semicolon after it.

The benefit of using self-executing anonymous functions is that the variables you create inside of them are destroyed when the function exits. In this way, you can avoid conflicts between variable names, and you avoid holding variables in memory after they're no longer needed. Listing 7-10 demonstrates how to write and use self-executing anonymous functions.

Listing 7-10:   Using a Self-Executing anonymous function

```
var myVariable = "I live outside the function.";
(function() {
  var myVariable = "I live in this anonymous function";
  document.write(myVariable);
})();
document.write(myVariable);
```

Web application programmers use anonymous functions regularly to accomplish a wide variety of modern effects in web pages. You read more about how to use them in Chapters 15 and 16.

Do it Again with Recursion

You can call functions from outside of the function or from within other functions. You can even call a function from within itself. When a function calls itself, it's using a programming technique called *recursion*.

You can use recursion in many of the same cases where you would use a loop, except that it repeats the statements within a function.

Listing 7-11 shows a simple recursive function. This recursive function has one big problem, however. Can you spot it?

Listing 7-11:   A Fatally Flawed Recursive Function

```
function squareItUp(startingNumber) {
  var square = startingNumber * startingNumber;
  console.log(square);
  squareItUp(square);
}
```

Do you see the issue with this function? It never ends. It will just keep on multiplying numbers together until you stop it.

Running this function will probably crash your browser, if not your computer. No permanent damage will be done, of course, but it's enough for you to just read the code and notice the problem here.

Listing 7-12 improves upon the `squareItUp()` function by providing what's called a *base case*. A base case is the condition under which a recursive function's job is done and it should halt. Every recursive function must have a base case.

Listing 7-12:   A Recursive Function to Square Numbers Until the Number Is Greater Than 1,000,000

```
function squareItUp(startingNumber) {
  square = startingNumber * startingNumber;
```

(continued)

Listing 7-12 *(continued)*

```
if (square > 1000000) {
  console.log(square);
} else {
  squareItUp(square);
}
}
```

There. That's better! But, this function still has a big problem. What if some-one passes a negative number, zero or 1 into it? The result of any of these cases would still be an infinite loop. To protect against such a situation, we need a termination condition. In Listing 7-13, a check to make sure that the argument isn't less than or equal to 1 and that it isn't something other than a number has been added. In both cases, the function will stop immediately.

Listing 7-13:   A Recursive Function with Termination and Base Conditions

```
function squareItUp(startingNumber) {

  // Termination conditions, invalid input
  if ((typeof startingNumber != 'number') ||
      (startingNumber <= 1)) {
    return - 1; // exit the function
  }

  square = staringNumber * startingNumber;

  //Base condition
  if (square > 1000000) {
    console.log(square); // Print the final value
  } else { // If the base condition isn't met, do it
      again.
    squareItUp(square);
  }

}
```

Functions within Functions

Functions can be declared within functions. Listing 7-14 demonstrates how this technique works and how it affects the scope of variables created within the functions.

Listing 7-14:   Declaring Functions within Functions

```
function turnIntoAMartian(myName) {

  function recallName(myName) {
    var martianName = myName + " Martian";
  }
  recallName(myName);
  console.log(martianName); // returns undefined

}
```

The preceding example demonstrates how nesting a function within a function creates another layer of scope. Variables created in the inner function aren't directly accessible to the containing function. In order to get their values, a return statement is needed, as shown in Listing 7-15.

Listing 7-15:   Returning Values from an Inner Function

```
function turnIntoAMartian(myName) {

  function recallName(myName) {
    var martianName = myName + " Martian";
    return martianName;
  }
  var martianName = recallName(myName);
  console.log(martianName);

}
```

Chapter 8

Making and Using Objects

· ·

In This Chapter

▶ Understanding objects

▶ Using properties and methods

▶ Creating objects

▶ Using dot notation

▶ Working with objects

· ·

"We cannot do anything with an object that has no name."

— Maurice Blanchot "Literature and the Right to Death"

In this chapter, we show you why you should use objects, how to use them, and what special powers they have to make your programs and your programming better.

Don't forget to visit the website to check out the online exercises relevant to this chapter!

Object of My Desire

In addition to the five primitive data types (see Chapter 3,) JavaScript also has a data type called *object*. JavaScript *objects* encapsulate data and functionality in reusable components.

To understand what objects are and how they work, it's helpful to compare JavaScript objects with physical, real-life things. Take a guitar, for example.

A guitar has things that make up what it is and has things that it does. Here are a few facts about the guitar we're using for this example:

✔ It has six strings.

✔ It's black and white.

✔ It's electric.

✔ Its body is solid.

Some of the things this guitar can do (or that can be done to the guitar) are

✔ Strum strings

✔ Increase the volume

✔ Decrease the volume

✔ Tighten the strings

✔ Adjust the tone

✔ Loosen the strings

If this guitar were a JavaScript object instead of a real-life object, the things that it does would be called its *methods,* and the things that make up the guitar, such as its strings and body type, would be its properties.

Methods and properties in objects are both written the same way; as name-value pairs, with a colon separating the name and the value. When a property has a function as its value, it's known as a method.

In reality, everything within an object is a property. We just call a property with a function value by a different name: a method.

Listing 8-1 shows what our guitar's properties might look like as a JavaScript object.

Listing 8-1:   A JavaScript Guitar Object

```
var guitar = {
  bodyColor: "black",
  scratchPlateColor: "white",
  numberOfStrings: 6,
  brand: "Yamaha",
  bodyType: "solid",
  strum: function() {...},
  tune: function() {...}
};
```

Creating Objects

JavaScript has two ways to create objects:

- ✔ By writing an object literal
- ✔ By using the object constructor method

Which one you choose depends on the circumstances. In the next sections, you discover the pros and cons of each and when one is preferred over the other.

Defining objects with object literals

The object literal method of creating objects starts with a standard variable definition, using the `var` keyword, followed by the assignment operator:

```
var person =
```

In the right side of the statement, however, you'll use curly braces with comma-separated name/value pairs:

```
var person = {eyes: 2, feet: 2, hands: 2, eyeColor:
        "blue"};
```

If you don't know the properties that your object will have when you create it or if your program requires that additional properties be added a later time, you can create the object with few, or even no properties, and then add properties to it later:

```
var person = {};
person.eyes = 2;
person.hair = "brown";
```

The methods in the examples earlier in this book have mostly been used to output text. `document.write` and `console.log` both use this method of separating properties with a period, so it may look familiar to you. The dot between the object name and the property indicates that the property belongs to that object. Dot notation is covered in more detail in the "Retrieving and Setting Object Properties" section, later of this chapter.

Another thing to notice about objects is that, like arrays, objects can contain multiple different data types as the values of properties.

The not-so-well-kept secret to really understanding JavaScript is in knowing that arrays and functions are types of objects and that the number, string, and Boolean primitive data types can also be used as objects. What this means is that they have all the properties of objects and can be assigned properties in the same way as objects.

Defining objects with an Object constructor

The second way to define an object is by using an `Object` constructor. This method declares the object using `new Object` and then populates it with properties. An example of using an `Object` constructor is shown in Listing 8-2.

Listing 8-2:   Using an Object Constructor

```
var person = new Object();
person.feet = 2;
person.name = "Sandy";
person.hair = "black";
```

The `Object` constructor method of creating objects can be used, but it's generally regarded as the inferior way to create objects. The main reasons are

✔ It requires more typing than the object literal method.

✔ It doesn't perform as well in web browsers

✔ It's more difficult to read than the object literal method.

Retrieving and Setting Object Properties

After you create an object and define its properties, you'll want to be able to retrieve and change those properties. The two ways to access object properties are by using dot notation or square brackets notation.

Dot notation

In dot notation, the name of an object is followed by a period (or dot), followed by the name of the property that you want to get or set.

To create a new property called `firstName` in the person object or to modify the value of an existing `firstName` property, you would use a statement like the following:

```
person.firstName = "Glenn";
```

If the `firstName` property doesn't already exist, this statement will create it. If it does exist, it will update it with a new value.

To retrieve the value of a property using dot notation, you would use the exact same syntax, but you would move the object and property names (called the *property accessor*) into a different position in the statement. For example, if you want to concatenate the values of `person.firstName` and `person.lastName` and assign them to a new variable called `fullName`, you would do the following:

```
var fullname = person.firstName + person.lastName;
```

Or, to write out the value of a `person.firstName` to your html document, just use the property accessor as you would any variable; such as

```
document.write (person.firstName);
```

Dot notation is generally the faster to type and easier to read way to set and retrieve object property values.

Square bracket notation

Square bracket notation uses, you guessed it, square brackets after the object name in order to get and set property values. To set a property value with square bracket notation, put the name of the property in quotes inside square brackets, like this:

```
person["firstName"] = "Iggy";
```

Square bracket notation has a couple of capabilities that dot notation doesn't. The main one is that you can use variables inside of square bracket notation for cases where you don't know the name of the property that you want to retrieve when you're writing your program.

The following example does the exact same thing as the preceding example, but with a variable inside of the square brackets rather than a literal string. Using this technique, you can make a single statement that can function in many different circumstances, such as in a loop or a function:

```
var personProperty = "firstName";
person[personProperty] = "Iggy";
```

Listing 8-3 shows a simple program that creates an object called `chair`, then loops through each of the object's properties, and asks the user to input values for each. Once the user has entered a value for each of the properties, the `writeChairReceipt` function is called, which prints out each properties along with the value the user entered.

Listing 8-3:   Chair Configuration Script

```html
<html>
<head>
 <title>The WatzThis? Chair Configurator</title>
</head>
<body>
 <script>
   var myChair = {
     "cushionMaterial" : "",
     "numberOfLegs" : "",
     "legHeight" : ""
   };

   function configureChair() {
    var userValue;
    for (var property in myChair) {
      if (myChair.hasOwnProperty(property)) {
        userValue = prompt("Enter a value for " +
          property);
        myChair[property] = userValue;
      }
     }
    }

   function writeChairReceipt() {
    document.write("<h2>Your chair will have the following
        configuration:</h2>");
    for (var property in myChair) {
      if (myChair.hasOwnProperty(property)) {
        document.write(property + ": " + myChair[property]
          + "<br>");
      }
     }
    }

   configureChair();
   writeChairReceipt();
 </script>
</body>
</html>
```

Deleting Properties

You can delete properties from objects by using the delete operator. Listing 8-4 demonstrates how this operator works.

Listing 8-4:   Using the delete Operator

```
var myObject = {
  var1 : "the value",
  var2 : "another value",
  var3 : "yet another"
};

// delete var2 from myObject
delete myObject.var2;

// try to write the value of var2
document.write(myObject.var2); // result is an error
```

Working with Methods

Methods are properties with functions for their values. You define a method the same way that you define any function. The only difference is that a method is assigned to a property of an object. Listing 8-5 demonstrates the creation of an object with several properties, one of which is a method.

Listing 8-5:   Creating a Method

```
var sandwich = {
meat:"",
cheese:"",
bread:"",
condiment:"",
makeSandwich: function (meat,cheese,bread,condiment) {
  sandwich.meat = meat;
  sandwich.cheese = cheese;
  sandwich.bread = bread;
  sandwich.condiment = condiment;
  var mySandwich = sandwich.bread + ", " + sandwich.meat +
          ", " + sandwich.cheese + ", " + sandwich.
          condiment;
  return mySandwich;
}
}
```

To call the `makeSandwich` method of the `sandwich` object, you can then use dot notation just as you would access a property, but with parentheses and parameters supplied after the method name, as shown in Listing 8-6.

Listing 8-6: Calling a Method

```html
<html>
<head>
 <title>Make me a sandwich</title>
</head>
<body>
 <script>

    var sandwich = {
    meat:"",
    cheese:"",
    bread:"",
    condiment:"",
    makeSandwich: function (meat,cheese,bread,condiment) {
      sandwich.meat = meat;
      sandwich.cheese = cheese;
      sandwich.bread = bread;
      sandwich.condiment = condiment;
      var mySandwich = sandwich.bread +
        ", " + sandwich.meat + ", " +
        sandwich.cheese + ", " +
        sandwich.condiment;
      return mySandwich;
      }
    }

    var sandwichOrder =
          sandwich.makeSandwich("ham","cheddar","wheat","
          spicy mustard");
    document.write (sandwichOrder);

 </script>
</body>
</html>
```

Using this

The `this` keyword is a shorthand for referencing the containing object of a method. For example, in Listing 8-7, every instance of the object name, `sandwich`, has been replaced with `this`. When the `makeSandwich` function is called as a method of the sandwich object, JavaScript understands that `this` refers to the `sandwich` object.

Listing 8-7:   Using `this` Inside a Method

```html
<html>
<head>
 <title>Make a sandwich</title>
</head>
<body>
 <script>

   var sandwich = {
     meat:"",
     cheese:"",
     bread:"",
     condiment:"",
     makeSandwich: function(meat,cheese,bread,condiment){
       this.meat = meat;
       this.cheese = cheese;
       this.bread = bread;
       this.condiment = condiment;
       var mySandwich = this.bread + ", " + this.meat + ",
           " + this.cheese + ", " + this.condiment;
       return mySandwich;
       }
     }

   var sandwichOrder =
         sandwich.makeSandwich("ham","cheddar","wheat","
         spicy mustard");
   document.write (sandwichOrder);

 </script>
</body>
</html>
```

The result of using the `this` keyword instead of the specific object name is exactly the same in this case.

Where `this` becomes very useful is when you have a function that may apply to multiple different objects. In that case, the `this` keyword will reference the object that it's called within, rather than being tied to a specific object.

In the next sections, you find out about constructor functions and inheritance, both of which are enabled by the humble `this` statement.

An Object-Oriented Way to Become Wealthy: Inheritance

When you create objects, you're not just limited to creating specific objects, such as your guitar, your car, your cat, or your sandwich. The real beauty of objects is that you can use them to create types of objects, from which other objects can be created.

If you read the earlier sections in the chapter, every object created has been constructed directly from the Object type of object.

The examples of the constructor method of creating an object from the "Creating Objects" section, earlier in this chapter, demonstrates this clearly:

```
var person = new Object();
```

Here, a new person object of the type Object is created. This new person object contains all the default properties and methods of the Object type, but with a new name. You can then add your own properties and methods to the person object to make it specifically describe what you mean by person.

```
var person = new Object();
person.eyes = 2;
person.ears = 2;
person.arms = 2;
person.hands = 2;
person.feet = 2;
person.legs = 2;
person.species = "Homo sapien";
```

So, now you've set some specific properties of the person object. Imagine that you want to create a new object that's a specific person, like Willie Nelson. You could simply create a new object called willieNelson and give it all the same properties as the person object, plus the properties that make Willie Nelson unique.

```
var willieNelson = new Object();
willieNelson.eyes = 2;
willieNelson.ears = 2;
willieNelson.arms = 2;
willieNelson.hands = 2;
willieNelson.feet = 2;
willieNelson.legs = 2;
willieNelson.species = "Homo sapien";
willieNelson.occupation = "musician";
willieNelson.hometown = "Austin";
willieNelson.hair = "Long";
willieNelson.genre = "country";
```

This method of defining the willieNelson object is wasteful, however. It requires you to do a lot of work, and there's no indication here that Willie Nelson is a person. He just happens to have all the same properties as a person.

The solution is to create a new type of object, called `Person` and then make the `willieNelson` object be of the type `Person`.

Notice that when we talk about a type of object, we always capitalize the name of the object type. This isn't a requirement, but it is a nearly universal convention. For example, we say

```
var person = new Object();
```

or

```
var willieNelson = new Person();
```

Constructing Objects with constructor functions

To create a new type of object, you define a new constructor function. Constructor functions are formed just like any function in JavaScript, but they use the `this` keyword to assign properties to a new object. The new object then inherits the properties of the object type.

Here is a constructor function for our `Person` object type:

```
function Person(){
  this.eyes = 2;
  this.ears = 2;
  this.arms = 2;
  this.hands = 2;
  this.feet = 2;
  this.legs = 2;
  this.species = "Homo sapien";
}
```

To create a new object of the type `Person` now, all you need to do is to assign the function to a new variable. For example:

```
var willieNelson = new Person()
```

The `willieNelson` object inherits the properties of the `Person` object type. Even though you haven't specifically created any properties for the `willieNelson` object, it contains all the properties of `Person`.

To test this out, run the code in Listing 8-8 in a web browser.

Listing 8-8:   Testing Inheritance

```html
<html>
<head>
 <title>Inheritance demo</title>
</head>
<body>
 <script>

   function Person(){
      this.eyes = 2;
      this.ears = 2;
      this.arms = 2;
      this.hands = 2;
      this.feet = 2;
      this.legs = 2;
      this.species = "Homo sapien";
   }
   var willieNelson = new Person();
   alert("Willie Nelson has " + willieNelson.feet + "
         feet!");
 </script>
</body>
</html>
```

The result of running Listing 8-8 in a browser is shown in Figure 8-1.

Figure 8-1:
Willie
Nelson
is a
`Person`

Modifying an object type

Suppose that you have your `Person` object type, which serves as the prototype for several objects. At some point you realize that the person, as well as all the objects that inherit from it, ought to have a few more properties.

To modify a prototype object, use the `prototype` property that every object inherits from `Object`. Listing 8-9 shows how this works.

Listing 8-9:   Modifying a prototype Object

```
function Person(){
  this.eyes = 2;
  this.ears = 2;
  this.arms = 2;
  this.hands = 2;
  this.feet = 2;
  this.legs = 2;
  this.species = "Homo sapien";
}

var willieNelson = new Person();
var johnnyCash = new Person();
var patsyCline = new Person();

// Person needs more properties!
Person.prototype.knees = 2;
Person.prototype.toes = 10;
Person.prototype.elbows = 2;

// Check the values of existing objects for the new
          properties
document.write (patsyCline.toes); // outputs 10
```

Creating Objects with Object.create

Yet another way to create objects from other objects is to use the `Object.create` method. This method has the benefit of not requiring you to write a constructor function. It just copies the properties of a specified object into a new object. When an object inherits from another object, the object it inherits from is called the prototype.

Listing 8-10 shows how `Object.create` can be used to create the `willieNelson` object from a prototype.

Listing 8-10: Using Object.create to Create an Object from a Prototype

```
// create a generic Person
var Person = {
  eyes: 2,
  arms: 2,
  feet: 2
}

// create the willieNelson object, based on Person
var willieNelson = Object.create(Person);

// test an inherited property
document.write (willieNelson.feet); // outputs 2
```

Part III
JavaScript on the Web

In this part . . .

- Find out how to use the Window object to control the browser.
- Master manipulating documents with the DOM.
- Get the inside scoop on using events in JavaScript.
- Figure out how to integrate input and output.
- Discover how to work with CSS and graphics.
- Find out how to deal with slow web pages in the article "Deferred Loading with JavaScript" at `www.dummies.com/extras/codingwithjavascript`.

Chapter 9

Controlling the Browser with the Window Object

"In making theories, always keep a window open so that you can throw one out if necessary."

— Bela Lugosi

The Browser Object Model (BOM) allows JavaScript to interact with the functionality of the web browser. Using the BOM, you can create and resize windows, display alert messages, and change the current page being displayed in the browser.

In this chapter, you discover what can be done with the browser window and how to use it to write better JavaScript programs.

Understanding the Browser Environment

Web browsers are complicated pieces of software. When they work well, they operate seamlessly and integrate all their functions into a smooth and seemingly simple web browsing experience. We all know that web browsers have an occasional hiccup and sometimes even crash. To understand why this happens, and to be able to make better use of browsers, it's important to know the many different parts of the web browser and how these parts interact with each other.

The user interface

The part of the web browser that you interact with when you type in a URL, click the home button, create or use a bookmark, or change your browser settings is called the user interface, or browser chrome (not to be confused with Google's Chrome browser).

The browser chrome consists of the web browser's menus, window frames, toolbars, and buttons that are outside of the main content window where web pages load, as shown in Figure 9-1.

Loader

The *loader* is the part of a web browser that communicates with web servers and downloads web pages, scripts, CSS, graphics, and all the other components of a web page. Most often, loading is the part of displaying a web page that creates the longest wait time for the user.

Figure 9-1:
The browser chrome.

The *HTML page* is the first part of a web page that must be downloaded, as it contains links and embedded scripts and styles that need to be processed in order to display the page.

Figure 9-2 shows the Chrome Developer Tools' Network tab. It displays a graphical view of everything that happens during the loading of a web page, along with a timeline showing how long the loading of each part takes.

Once the HTML document is downloaded, browsers will open several connections to the server in order to download the other parts of the web page as quickly as possible. Generally, the parts of a web page that are linked from an HTML document (also known as the *resources*) are loaded in the order in which they appear in the HTML document. For example, a script that is linked in the head element of the page will be loaded before one that's linked at the bottom of the page.

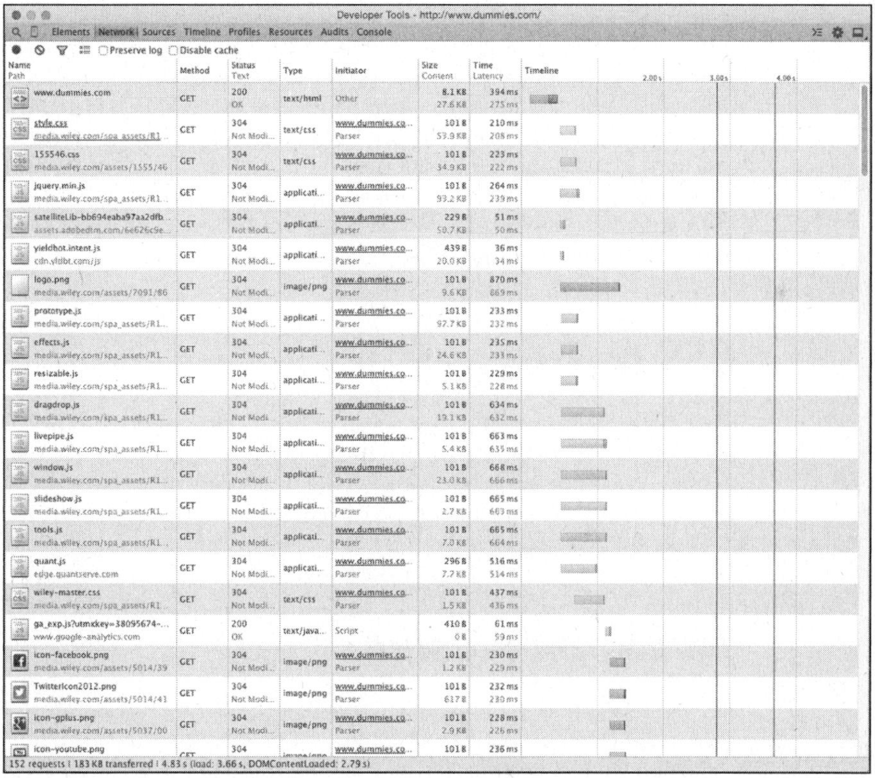

Figure 9-2: Web browser loading.

The load order of resources is critical to the efficiency and speed at which the page can be displayed to the user. In order for a web page to be displayed correctly, the CSS styles that apply to that page need to be loaded and parsed. Because of this, CSS should always be loaded in the head element at the top of the web page.

JavaScript sometimes affects the display of a web page as well, but more often, it affects only the functionality. When a script will affect the display of a web page, it should be loaded in the head of the document (after the CSS). Scripts that aren't critical to how the web page appears should be linked from the very end of the body element (right before the `</body>`), so as to not create a blocking scenario in which the browser waits for scripts to load before displaying anything to the user.

HTML parsing

After a web page is downloaded, the HTML parsing component of the browser goes to work parsing the HTML to create a model (called the Document Object Model or DOM) of the web page. The DOM, which is covered in detail in Chapter 10, is like a map of your web page. JavaScript programmers use this map to manipulate and access all the different parts of a web page.

Upon completion of the HTML parsing, the browser begins downloading the other components of the web page.

CSS parsing

Once the CSS for a web page is completely downloaded, the web browser will parse the styles and figure out which ones apply to the HTML document. CSS parsing is a complex process involving multiple passes over a document in order to apply each style correctly and to take into account how the styles impact each other.

JavaScript parsing

The next step in displaying a web page is the JavaScript parsing. The JavaScript parser compiles and runs every script in your web page in the order in which it appears in the document. If your JavaScript code adds or removes elements, text, or styles within the HTML DOM, the browser will update the HTML and CSS renderings accordingly.

Layout and rendering

Finally, once all the web page's resources have been loaded and parsed, the browser determines how to display the page and then displays it. Unless you've specified that a script included earlier in the document should wait until the end to be executed, the layout and rendering of your scripts will occur in the order they're included in the document.

In general, it's better to display a web page to the user as quickly as possible, even if the page may not be fully functional when it first appears. Modern websites frequently employ this strategy specifically (called *deferred loading*) to improve the perceived performance of their pages. If you've ever opened a web page and had to wait for a moment before you can use a form or interactive element, you've seen deferred loading in action.

Igniting the BOM

JavaScript programmers can find out information about a user's web browser and control aspects of the user's experience through an API called the Browser Object Model.

There is no official standard for the Browser Object Model. Different browsers implement it in different ways. However, there are some generally accepted standards for how JavaScript interacts with web browsers.

The Navigator object

The Navigator object provides JavaScript with access to information about the user's web browser. The Navigator object takes its name from the first web browser to implement it, Netscape Navigator. The Navigator object isn't built into JavaScript. Rather, it's a feature of web browsers that is accessible using JavaScript. Nearly every web browser (and every modern web browser) has adopted the same terminology to refer to this highest-level browser object.

The Navigator object accesses helpful information such as

✔ The name of the web browser

✔ The version of the web browser

✔ The physical location of the computer the browser is running on (if the user allows the browser to access geolocation data).

✔ The language of the browser

✔ The type of computer the browser is running on

Table 9-1 shows all the properties of the browser `Navigator` object.

Table 9-1 The Properties of the Navigator Object

Property	Use
appCodeName	Gets the code name of the browser
appName	Gets the name of the browser
appVersion	Gets the browser version information
cookieEnabled	Tells whether cookies are enabled in the browser
geolocation	Can be used to locate the user's physical location
language	Gets the language of the browser
onLine	Identifies whether the browser is online
platform	Gets the platform the browser was compiled for
product	Gets the browser engine name of the browser
userAgent	Gets the user-agent the browser sends to web servers.

To get the properties of the `Navigator` object, you use the same syntax used to get the properties of any object — namely, dot notation or brackets notation. Listing 9.1, when opened in a web browser, will display all the current properties and values of the `Navigator` object.

Listing 9-1: Properties of the Navigator Object and Their Values

```html
<html>
<head>
  <style>
    .columns {
      -webkit-column-count: 6; /* Chrome, Safari, Opera */
      -moz-column-count: 6; /* Firefox */
      column-count: 6;
      }
  </style>
</head>
<body>
  <div class="columns">
    <script>
      for (var prop in navigator){
        document.write (prop + ": " + navigator[prop] +
          "<br>");
      }
    </script>
  </div>
</body>
</html>
```

Figure 9-3 shows the output of Listing 9.1 when opened in a web browser.

If you run Listing 9.1 yourself, you'll notice something interesting about the output: The values for the AppName properties are seemingly just plain wrong. For example, the browser used to generate the Figure 9-3 was Google Chrome, but AppName lists it as Netscape.

This misleading value is a relic from the days when programmers used the properties of the Navigator object to detect whether a user was using a particular browser and supported certain features.

When new browsers, such as Chrome and Firefox, came along, those browsers adopted the Netscape browser AppName value in order to make sure they were compatible with websites that detected features in this way.

Today, browser detection isn't recommended, and you can use better ways to detect browser support for particular functionality than by looking at the AppName property. The most common way to detect features today is by examining the DOM for objects associated with the feature you want to use. For example, if you want to find out if a browser supports the HTML5 audio element, you can use the following test:

```
var test_audio= document.createElement("audio");
if (test_audio.play) {
  console.log ("Browser supports HTML5 audio");
  } else {
  console.log ("Browser doesn't support HTML5 audio");
  }
```

The Window object

The main area of a web browser is called the *window*. This is the area into which HTML documents (and associated resources) load. Each tab in a web browser is represented in JavaScript by an instance of the `Window` object. The `Window` object's properties are listed in Table 9-2.

Table 9-2	The Window Object's Properties
Property	**Use**
closed	A Boolean value indicating whether a window has been closed or not
defaultStatus	Gets or sets the default text in the status bar of a window
document	Refers to the `Document` object for the window
frameElement	Gets the element, such as `<iframe>` or `<object>`, that the window is embedded in
frames	Lists all the subframes in the current window
history	Gets the user's browser history for the current window.
innerHeight	Gets the inner height of the window
innerWidth	Gets the inner width of the window
length	Gets the number of frames in the window
location	Gets the `Location` object for the window
name	Gets or sets the name of the window
navigator	Gets the `Navigator` object for the window
opener	Gets the `Window` object that created the current window
outerHeight	Gets the outer height of the window, including scrollbars and toolbars
pageXOffset	Gets the number of pixels that have been scrolled horizontally in the window
pageYOffset	Gets the number of pixels that have been scrolled vertically in the window
parent	Refers to the parent of the current window
screen	Refers to the `Screen` object of the window

Property	Use
`screenLeft`	Gets the horizontal pixel distance from the left side of the main screen to the left side of the current window
`screenTop`	Gets the vertical pixel distance from the top of the window relative to the top of the screen
`screenX`	Gets the horizontal coordinate relative to the screen
`screenY`	Gets the vertical coordinate relative to the screen
`self`	Refers to the current window
`top`	Refers to the topmost browser window

Some of the most common uses for the window properties include

✔ Opening a new location in the browsers window

✔ Finding the size of a browser window

✔ Returning to a previously open page (as in the back button functionality)

Opening a web page with the window.location property

Getting the value of the `window.location` property will return the URL of the current page. Setting the value of the `window.location` property with a new URL causes the browser to load the web page at that URL in the window.

Listing 9.2 is a web page with a script that requests a web page address from the user and then loads that page in the current browser window.

Listing 9-2: A Script for Loading a Web Page in the Browser Window Using the window.location Property

```
<html>
<head>
  <script>
    function loadNewPage (url){
      window.location = url;
    }
  </script>
</head>
<body>
  <script>
    var newURL = prompt("Please enter a web page
          address!");
    loadNewPage(newURL);
  </script>
</body>
</html>
```

Figure 9-4 shows the output of Listing 9-2.

Figure 9-4:
The
window.
location
property in
action.

Determining the size of a browser window

When you're designing a website or a web application to work and function on different types of devices (a technique known as *responsive design*), knowing the size of the web browser, particularly the width, is critical.

The `window.innerWidth` and `window.innerHeight` properties give you this information, in pixels, for the current web browser window.

Using CSS to determine the size of a browser window is also possible and quite common. However, there are some differences in how CSS and JavaScript treat scrollbars that may influence which technique you decide to use.

Try a simple responsive design example using JavaScript. Run the program in Listing 9-3 in your web browser. If your web browser window width is below 500 pixels, one message will be displayed. If your window's width is greater than 500 pixels, a different message will be displayed.

Listing 9-3: Changing a Web Page Based on the Width of the Window

```html
<html>
<head>
  <title>Adapting to the window.innerWidth</title>
</head>
<body>
  <script>
    var currentWidth = window.innerWidth;
    if (currentWidth > 500) {
      document.write("<h1>Your window is big.</h1>");
    } else {
      document.write("<h1>Your window is small.</h1>");
    }
  </script>
</body>
</html>
```

To test out the responsive design example in Listing 9.3, follow these steps:

1. **In your web browser, open an HTML document containing the code in Listing 9-3.**

   If your window is more than 500px wide when you open your page, you'll see a message that your window is big.

2. **Drag the lower right corner of your browser to make the window as narrow as you can, as shown in Figure 9-5.**

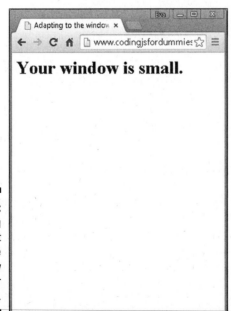

Figure 9-5:
Displaying a different message for narrow browser width.

3. Click your browser's refresh button, or press Command+R (on Mac) or Ctrl+R (on Windows), to reload the page.

Notice that the message on the page now says your browser's window is small.

Creating a Back button using location and history

The history property of the window object is a read-only reference to the history object, which stores information about the pages the user has accessed in the current browser window. By far the most common use of the history object is to enable buttons that return the user to a previously viewed page.

Listing 9-4:   Implementing a Back Button in a Web Application

```
<html>
<head>
  <title>Creating a Back button</title>
  <script>
    function takeMeBack () {
      window.location(window.history.go(-1));
    }
    function getHistoryLength () {
      var l = window.history.length;
      return l;
    }
  </script>
</head>
<body>
  <script>
    var historyLength = getHistoryLength();
    document.write ("<p>Welcome! The number of pages
          you've visited in this window is: " +
          historyLength + ".</p> ");
  </script>
  <br>
  <a href="javascript:void(0);" onclick="takeMeBack();">Go
          Back</a>
</body>
</html>
```

To use the back button in Listing 9-4, follow these steps:

1. Open a new browser window and visit any page you like, such as www.watzthis.com.

2. While in that same browser window, open an HTML document containing the code in Listing 9-4.

3. Click the Go Back link.

Your browser will take you back to the last page you visited before the one containing the Back button.

Care to guess what happens if you open Listing 9-4 in a new browser tab before accessing any other web pages in that tab? If you guessed that nothing will happen, you're correct! If only ONE page (the current one) has been displayed in a window, there's nothing to go back to.

Using the `Window` object's methods

In addition to its properties, the `Window` object also has some useful methods that JavaScript programmers should know and use. Table 9-3 shows the complete list of these methods.

A method is just another name for a function that's contained within an object.

Table 9-3	The Window Object's Methods
Method	*Use*
`alert()`	Displays an alert box with a message and an OK button
`atob()`	Decodes a base-64 encoded string
`blur()`	Causes the current window to lose focus
`clearInterval()`	Cancels the timer set using setInterval()
`clearTimeout()`	Cancels the timer set using setTimeout()
`close()`	Closes the current window or notification
`confirm()`	Displays a dialogue box with an optional message and two buttons; OK and Cancel
`createPopup()`	Creates a pop-up window
`focus()`	Sets the current window into focus
`moveBy()`	Moves the current window by a specified amount
`moveTo()`	Relocates a window to a specified position
`open()`	Opens a new window
`print()`	Prints the contents of the current window
`prompt()`	Displays a dialogue box prompting the user for input
`resizeBy()`	Resizes the window by a specified number of pixels
`resizeTo()`	Resizes a window to a specified height and width.
`scrollBy()`	Scrolls the document by a specified amount
`scrollTo()`	Scrolls the document to a specific set of coordinates

Table 9-3 *(continued)*

Method	Use
`setInterval()`	Calls a function or executes an expression repeatedly at specified intervals (in milliseconds)
`setTimeout()`	Calls a function or executes an expression after a specified interval (in milliseconds)
`stop()`	Stops the current window from loading

Chapter 10

Manipulating Documents with the DOM

"No object is mysterious. The mystery is your eye."

— Elisabeth Bowen

*U*nderstanding the DOM is key to being able to manipulate the text or HTML in a web page. Using the DOM, you can create animations, update data without refreshing web pages, move objects around in a browser, and much more!

Understanding the DOM

The Document Object Model is the interface for JavaScript to talk to and work with HTML documents inside of browser windows. The DOM can be visualized as an inverted tree, with each part of the HTML document branching off of its containing part.

Listing 10-1 is the markup for a web page. The DOM representation is shown in Figure 10-1.

Listing 10-1:   An HTML Document

```
<html>
<head>
  <title>Bob's Appliances</title>
</head>
<body>
  <header>
    <img src="logo.gif" width="100" height="100" alt="Site
         Logo">
  </header>
  <div>
    <h1>Welcome to Bob's</h1>
    <p>The home of quality appliances</p>
  </div>
  <footer>
    copyright &copy; Bob
  </footer>
</body>
</html>
```

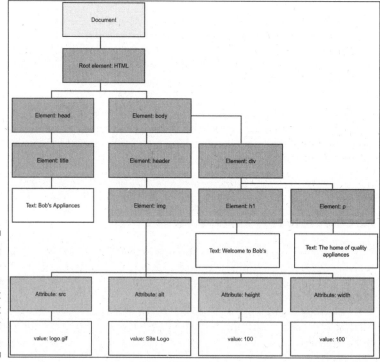

Figure 10-1:
A represen-
tation of the
Document
Object
Model for
Listing 10-1.

A DOM tree is made up of individual components, called *nodes*. The main node, from which every other node springs, is called the *document node*. The node under the document node is the *root element node*. For HTML documents, the root node is HTML. After the root node, every element, attribute, and piece of content in the document is represented by a node in the tree that comes from another node in the tree.

The DOM has several different types of nodes:

- ✔ **Document node:** The entire HTML document is represented in this node
- ✔ **Element nodes:** The HTML elements
- ✔ **Attribute nodes:** The Attributes associated with elements
- ✔ **Text nodes:** The text content of elements
- ✔ **Comment nodes:** The HTML comments in a document

Node Relationships

HTML DOM trees resemble family trees in the hierarchical relationship between nodes. In fact, the technical terms used to describe relationships between nodes in a tree take their names from familial relationships.

- ✔ Every node, except the root node, has one *parent*.
- ✔ Each node may have any number of *children*.
- ✔ Nodes with the same parent are *siblings*.

Because HTML documents often have multiple elements that are of the same type, the DOM allows you to access distinct elements in a node list using an index number. For example, you can refer to the first <p> element in a document as p[0], and the second <p> element node as p[1].

Although a node list may look like an array, it's not. You can loop through the contents of a node list, but you can't use array methods on node lists.

In Listing 10-2, the three <p> elements are all children of the <div> element. Because they have the same parent, they are siblings.

In Listing 10-2, the HTML comments are also children of the section element. The last comment before the closing section tag is called the *last child* of the section.

By understanding the relationships between document nodes, you can use the DOM tree to find any element within a document.

Listing 10-2: Demonstration of Parent, Child, and Sibling Relationships in an HTML Document

```
<html>
<head>
  <title>The HTML Family</title>
</head>
<body>
  <section> <!-- proud parent of 3 p elements, child of
        body -->
    <p>First</p> <!-- 1st child of section element,
        sibling of 2 p elements -->
    <p>Second</p> <!-- 2nd p child of section element,
        sibling of 2 p elements -->
    <p>Third</p> <!-- 3rd p child of section element,
        sibling of 2 p elements -->
  </section>
</body>
</html>
```

Listing 10-3 is an HTML document containing a script that outputs all the child nodes of the `section` element.

Listing 10-3: Displaying the Child Nodes of the section Element

```
<html>
<head>
  <title>The HTML Family</title>
</head>
<body>
  <section> <!-- proud parent of 3 p elements, child of
        body -->
    <p>First</p> <!-- 1st child of section element,
        sibling of 2 p elements -->
    <p>Second</p> <!-- 2nd p child of section element,
        sibling of 2 p elements -->
    <p>Third</p> <!-- 3rd p child of section element,
        sibling of 2 p elements -->
  </section>
  <h1>Nodes in the section element</h1>
  <script>
    var myNodelist =
        document.body.childNodes[1].childNodes;
    for (i = 0; i < myNodelist.length; i++){
      document.write (myNodelist[i] + "<br>");
    }
  </script>
</body>
</html>
```

Figure 10-2 shows what the output of Listing 10-3 looks like in a browser. Notice that the first child node of the `section` element is a text node. If you look closely at the HTML markup in Listing 10-3, you'll see that there is a single space between the opening `section` tag and the comment. Even something as simple as this single space creates an entire node in the DOM tree. This fact needs to be taken into consideration when you're navigating the DOM using relationships between nodes.

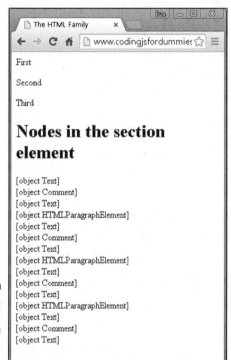

Figure 10-2:
Viewing the output of Listing 10-3.

The HTML DOM also provides a couple keywords for navigating nodes using their positions relative to their siblings or parents. The relative properties are

- `firstChild`: References the first child of a node
- `lastChild`: References the last child of the node
- `nextSibling`: References the next node with the same parent node
- `previousSibling`: References the previous node with the same parent node

Listing 10-4 shows how you can use these relative properties to traverse the DOM.

Listing 10-4:   Using firstChild and lastChild to Highlight Navigation Links

```html
<html>
<head>
  <title>Iguanas Are No Fun</title>
  <script>
    function boldFirstAndLastNav() {
      document.body.childNodes[1].firstChild.style.
          fontWeight="bold";
      document.body.childNodes[1].lastChild.style.
          fontWeight="bold";
    }
  </script>

</head>
<body>
  <nav><a href="home.html">Home</a> | <a
        href="why.html">Why Are Iguanas No Fun?</a> |
        <a href="what.html">What Can Be Done?</a> | <a
        href="contact.html">Contact Us</a></nav>
  <p>Iguanas are no fun to be around. Use the links above
        to learn more.</p>
  <script>
    boldFirstAndLastNav();
  </script>
</body>
</html>
```

Notice in Listing 10-4 that all the spacing must be removed between the elements within the <nav> element in order for the firstChild and lastChild properties to access the correct elements that we want to select and style.

Figure 10-3 shows what the document in Listing 10-4 looks like when previewed in a browser. Notice that just the first and last links in the navigation are bold.

This is the first example in which we use the DOM to make a change to existing elements within the document. However, this method of selecting elements is almost never used. It's too prone to mistakes and too difficult to interpret and use.

In the next section, you see that the DOM provides us with a much better means of traversing and manipulating the DOM than counting its children.

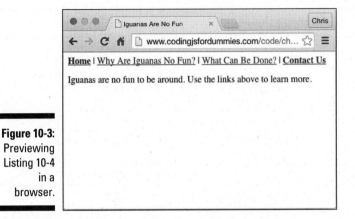

Figure 10-3:
Previewing
Listing 10-4
in a
browser.

Using the Document Object's Properties and Methods

The Document object provides properties and methods for working with HTML documents. The complete list of Document object properties is shown in Table 10-1. The Document object's methods are shown in Table 10-2.

Table 10-1	The Document Object's Properties
Property	*Use*
anchors	Gets a list of all anchors (`<a>` elements with name attributes) in the document
applets	Gets an ordered list of all the applets in the document
baseURI	Gets the base URI of the document
body	Gets the `<body>` or `<frameset>` node of the document body
cookie	Gets or sets the name/value pairs of cookies in the document
doctype	Gets the Document Type Declaration associated with the document
documentElement	Gets the element that is the root of the document (for example, the `<html>` element of an HTML document)
documentMode	Gets the mode used by the browser to render the document

(continued)

Table 10-1 *(continued)*

Property	Use
documentURI	Gets or sets the location of the document
domain	Gets the domain name of the server that loaded the document
embeds	Gets a list of all `<embed>` elements in the document
forms	Gets a collection of all `<form>` elements in the document
head	Gets the `<head>` element in the document
images	Gets a list of all `<img>` elements in the document
implementation	Gets the `DOMImplementation` object that handles the document
lastModified	Gets the date and time the current document was last modified
links	Gets a collection of all `<area>` and `<a>` elements in the document that contain the `href` attribute
readyState	Gets the loading status of the document. Returns `loading` while the document is loading, `interactive` when it has finished parsing, and `complete` when it has completed loading
referrer	Gets the URL of the page that the current document was linked from
scripts	Gets a list of `<scripts>` elements in the document
title	Gets or sets the title of the document
URL	Gets the full URL of the document

Table 10-2	The Document Object's Methods
Method	*Use*
addEventListener()	Assigns an event handler to the document
adoptNode()	Adopts a node from an external document
close()	Finishes the output writing stream of the document that was previously opened with `document.open()`
createAttribute()	Creates an attribute node
createComment()	Creates a comment node

Method	Use
createDocumentFragment()	Creates an empty document fragment
createElement()	Creates an element node
createTextNode()	Creates a text node
getElementById()	Gets the element that has the specified ID attribute
getElementByClassName()	Gets all elements with specified class name
getElementByName()	Gets all elements with the specified name
getElementsByTagName()	Gets all elements with the specified tag name
importNode()	Copies and imports a node from an external document
normalize()	Clears the empty text nodes and joins adjacent nodes
open()	Opens a document for writing
querySelector()	Gets the first element that matches the specified group of selector(s) in the document
querySelectorAll()	Gets a list of all the elements that match the specified selector(s) in the document
removeEventListener()	Clears an event handler that had been added using the .addEventListener() method from the document
renameNode()	Renames an existing node
write()	Writes JavaScript code or HTML expressions to a document
writeIn()	Writes JavaScript code or HTML expressions to a document and adds a new line character after each statement

Using the Element Object's Properties and Methods

The Element object provides properties and methods for working with HTML elements within a document. Table 10-3 shows all the properties of the Element object. Table 10-4 lists all the methods of the Element object.

Table 10-3	The Element Object's properties
Method	*Use*
accessKey	Gets or sets the accesskey attribute of the element
attributes	Gets a collection of all the element's attribute registered to the specified node (returns a NameNodeMap)
childElementCount	Gets the number of child elements in the specified node
childNodes	Gets a list of the element's child nodes
children	Gets a list of the element's child elements
classList	Gets the class name(s) of the element
className	Gets or sets the value of the class attribute of the element
clientHeight	Gets the inner height of an element, including padding
clientLeft	Gets the left border width of the element
clientTop	Gets the top border width of the element
clientWidth	Gets the width of the element, including padding
contentEditable	Gets or sets whether the element is editable
dir	Gets or sets the value of the dir attribute of the element
firstChild	Gets the first child node of the element
firstElementChild	Gets the first child element of the element
id	Gets or sets the value of the id attribute of the element
innerHTML	Gets or sets the content of the element
isContentEditable	Returns true if the content of an element is editable; returns false if it is not editable
lang	Gets or sets the base language of the elements attribute
lastChild	Gets the last child node of the element
lastElementChild	Gets the last child element of the element
namespaceURI	Gets the namespace URI for the first node in the element
nextSibling	Gets the next node at the same node level

Method	Use
nextElement Sibling	Gets the next element at the same node level
nodeName	Gets the current node's name
nodeType	Gets the current node's type
nodeValue	Gets or sets the value of the node
offsetHeight	Gets the height of the element, including vertical padding, borders, and scrollbar
offsetWidth	Gets the width of the element, including horizontal padding, borders, and scrollbar
offsetLeft	Gets the horizontal offset position of the element.
offsetParent	Gets the offset container of the element
offsetTop	Gets the vertical offset position of the element
ownerDocument	Gets the root element (document node) for an element
parentNode	Gets the parent node of the element
parentElement	Gets the parent element node of the element
previousSibling	Gets the previous node at the same node tree level
previousElement Sibling	Gets the previous element node at the same node tree level
scrollHeight	Gets the entire height of the element, including padding
scrollLeft	Gets or sets the number of pixels the element's content is scrolled horizontally
scrollTop	Gets or sets the number of pixels the element's content is scrolled vertically
scrollWidth	Gets the entire width of the element, including padding
style	Gets or sets the value of the style attribute of the element
tabIndex	Gets or sets the value of the tabindex attribute of the element
tagName	Gets the tag name of the element
textContent	Gets or sets the textual content of the node and its descendants
title	Gets or sets the value of the title attribute of the element
length	Gets the number of nodes in the NodeList

Table 10-4	The Element Object's Methods
Method	**Use**
`addEventLIstener()`	Registers an event handler to the element
`appendChild()`	Inserts a new child node to the element (as a last child node)
`blur()`	Eliminates focus from the element
`click()`	Replicates a mouse-click on the element
`cloneNode()`	Clones the element
`compareDocumentPosition()`	Compares the document position of two elements
`contains()`	Yields `true` if the node is a descendant of a node; otherwise, yields `false`
`focus()`	Gives focus to the element
`getAttribute()`	Gets the specified attribute value of the element node
`getAttributeNode()`	Gets the specified attribute node
`getElementsByClassName()`	Gets a collection of all child elements with the stated class name.
`getElementByTagName()`	Gets a collection of all the child elements with the stated tag name
`getFeature()`	Gets an object that implements the API's of the stated feature
`hasAttribute()`	Yields `true` if the element has the stated attribute; otherwise, yields `false`
`hasAttributes()`	Yields `true` if the element has any attributes; otherwise, yields `false`
`hasChildNodes()`	Yields `true` if the element has any child nodes; otherwise, yields `false`
`insertBefore()`	Enters a new child node before the stated existing node
`isDefaultNamespace()`	Yields `true` if the stated `namespaceURI` is the default; otherwise, yields `false`
`isEqualNode()`	Evaluates to see whether two elements are equal

Method	Use
isSameNode()	Evaluates to see whether two elements are the same node
isSupported()	Yields true if the stated feature is supported on the element
normalize()	Joins the specified nodes with their adjacent nodes and removes any empty text nodes
querySelector()	Gets the first child element that matches the stated CSS selector(s) of the element
querySelectorAll()	Gets all the child elements that match the stated CSS selector(s) of the element
removeAttribute()	Takes the stated attribute out of the element
removeAttributeNode()	Takes the stated attribute node out of the element and retrieves the removed node
removeChild()	Removes the stated child node
replaceChild()	Replaces specified child node with another
removeEventListener()	Removes the specified event handler
setAttribute()	Changes or sets the stated attribute to the specified value
setAttributeNode()	Changes or sets the stated attribute node
toString()	Changes an element to a string
item()	Get the node at the stated index in the NodeList

Working with the Contents of Elements

You can display node types and node values by using the HTML DOM. You also can set property values of elements within the DOM using the Element object. When you use JavaScript to set the properties of DOM elements, the new values are reflected in real-time within the HTML document.

Changing the properties of elements in a web document in order to reflect them instantly in the browser, without needing to refresh or reload the web page, is a cornerstone of what used to be called Web 2.0.

innerHTML

The most important property of an element that you can modify through the DOM is the innerHTML property.

The innerHTML property of an element contains everything between the beginning and ending tag of the element. For example, in the following code, the innerHTML property of the div element contains a p element and its text node child:

```
<body><div><p>This is some text.</p></div></body>
```

It's very common in web programming to create empty div elements in your HTML document and then use the innerHTML property to dynamically insert HTML into the elements.

To retrieve and display the value of the innerHTML property, you can use the following code:

```
var getTheInner = document.body.firstChild.innerHTML;
document.write (getTheInner);
```

In the preceding code, the value that will be output by the document.write() method is

```
<p>This is some text.</p>
```

Setting the innerHTML property is done in the same way that you set the property of any object:

```
document.body.firstChild.innerHTML = "Hi there!";
```

The result of running the preceding JavaScript will be that the p element and the sentence of text in the original markup will be replaced with the words "Hi There!" The original HTML document remains unchanged, but the DOM representation and the rendering of the web page will be updated to reflect the new value. Because the DOM representation of the HTML document is what the browser displays, the display of your web page will also be updated.

Setting attributes

To set the value of an HTML attribute, you can use the setAttribute() method:

```
document.body.firstChild.innerHTML.setAttribute("class",
        "myclass");
```

The result of running this statement is that the first child element of the body element will be given a new attribute named "class" with a value of "myclass".

Getting Elements by ID, Tag Name, or Class

The getElementBy methods provide easy access to any element or groups of elements in a document without relying on parent/child relationships of nodes. The three most commonly used ways to access elements are

✔ getElementById

✔ getElementsByTagName

✔ getElementsByClassName

getElementById

By far the most widely used method for selecting elements, getElementById is essential to modern web development. With this handy little tool, you can find and work with any element simply by referencing a unique id attribute. No matter what else happens in the HTML document, getElementById will always be there for you and will reliably select the exact element that you want.

Listing 10-5 demonstrates the awesome power of getElementById to enable you to keep all your JavaScript together in your document or to modularize your code. By using getElementById, you can work with any element, anywhere in your document just as long as you know its id.

Listing 10-5:   Using getElementById to Select Elements

```html
<html>
<head>
  <title>Using getElementById</title>
  <script>
    function calculateMPG(miles,gallons){
      document.getElementById("displayMiles").innerHTML =
          parseInt(miles);
      document.getElementById("displayGallons").innerHTML
          = parseInt(gallons);
      document.getElementById("displayMPG").innerHTML =
          miles/gallons;
    }
  </script>
</head>
<body>
  <p>You drove <span id="displayMiles">___</span>
          miles.</p>
  <p>You used <span id="displayGallons">___</span>
          gallons of gas.</p>
  <p>Your MPG is <span id="displayMPG">___</span>.
  <script>
    var milesDriven = prompt("Enter miles driven");
    var gallonsGas = prompt("Enter the gallons of gas
          used");
    calculateMPG(milesDriven,gallonsGas);
  </script>
</body>
</html>
```

getElementsByTagName

The `getElementsByTagName` method returns a node list of all the elements with the specified tag name. For example, in Listing 10-6, `getElementsByTag Name` is used to select all `h1` elements and change their `innerHTML` properties to sequential numbers.

Listing 10-6:   Using getElementsByTagName to Select and Change Elements

```html
<html>
<head>
  <title>Using getElementsByTagName</title>
  <script>
    function numberElements(tagName){
      var getTags =
          document.getElementsByTagName(tagName);
```

```
        for(i=0; i < getTags.length; i++){
          getTags[i].innerHTML = i+1;
        }
      }
    </script>
  </head>
  <body>
    <h1>this text will go away</h1>
    <h1>this will get overwritten</h1>
    <h1>JavaScript will erase this</h1>
    <script>
      numberElements("h1");
    </script>
  </body>
  </html>
```

getElementsByClassName

The getElementsByClassName method works in much the same way as
the getElementsByTagName, but it uses the values of the class attribute to
select elements. The function in Listing 10-7 selects elements with a class of
"error" and will change the value of their innerHTML property.

**Listing 10-7:   Using getElementsByClassName to Select and
Change Elements**

```
<html>
<head>
  <title>Using getElementsByClassName</title>
  <script>
    function checkMath(result){
      var userMath =
          document.getElementById("answer1").value;
      var errors =
          document.getElementsByClassName("error");
      if(parseInt(userMath) != parseInt(result)) {
        errors[0].innerHTML = "That's wrong. You entered "
          + userMath + ". The answer is " + result;
      } else {
        errors[0].innerHTML = "Correct!";
      }
    }
  </script>
  </head>
<body>
```

(continued)

Listing 10-7 *(continued)*

```
    <label for = "number1">4+1 = </label><input type="text"
        id="answer1" value="">
    <button id="submit" onclick="checkMath(4+1);">Check
        your math!</button>
    <h1 class="error"></h1>
</body>
</html>
```

The result of running Listing 10-7 in a web browser and entering a wrong answer is shown in Figure 10-4.

Notice that Listing 10-7 uses an `onclick` attribute inside the `button` element. This is an example of a DOM event handler attribute. You can find out more about event handlers in Chapter 11.

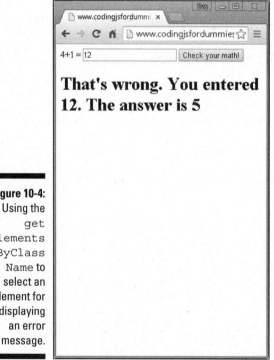

Figure 10-4:
Using the `get Elements ByClass Name` to select an element for displaying an error message.

Using the Attribute Object's Properties

The `Attribute` object provides properties for working with attributes within the HTML elements. Table 10-5 lists all the `Attribute` object's properties.

Table 10-5	The Attribute Object's Properties
Property	**Use**
`isId`	Yields `true` if the attribute is an Id; otherwise, yields `false`
`name`	Gets the name of the attribute
`value`	Gets or sets the value of the attribute
`specified`	Yields `true` if the attribute has been specified; otherwise, yields `false`

Creating and appending elements

To create a new element in an HTML document, use the `document.create Element()` method. When you use `createElement()`, a new beginning and end tag of the type you specify will be created.

Listing 10-8 shows an example of how you can use this method to dynamically create a list in an HTML document from an array.

Listing 10-8:   Using document.createElement() to Generate a Table from an Array

```
<html>
<head>
  <title>Generating a list</title>
</head>
<body>
  <h1>Here are some types of balls</h1>
  <ul id="ballList">
  </ul>

  <script>
    var typeOfBall = ["basket", "base", "soccer", "foot",
          "hand"];
    for (i=0; i<typeOfBall.length; i++) {
      var listElement = document.createElement("li");
      listElement.innerHTML = typeOfBall[i];
```

(continued)

Listing 10-8 *(continued)*

```
        document.getElementById("ballList").appendChild
            (listElement);
    }
  </script>

</body>
</html>
```

Removing elements

For all the great things that it lets you do with HTML documents, the HTML DOM is not highly regarded by professional JavaScript programmers. It has a number of oddities and tends to make some things more difficult than they should be.

One of the big faults with the DOM is that it doesn't provide any way to directly remove an element from a document. Instead, you have to tell the DOM to find the parent of the element you want to remove and then tell the parent to remove its child. It sounds a little confusing, but Listing 10-9 should clear it all up.

Listing 10-9:   Removing an Element from a Document

```
<html>
<head>
  <title>Remove an element</title>
  <script>
    function removeFirstParagraph(){
      var firstPara =
          document.getElementById("firstparagraph");
      firstPara.parentNode.removeChild(firstPara);
    }
  </script>
</head>
<body>
  <div id="gibberish">
    <p id="firstparagraph">Lorem ipsum dolor sit amet,
        consectetur adipiscing elit. Vestibulum
        molestie pulvinar ante, a volutpat est
        sodales et. Ut gravida justo ac leo euismod,
        et tempus magna posuere. Cum sociis natoque
        penatibus et magnis dis parturient montes,
        nascetur ridiculus mus. Integer non mi iaculis,
        facilisis risus et, vestibulum lorem. Sed quam
        ex, placerat nec tristique id, mattis fringilla
        ligula. Maecenas a pretium justo. Suspendisse
```

```
              sit amet nibh consectetur, tristique tellus
              quis, congue arcu. Etiam pellentesque dictum
              elit eget semper. Phasellus orci neque, semper
              ac tortor ac, laoreet ultricies enim.</p>
    </div>
    <button onclick="removeFirstParagraph();">That's
              Gibberish!</button>
  </body>
</html>
```

When you run Listing 10-9 in a browser and press the button, the `onclick` event calls the `removeFirstParagraph()` function.

The first thing `removeFirstParagraph()` does is to select the element that we actually want to remove, the element with the `id = "firstparagraph"`. Then, the script selects the parent node of the first paragraph. It then uses the `removeChild()` method to remove the first paragraph.

Chapter 11

Using Events in JavaScript

"And now, the sequence of events in no particular order:"

— Dan Rather

*W*eb pages are much more than just static displays of text and graphics. JavaScript gives web pages interactivity and the ability to perform useful work. An important part of JavaScript's ability to perform useful functions in the browser is its ability to respond to events.

Knowing Your Events

Events are the things that happen within the browser (such as a page loading) and things the user does (such as clicking, pressing keys on the keyboard, moving the mouse, and so on). Events happen all the time in the browser.

The HTML DOM gives JavaScript the ability to identify and respond to events in a web browser. Events can be divided into groups according to what HTML elements or browser objects they apply to. Table 11-1 lists events that are supported by every HTML element.

Other types of events are supported by every element other than the body and frameset elements. These are listed in Table 11-2.

Table 11-1	Events Supported by All HTML elements
Event	**Occurs When . . .**
abort	The loading of a file is aborted.
change	An elements value has changed since losing and regaining focus.
click	A mouse has been clicked on an element.
dbclick	A mouse has been clicked twice on an element.
input	The value of an `<input>` or `<textarea>` element is changed.
keydown	A key is pressed down.
keyup	A key is released after being pressed.
mousedown	A mouse button has been pressed down on an element.
mouseenter	A mouse pointer is moved onto the element that has the listener attached.
mouseleave	A mouse pointer is moved off of the element that has the listener attached.
mousemove	A mouse pointer is moved over an element.
mouseout	A mouse pointer is moved off of the element or one of its children that has the listener attached.
mouseover	A mouse pointer is moved onto the element or one of its children that the listener is attached to.
mouseup	A mouse button is released over an element.
mousewheel	A wheel button of a mouse is rotated.
onreset	A form is reset.
select	Text has been selected.
submit	A form is submitted.

Table 11-2	Events Supported by Every Element Except `<body>` and `<frameset>`
Event	**Occurs When . . .**
blur	An element has gone out of focus.
error	A file failed to load.
focus	An element has come into focus.
load	A file and its attached files have finished loading.
resize	The document has been resized.
scroll	The document or an element has been scrolled.

Table 11-3 shows the events that are supported by the Window object.

Table 11-3	Events supported by the Window Object
Event	*Occurs When . . .*
afterprint	The document print preview has been closed or the document has started printing.
beforeprint	The document print preview is open or the document is about to the printed.
beforeunload	The window, the document, and its included files are about to be unloaded.
hashchange	The part of the URL after the number sign (#) changes.
pagehide	The browser leaves a page in the browser history.
pageshow	The browser goes to a page in the session history.
popstate	The active session history item changes.
unload	The document or included file is being unloaded.

In addition to these events, many other specifications define events that can happen. For example, the File API has a series of events related to file loading, and the HTML5 Media specification contains events related to audio and video playback. As you can see, a lot of things are going on (or can go on) in your browser!

For a complete list of events, you can visit https://developer.mozilla.org/en-US/docs/Web/Events.

Handling Events

When JavaScript does something in response to these events, it's called *event handling.*

Over the years, browser makers have implemented several ways for JavaScript programs to handle events. As a result, the landscape of JavaScript events has been one of incompatibilities between browsers.

Today, JavaScript is getting to the point where the old, inefficient techniques for handling events can soon be discarded. However, because these older techniques are still widely used, it's important that they are covered here.

Using inline event handlers

The first system for handling events was introduced along with the first versions of JavaScript. It relies on special event handler attributes, including the `onclick` event handler.

The inline event handler attributes are formed by adding the prefix on to an event. To use them, add the event attribute to an HTML element. When the specified event occurs, the JavaScript within the value of the attribute will be performed. For example, Listing 11-1 pops up an alert when the link is clicked.

Listing 11-1: Attaching an onclick Event Handler to a Link Using Inline Method

```
<a href="home.html" onclick="alert('Go Home!');">Click
          Here To Go Home</a>
```

If you put this markup into an HTML document and click the link, you see an alert window with the words Go Home! When you dismiss the alert window, the link proceeds with the default event handler associated with the a element — namely, following the link in the `href` attribute.

In many cases, you may not want the default action associated with an element to happen. For example, what if you just wanted the alert window in Listing 11-1 to pop up without doing anything else?

JavaScript programmers have come up with several different methods to prevent default actions. One technique is to make the default action be something that is inconsequential. For example, by changing the value of the `href` attribute to a #, the link will point to itself:

```
<a href="#" onclick="alert('Go Home!');">Click Here</a>
```

A better method, however, is to tell the event handler to return a boolean false value, which tells the default action not to run:

```
<a href="homepage.html" onclick="alert('Go Home!')
          ;return false'>Click Here</a>
```

Event handling using element properties

One of the biggest problems with the older, inline technique of assigning events to elements is that it violates one of the best practices of programming: keeping presentation (how something looks) separate from functionality (what it does). Mixing up your event handlers and HTML tags makes your web pages more difficult to maintain, debug, and understand.

With version 3 of their browser, Netscape introduced a new event model that allows programmers to attach events to elements as properties. Listing 11-2 shows an example of how this model works.

Listing 11-2: Attaching Events to Elements Using Event Properties

```html
<html>
<head>
 <title>Counting App</title>
 <script>
 // wait until the window is loaded before registering the
         onclick event
 window.onload = initializer;
 // create a global counting variable
 var theCount = 0;
 /**
 Registers onclick event
 */
 function initializer(){
 document.getElementById("incrementButton").onclick =
         increaseCount;
 }
 /**
 Increments theCount and displays result.
 */
 function increaseCount(){
 theCount++;
 document.getElementById("currentCount").innerHTML =
         theCount;
 }
 </script>
</head>
<body>
 <h1>Click the button to count.</h1>
 <p>Current Number: <span id="currentCount">0</span></p>
 <button id="incrementButton">Increase Count</button>
</body>
</html>
```

One thing to notice about Listing 11-2 is that function names that are assigned to the event handler don't have parentheses after them. What's going on here is that the whole function is assigned to the event handler and is telling it "run this when this event happens," rather than actually using a function call. If you add the parentheses after the function name, the function will be executed, and its result will be assigned to the `onclick` event, which is not what we want.

Event handling using addEventListener

Although the previous two methods of event handling are very commonly used and are supported by every browser, a more modern and flexible way to handle events (and the recommended way for new browsers) is to use the `addEventListener()` method.

The `addEventListener` method listens for events on any DOM node and triggers actions based on those events. When the function specified as an action for the event runs, it automatically receives a single argument, the `Event` object. By convention, we name this argument `e`.

`addEventListener()` has several benefits over using the DOM event attributes:

- ✔ You can apply more than one event listener to an element.
- ✔ It works on any node in the DOM tree, not just on elements.
- ✔ It gives you more control over when it's activated.

Listing 11-3 demonstrates the use of the `addEventListener()` method. This example has the same counting function as Listing 11-2, but it adds a second event handler to the button that increases the size of the number each time it's clicked.

Listing 11-3:   Assigning an Event with addEventListener()

```
<html>
<head>
 <title>Counting App</title>
 <script>
 // wait until the window is loaded before registering
          the onclick event
 window.addEventListener('load',registerEvents,false);
 // create a global counting variable
 var theCount = 0;
 /**
```

```
Registers onclick events
*/
function registerEvents(e){
document.getElementById("incrementButton").addEventListener
        ('click',increaseCount,false);
document.getElementById("incrementButton").addEventListener
        ('click',changeSize,false);
}

/**
Increments theCount and displays result.
*/
function increaseCount(e){
theCount++;
document.getElementById("currentCount").innerHTML =
        theCount;
}
/**
Change the font size of the count text
*/
function changeSize(e){
document.getElementById("currentCount").style.fontSize =
        theCount;
}
</script>
</head>
<body>
<h1>Click the button to count.</h1>
<p>Current Number: <span id="currentCount">0</span></p>
<button id="incrementButton">Increase Count</button>
</body>
</html>
```

Figure 11-1 shows what the page created by Listing 11-3 looks like after an exciting afternoon of clicking the button.

The `addEventListener()` method is implemented by using three arguments.

The first argument is the event type. Unlike the other two event handling methods, `addEventListener()` just wants the name of the event, without the on prefix.

The second argument is the function to call when the event happens. As with the event properties method of event handling, it's important to not use the parentheses here in order for the function to be assigned to the event handler, rather than the result of running the function.

Figure 11-1:
Attaching
two events
to the same
element
increases
the possi-
bilities!

The third argument is a Boolean value (`true` or `false`) that indicates the order in which event handlers execute when an element with an event has a parent element that also is associated with an event.

When elements are nested, it's important to know which one will happen first. Figure 11-2 illustrates a common problem: The outer square is clickable, but so is the inner circle. When you click on the inner circle, should the event attached to the square happen first, or should the event attached to the circle happen first?

Most people would say that it makes sense that the circle event should happen first. However, when Microsoft implemented its version of events in Internet Explorer, it decided that the outer event (the square) should happen first.

Figure 11-2:
Events
within
events.

The most common way for events to be handled in a situation like the one in Figure 11-2 is called *bubbling up*. Events on the inside-most element happen first and then bubble up to the outermost elements. To use the bubble up method, set the last argument of the addEventListener() method to false, which is also the default value.

The other way to handle this scenario is called the *capture* method. In capture mode, the outermost events happen first, and the innermost events happen last.

Listing 11-4 shows an example demonstrating why knowing the order in which event handlers execute is important. The h1 elements have click events, but so do words within that header.

Listing 11-4:   Demonstrating Event Capture and Event Bubbling

```
<html>
<head>
 <title>Event capturing vs. Event bubbling</title>
 <style>
 #theText {font-size: 18px;}
 h1 {
 border:1px solid #000;
 background-color: #dadada;
 }
 #capEvent, #bubEvent {
 background-color: #666;
 }
 </style>
 <script>
 // wait until the window is loaded before registering
          the events
 window.addEventListener('load',registerEvents,false);
 /**
 Registers onclick events
 */
 function registerEvents(e){
document.getElementById("capTitle").addEventListener
          ('click',makeTiny,true);
document.getElementById("capEvent").addEventListener
          ('click',makeHuge,true);
document.getElementById("bubTitle").addEventListener
          ('click',makeTiny,false);
document.getElementById("bubEvent").addEventListener
          ('click',makeHuge,false);
 }
 function makeHuge(e){
 console.log("making the text huge");
 document.getElementById("theText").style.fontSize =
          "80px";
```

(continued)

Listing 11-4 *(continued)*

```
}
function makeTiny(e){
console.log("making the text tiny");
document.getElementById("theText").style.fontSize =
        "10px";
}
</script>
</head>
<body>
<h1 id="capTitle">Event <span id="capEvent">capturing
        </span></h1>
<h1 id="bubTitle">Event <span id="bubEvent">bubbling
        </span></h1>
<p id="theText">Hello, Events!</p>
</body>
</html>
```

Figure 11-3 shows what Listing 11-4 looks like in a web browser.

In Figure 11-3, when the word capturing is clicked, the event registered to the larger container fires first, followed by the event registered to the event containing the word capturing.

When you click the word bubbling, the event registered to that span fires first, followed by the event on its parent element.

Figure 11-3:
Handling
nested
events.

Stopping propagation

In addition to bubbling and capturing, you can handle nested events in a third way: just do the single event and then stop. You can turn off bubbling and capturing for an event (or even for all events) by using the stopPropagation() method.

If you don't need event propagation in your script, it's a good idea to just turn it off because all that bubbling and capturing does use system resources and can make your website slower.

Listing 11-5 demonstrates how to turn off event propagation.

Listing 11-5: Turning Off Event Propagation

```
function load(e){
  if (!e) var e = window.event;
  // set cancelBubble for IE 8 and earlier
  e.cancelBubble = true;

  if (e.stopPropagation) e.stopPropagation();

document.getElementById("capTitle").addEventListener
          ('click',makeTiny,true);
document.getElementById("capEvent").addEventListener
          ('click',makeHuge,true);
document.getElementById("bubTitle").addEventListener
          ('click',makeTiny,false);
document.getElementById("bubEvent").addEventListener
          ('click',makeHuge,false);
}
```

Chapter 12

Integrating Input and Output

In This Chapter

▶ Working with forms

▶ Using input

▶ Sending output

"Malfunction. Need Input."

— Number 5, Short Circuit (1986)

*H*andling user input and sending back results are basic and necessary functions for any computer program. In this chapter, you find out how JavaScript and HTML can work together to receive and output data.

Understanding HTML Forms

The primary way to get input from users of web applications is through HTML forms. HTML forms give web developers the ability to create text fields, drop-down selectors, radio buttons, checkboxes, and buttons. With CSS, you can adjust the look of a form to fit your particular website. JavaScript gives you the ability to enhance the functionality of your form.

The form element

All HTML forms are contained within a `form` element. The `form` element is the container that holds the input fields, buttons, checkboxes and labels that make up a user input area. The `form` element acts much like any container element, such as a `div`, `article`, or `section`. But it also contains some attributes that tell the browser what to do with the user input from the form fields it contains.

Listing 12-1 shows an HTML form containing two input fields and a submit button.

Listing 12-1:   Example of an HTML Page Containing a Form

```
<html>
<head>
  <title>HTML form</title>
</head>
<body>

  <form action="subscribe.php" name="newsletterSubscribe"
        method="post">
    <label for="firstName">First Name: </label>
    <input type="text" name="firstName"
        id="firstName"><br>
    <label for="email">Email: <input type="text"
        name="email" id="email"></label><br>
    <input type="submit" value="Subscribe to our
        newsletter!">
  </form>

</body>
</html>
```

When you view this form in a web browser, it looks like Figure 12-1.

Figure 12-1:
An HTML
form.

In the preceding example, the `form` element has three attributes:

- ✔ `action`: Tells the browser what to do with the user input. Often, the action is a server-side script.

- ✔ `name`: Specifies the name that the programmer assigned to this form. The name attribute of the form is useful for accessing the form using the DOM.

✔ method: Takes a value of either get or post, indicating whether the browser should send the data from the form in the URL or in the HTTP header.

In addition to these three attributes, the form element can also contain several other attributes:

✔ accept-charset: Indicates the character sets that the server accepts. Unless you're working with multilingual content (and even then), you can safely leave this attribute out.

✔ autocomplete: Indicates whether the input elements of the form should use autocomplete in the browser.

✔ enctype: Indicates the type of content that the form should submit to the server. For forms that are submitting only text data to the server, this should be set to text/html. If your form is submitting a file to the server (such as an uploaded graphic), the enctype should be multipart/form-data. The default value is application/x-www-form-urlencoded.

✔ novalidate: A Boolean value indicating whether the input from the form should be validated by the browser on submit. If this attribute isn't specified, forms are validated by default.

✔ target: Indicates where the response from the server should be displayed after the form is submitted. The default ("_self") is to open the response in the same browser window where the form was. Another option is to open the response in a new window ("_blank").

The label element

You can use the label element to associate an input field's description (label) with the input field. The for attribute of the label element takes the value of the id attribute of the element that the label should be associated with, as shown in this example:

```
<label for="firstName">First Name: </label>
<input type="text" name="firstName">
```

Another method for associating a label with a form field is to nest the form field within the label element, as shown in this example:

```
<label>First Name: <input type="text"
        name="firstName"></label>
```

This method has the advantage of not requiring the input field to have an id (which is often just a duplicate of its name attribute).

The input element

The HTML `input` element is the most fundamental form-related HTML element. Depending on the value of its type attribute, it causes the browser to display (or not display) several types of input fields.

Most commonly, the `input` element's type is set to `"text"`, which creates a text input in the browser. The optional `value` attribute assigns a default value to the element, and the `name` attribute is the name that is paired with the value to form the name/value pair that can be accessed through the DOM and that is submitted along with the rest of the form values when the form is submitted.

A basic `text` input field looks like this:

```
<input type="text" name="streetAddress">
```

With HTML5, the `input` element gained a bunch of new possible `type` attribute values. These new values allow the web developer to more pre-cisely specify the type of value that should be provided in the input. They also allow the web browser to provide controls that are better suited to the type of input that's required to do input validation and results in better web applications.

It may seem odd that this chapter focuses so much on the form capabilities of HTML, rather than jumping right into JavaScript. However, forms are an area where HTML can really reduce the workload of programmers, so it's vital that JavaScript programmers learn what can be accomplished with forms through HTML.

The `input` element's possible values for the type attribute are shown in Table 12-1.

Table 12-1	Possible Values for the input Element's Type Attribute
Value	**Description**
`button`	A clickable button
`checkbox`	A checkbox
`color`	A color picker
`date`	A date control (year, month, and day)
`datetime`	A date and time control (year, month, day, hour, minute, second, and fraction of a second based on the UTC time zone)

Value	Description
`datetime-local`	A date and time control (year, month, day, hour, minute, second, and fraction of a second; no time zone)
`email`	A field for an email address
`file`	A file-select field and a Browse button
`hidden`	A hidden input filed
`image`	A submit button using an image, rather that the default button
`month`	A month and year control
`number`	A number input field
`password`	A password filed
`radio`	A radio button
`range`	An input using a range of numbers, such as a slider control
`reset`	A reset button
`search`	A text field for entering a search string
`submit`	A submit button
`tel`	A filed for entering a telephone number
`text`	Default; a single-line text field
`time`	A control for entering a time (no time zone)
`url`	A field for entering a URL
`week`	A week and year control (no time zone)

As of this writing, not all browsers support all possible values for the `input` element's `type` attribute. Using a `type` attribute that a browser doesn't understand will just result in the display of a text input field.

The select element

The HTML `select` element defines either a drop-down or a multiselect input. The `select` element contains option elements that are the choices that the user will have in the select control, as shown in Listing 12-2.

Listing 12-2:   A Drop-Down Form Control, Created Using the select Element

```
<select name="favoriteColor">
 <option value="red">red</option>
 <option value="blue">blue</option>
 <option value="green">green<option>
</select>
```

The form created by the markup in Listing 12-2 is shown in Figure 12-2.

The textarea element

The textarea element defines a multiline text input field:

```
<textarea name="description" rows="4"
          cols="30"></textarea>
```

The button element

The button element defines another way to create a clickable button:

```
<button name="myButton">Click The Button</button>
```

The button element can be used in place of input elements with the type attribute set to 'submit'. Or, you can use button elements anywhere you need a button, but where you don't want the submit action to happen.

If you don't want the button to submit the form when clicked, you need to add a type attribute to it with the value of 'button'.

Working with the Form Object

The HTML DOM represents forms using the Form object. Through the Form object, you can get and set values of form fields, control the action that's taken when a user submits a form, and change the behavior of the form.

Using Form properties

The properties of the Form object match up with the attributes of the HTML form element (see the section earlier in this chapter). They're used for getting or setting the values of the HTML form element attributes with JavaScript. Table 12-2 lists all the properties of the Form object.

DOM objects are representations of HTML pages. Their purpose is to give you access (also known as *programming interface*) to the different parts of the document through JavaScript. Anything within an HTML document can be accessed and changed with JavaScript by using the DOM.

Table 12-2	Form Object Properties
Property	*Use*
acceptCharset	Gets or sets a list of character sets that are supported by the server.
action	Gets or sets the value of the action attribute of the form element.
autocomplete	Gets or sets whether input elements can have their values automatically completed by the browser.
encoding	Tells the browser how to encode the form data (either as text or as a file). This property is synonymous with enctype.
enctype	Tells the browser how to encode the form data (either as text or as a file).
length	Gets the number of controls in the form.
method	Gets or sets the HTTP method the browser uses to submit the form.
name	Gets or sets the name of the form.
noValidate	Indicates that the form does not need to be validated upon submittal.
target	Indicates the place to display the results of a submitted form.

Using the autocomplete attribute

The `autocomplete` attribute in an HTML `form` element sets the default autocomplete value for the `input` elements inside the form. If you want the browser to provide autocomplete functionality for every input in the form, set autocomplete to `'on'`. If you want to be able to select which elements the browser can autocomplete or if your document provides its own autocomplete functionality (through JavaScript), set the form's autocomplete attribute to `'off'`, and then you can set the `autocomplete` attribute for each individual `input` element within the form.

You can find techniques for setting or getting the value of a form's properties in Chapter 10. After referencing the form using one of these methods, you then access the property using dot notation or the square bracket method.

To get the value of the `name` property of the first form in a document, you could use the following statement:

```
document.getElementByTagName("form")[0].name
```

A more common way to access a form is by assigning it an `id` attribute and using `getElementById` to select it.

The DOM provides another, more convenient method for accessing forms: the forms collection. The forms collection lets you access the forms in a document in two different ways:

- ✔ **By index number:** When a `form` element is created in the document, it is assigned an index number, starting with zero. To access the first form in the document, use `document.forms[0]`.

- ✔ **By name:** You can also access forms using the value of the `name` attribute of the `form` element. For example, to get the value of the action property of a form with a name of `"subscribeForm"`, you would use `document.forms.subscribeForm.action`. Or you can use the square brackets method of accessing properties and write `document.forms["subscribeForm"].action`.

Using the Form object's methods

The `Form` object has two methods: `reset()` and `submit()`.

The reset () method

The `reset()` method clears any changes to the form's fields that were made after the page loaded and resets the default values. It does the same thing as the HTML reset button, which is created by using a `type="reset"` attribute with an `input` element, as shown in the following code:

```
<input type="reset" value="Clear the form">
```

The submit () method

The `submit()` method causes the form to submit its values according to the properties of the form (`action`, `method`, `target`, and so on). It does the same thing as the HTML submit button, which is created by using a `type="submit"` attribute with an `input` element, as shown in the following code:

```
<input type="submit" value="Submit the form">
```

Listing 12-3 demonstrates the use of the `submit()` and `reset()` methods, along with several of the form object's properties.

Listing 12-3:   Using the Form Object's Properties and Methods

```
<html>
<head>
  <title>Subscribe to our newsletter!</title>
  <script>
    function setFormDefaults(){
      document.forms.subscribeForm.method = "post";
      document.forms.subscribeForm.target = "_blank";
      document.forms.subscribeForm.action =
          "http://watzthis.us9.list-manage.com/subscribe/
          post?u=1e6d8741f7db587af747ec056&amp;
          id=663906e3ba";

      //register the button events
      document.getElementById('btnSubscribe').
          addEventListener('click', submitForm);
      document.getElementById('btnReset').
          addEventListener('click', resetForm);
    }
    function submitForm() {
      document.forms.subscribeForm.submit();
    }
    function resetForm() {
      document.forms.subscribeForm.reset();
    }
  </script>
</head>
<body onload="setFormDefaults();">
```

(continued)

Listing 12-3 *(continued)*

```
<form name="subscribeForm">
  <h2>Subscribe to our mailing list</h2>
  <label for="mce-EMAIL">Email Address </label>
  <input type="email" value="" name="EMAIL" id="mce-
      EMAIL">
  <button type="button" id="btnSubscribe">Subscribe!
      </button>
  <button type="button" id="btnReset">Reset</button>
</form>
</body>
</html>
```

Accessing form elements

JavaScript offers several different ways to access form input fields and their values. These ways are not all created equal, however, and differences of opinion exist among JavaScript programmers as to which technique is the best. The following list presents the different techniques and their benefits and drawbacks:

✔ **Use the index number of the form and of its input fields.** For example, to access the first input field in the first form, you could use the following code:

```
document.forms[0].elements[0]
```

Avoid the preceding technique because it relies on the structure of the document and the order of the elements within the form not to change. As soon as someone decides that the email field should come before the first name field in the form, your whole script will break.

✔ **Use the name of the form and the name of the input field.** For example:

```
document.myForm.firstName
```

This technique has the benefit of being easy to read and easy to use. It's supported by every browser (and has been since very early in the development of the DOM).

✔ **Use `getElementById` to select the form and the name of the input field to select the input.** For example:

```
document.getElementById("myForm").firstName
```

This technique requires you to assign an `id` attribute to the form of the element. For example, the preceding code would match an input field named `firstName` inside of the following form element.

```
<form id="myForm" action="myaction.php">
. . .
</form>
```

✔ **Use a unique `id` attribute value on the field to access the field directly.** For example:

```
document.getElementById("firstName")
```

Something to remember when using the preceding technique is that if you have multiple forms on your page, you need to make sure that each form field has a unique `id` attribute (`id` attribute values must be unique anyway, so it's not really an issue).

Getting and setting form element values

The DOM gives you access to form elements' names and values using the name and value properties.

Listing 12-4 demonstrates the getting and setting of form input fields using a simple calculator application.

Listing 12-4:   A Calculator App Demonstrating the Getting and Setting of Form Input Fields

```html
<html>
<head>
  <title>Math Fun</title>
  <script>

    function registerEvents() {
      document.mathWiz.operate.addEventListener('click',
          doTheMath,false);
    }

    function doTheMath() {
      var first =
          parseInt(document.mathWiz.numberOne.value);
      var second =
          parseInt(document.mathWiz.numberTwo.value);
      var operator = document.mathWiz.operator.value;

      switch (operator){
        case "add":
          var answer = first + second;
          break;
        case "subtract":
          var answer = first - second;
      break;
    case "multiply":
```

(continued)

Listing 12-4 *(continued)*

```
            var answer = first * second;
            break;
        case "divide":
            var answer = first / second;
            break;
    }

    document.mathWiz.theResult.value = answer;
    }
  </script>
</head>
<body onload="registerEvents();">
  <form name="mathWiz">
    <label>First Number: <input type="number"
            name="numberOne"></label><br>
    <label>Second Number: <input type="number"
            name="numberTwo"></label><br>
    <label>Operator:
     <select name="operator">
       <option value="add"> + </option>
       <option value="subtract"> - </option>
       <option value="multiply"> * </option>
       <option value="divide"> / </option>
     </select>
    </label>
    <br>
    <input type="button" name="operate" value="Do the
            Math!"><br>
    <label>Result: <input type="number" name="theResult">
            </label>
  </form>
</body>
</html>
```

Validating user input

One of the most common uses for JavaScript is to check, or validate, form input before submitting user input to the server. JavaScript form validation provides an extra safeguard against bad or potentially unsafe data making its way into a web application. It also provides users with instant feedback about whether they've made a mistake.

Some of the most common JavaScript input validation tasks have been replaced by HTML attributes in HTML5. However, due to browser incompatibilities, it's still a good practice to validate user-submitted data using JavaScript.

In the calculator program in Listing 12-4, the input type was set to number for the operand units. This should cause the browser to prevent the user from submitting non-numeric values into these fields. Because the number input type is relatively new, you can't always count on the browsers to support it, so using JavaScript user input validation is important.

Listing 12-5 demonstrates an input validation script. The important thing to notice here is that the action of the form has been set to the input validation function. The `submit()` method of the form runs only after the tests in the input validation function have finished.

The line in the preceding code that does the real magic is this strange-looking one inside of the `validate()` function:

```
if (/^\d+$/.test(first) && /^\d+$/.test(second)) {
```

The characters between / and / make up what's called a *regular expression*. A regular expression is a search pattern made up of symbols that represent groups of other symbols. In this case, we're using a regular expression to check whether the values the user entered are both numeric. You can find out more about regular expressions in Chapter 14.

Input validation is such a common use for JavaScript that many different techniques have been created for doing it. Before you reinvent the wheel for your particular JavaScript application, do a search for "open source JavaScript input validation" and see whether any existing libraries of code can save you some time and give you more functionality.

Listing 12-5:   Performing Input Validation with JavaScript

```html
<html>
<head>
  <title>Math Fun</title>
  <script>

    function registerEvents() {
      document.mathWiz.operate.addEventListener('click',
        validate,false);
    }

    function validate() {
      var first = document.mathWiz.numberOne.value;
      var second = document.mathWiz.numberTwo.value;
      var operator = document.mathWiz.operator.value;

      if (/^\d+$/.test(first) && /^\d+$/.test(second)) {

        doTheMath();

      } else {

        alert("Error: Both numbers must be numeric");
```

(continued)

Listing 12-5 *(continued)*

```
      }

    }

  function doTheMath() {
    var first =
        parseInt(document.mathWiz.numberOne.value);
    var second = parseInt(document.mathWiz.numberTwo.
        value);
    var operator = document.mathWiz.operator.value;
    switch (operator){
      case "add":
        var answer = first + second;
        break;
      case "subtract":
        var answer = first - second;
        break;
      case "multiply":
        var answer = first * second;
        break;
      case "divide":
        var answer = first / second;
        break;
    }

    document.mathWiz.theResult.value = answer;
  }
 </script>
</head>
<body onload="registerEvents();">
  <div id="formErrors"></div>
  <form name="mathWiz">
    <label>First Number: <input type="number"
        name="numberOne"></label><br>
    <label>Second Number: <input type="number"
        name="numberTwo"></label><br>
    <label>Operator:
      <select name="operator">
        <option value="add"> + </option>
        <option value="subtract"> - </option>
        <option value="multiply"> * </option>
        <option value="divide"> / </option>
      </select>
    </label>
    <br>
    <input type="button" name="operate" value="Do the
        Math!"><br>
    <label>Result: <input type="number" name="theResult">
        </label>
  </form>
</body>
</html>
```

Chapter 13

Working with CSS and Graphics

"To achieve style, begin by affecting none."

— E.B. White, The Elements of Style

Once you understand how to manipulate the DOM objects using JavaScript, web pages change from static documents into interactive applications that can respond to user input, change without reloading, and deliver live data to a variety of different computing devices.

Using the Style Object

The DOM's Style object is a powerful tool for making a web page change its look and adapt in real time to user input or current browser conditions. The Style object gives programmers access to CSS style properties for any selected element or collection of elements in a document. (For more on the basic rules and syntax of CSS, see Chapter 1.)

Some of the things that you can do with the Style object are

✔ Change text colors to highlight keywords entered into search boxes

✔ Animate an object after a user clicks on it

✔ Change the border and background color of the part of a form the user is currently editing

> ✔ Expand and collapse or hide and show different parts of a page
>
> ✔ Create tips or help boxes that appear above the content of the page when a user clicks a link

The `Style` object works the same way as other DOM objects. It includes a set of properties that you can use to get or set different aspects of a selected element.

The properties of the `Style` object mirror CSS properties. The difference between the two is that the DOM `Style` objects' properties are spelled using `camelCase` instead of using CSS's dashed format.

Table 13-1 shows a few of the most commonly used `Style` object properties, along with what CSS property they modify.

For a complete list of the `Style` object's properties, and of every other DOM objects properties, visit `http://overapi.com/html-dom`.

Getting the current style of an element

The `Style` object returns the currently applied inline styles of an element. It doesn't tell you what the actual style is that the browser will render because it doesn't include styles held in the external CSS files or styles inside of `style` elements.

For this reason, the `Style` object is not entirely useful for getting the style of an element. In Listing 13-1, the `div` element has an inline style and several style rules that are set within a `style` element.

Table 13-1	Common Style Object Properties and Their CSS Equivalents	
Property	**CSS Style**	**Description**
`backgroundColor`	background-color	Gets or sets the background color of an element
`borderWidth`	border-width	Sets the width of all four borders of an element
`fontFamily`	font-family	Gets or sets a list of font family names assigned to the text in an element
`lineHeight`	line-height	Gets or sets the distance between lines of text
`textAlign`	text-align	Gets or sets the horizontal alignment of text in a black element

When using the `Style` object to get the style properties of an element, only styles set using JavaScript or inline CSS are returned.

Listing 13-1:   The Wrong Way to Get an Element's Current Style

```
<html>
<head>
  <title>Getting Inline Styles</title>
  <style>
    #myText {
      color: white;
      background-color: black;
      font-family: Arial;
      margin-bottom: 20px;
    }
    #stylesOutput {
      font-size: 18px;
      font-family: monospace;
    }
  </style>
  <script>
    function getElementStyles(e){
      var colorOutput = "color: " + e.target.style.color;
      var fontSizeOutput = "font size: " + e.target.style.
          fontSize;
      document.getElementById("stylesOutput").innerHTML =
          colorOutput + "<br>" + fontSizeOutput;
    }

  </script>
</head>
<body>
  <div id="myText" style="font-size: 26px;"
        onclick="getElementStyles(event);">Here is
        some text.</div>
  <div id="stylesOutput"></div>
</body>
</html>
```

Figure 13-1 shows what happens when you load this page in a browser and click on the `div` element.

The two important things to notice about the results of this script are

- ✔ The value of the `Style` object's property is blank, even though the div's color was set to white using CSS in the head.

- ✔ The value of the `Style` object's font size is set correctly because the CSS `font-size` property was set using inline CSS.

Figure 13-1:
The result
of using the
Style
object to
get an ele-
ment's style.

The `style` object's properties behave like inline styles and will retrieve only the values of inline styles applied to an element.

A good way to get the current style of an element is by using `window.getComputedStyle()`, as shown in Listing 13-2.

Listing 13-2: The Correct Way to Get an Element's Current Style

```
<html>
<head>
  <title>Getting Computed Styles</title>
  <style>
    #myText {
      color: white;
      background-color: black;
      font-family: Arial;
      margin-bottom: 20px;
    }
    #stylesOutput {
      font-size: 18px;
      font-family: monospace;
    }
  </style>
  <script>
    function getElementStyles(e){
      var computedColor =
          window.getComputedStyle(e.target).
          getPropertyValue("color");
      var computedSize = window.getComputedStyle
          (e.target).getPropertyValue("font-size");

      var colorOutput = "color: " + computedColor;
      var fontSizeOutput = "font size: " + computedSize;
```

```
        document.getElementById("stylesOutput").innerHTML =
           colorOutput + "<br>" + fontSizeOutput;
      }

  </script>
</head>
<body>
  <div id="myText" style="font-size: 26px;"
           onclick="getElementStyles(event);">Here is some
           text.</div>
  <div id="stylesOutput"></div>
</body>
</html>
```

Figure 13-2 shows the output of Listing 13-2: showing the computed (and correct) `style` property values.

Notice in Listing 13-2, the `getPropertyValue` function takes the CSS property (`font-size`) rather than the `style` property (`fontSize`). The reason is that the script is querying the value of `font-size` directly from the element, rather than through the `Style` object (which will only tell us about the inline styles).

Figure 13-2:
Displaying
computed
styles.

Setting style properties

To set properties of the `Style` object, select the element you want the new style to apply to and then use dot notation or bracket notation to assign a new value to a property of the `Style` object.

To change the border-width of an element that has the id of
"borderedSquare", you would use the following code:

```
document.getElementById("borderedSquare").style.
        borderWidth = "15px";
```

Animating Elements with the Style Object

You can use CSS styles to control the look of elements, but you can also use
them to control the positioning of elements. By using JavaScript loops with
style property modifications, you can create basic animations fairly easily.

In Listing 13-3, a JavaScript function moves a square across the screen by
using a for loop to change the CSS 'left' property.

Listing 13-3:   Animating an Element with the Style Object

```
<html>
<head>
  <title>JavaScript animation</title>
  <style>
    #square {
      width: 100px;
      height: 100px;
      background-color: #333;
      position: absolute;
      left: 0px;
      top: 100px;
    }
  </style>
  <script>
    function moveSquare() {
      for (i=0; i<500; i++){
        document.getElementById("square").style.left =
          i+"px";
      }
    }
  </script>
</head>
<body onload="moveSquare();">
  <div id="square"></div>
</body>
</html>
```

If you open this script in a browser, it seemingly opens with animation already complete. In fact, the animation actually does run, but it happens so fast that you can't see it happening (unless you happen to have a very slow computer or very fast eyes).

What's needed in order to make this animation run at human speed is a pause between each iteration of the loop. The most common way to create a loop with pauses is by using the setTimeout() method of the Window object.

The setTimeout() method takes two arguments:

✔ A function or piece of code to run

✔ A number of milliseconds (thousandths of a second) to wait before running

By putting a call to setTimeout() within a function and calling the function recursively, we can gain control over how fast the animation runs. (For more on writing recursive functions, see Chapter 7.)

In Listing 13-4, the box is now moving at the much slower pace of 1 pixel per 1/100th second. This example also features a few other improvements over Listing 13-3:

✔ The square is now clickable. Clicking the square triggers the animation.

✔ The animation of the square is based on the position of the square when the click event happens. Clicking on the square causes it to move 100 pixels to the right of wherever it is when it is clicked.

Listing 13-4:   Animation with the Style Object, setTimeout(), and Recursion

```
<html>
<head>
  <title>JavaScript animation</title>
  <style>
    #square {
      width: 100px;
      height: 100px;
      background-color: #333;
      position: absolute;
      left: 0px;
      top: 100px;
    }
  </style>
  <script>
```

(continued)

Listing 13-4 *(continued)*

```
    // wait until the window is loaded
    window.addEventListener('load',initialize,false);

  function initialize(){

    //move the square when clicked
    document.getElementById("square").
        addEventListener('click',function(e){

      //get the starting position
      var left = window.getComputedStyle(e.target).
        getPropertyValue("left");

      //convert left to a base 10 number
      left = parseInt(left, 10);
      moveSquare(left,100);

    }, false);

  }

  function moveSquare(left,numMoves) {
    document.getElementById("square").style.left =
        left+"px";

    if (numMoves > 0) {
      numMoves--;
      left++;
      setTimeout(moveSquare,10,left,numMoves);
    } else {
      return;
    }
  }
  </script>
</head>
<body>
  <div id="square"></div>
</body>
</html>
```

Figure 13-3 shows the output of Listing 13-4 when run in a browser.

Look closely at the code that registers the click event on the square. An anonymous function is used as an event handler. Although it may look confusing at first glance, if you reduce it to its basic parts, it's still just the same basic `addEventListener()` method at work, with its three arguments: the event type, the listener (in this case, an anonymous function), and the Boolean value for whether to use event capture.

Figure 13-3:
JavaScript
enables
animations
based on
events.

Working with Images

HTML `img` elements are normally pretty static, unchanging things — unless the image is an animation, of course. With JavaScript, effects such as the resizing of images, repositioning images, lightbox effects, rollover effects, and more are all possible by manipulating the attributes of the `img` element and by changing CSS styles.

Using the Image object

The DOM's `Image` object gives you access to the properties of an HTML `img` element. Once you have that access, you can set and get values in order to change any of the valid attributes of the element. The properties of the `Image` object are shown in Table 13-2.

The most important and most widely used property of the `Image` object are the `src` property, the `width` property, and the `height` property. With these three properties, you can create image swap effects, amazing image size effects, cool rollover buttons, and a lot more!

Creating rollover buttons

A *rollover button* is a button that changes in some way when the mouse pointer is hovering over it. Rollover buttons are a great way to indicate to the user that an image can be clicked. You can also use them to reveal more information about what will happen if a button or a link is clicked. You can even use them just for fun or aesthetics. Some web designers like to put so-called *easter eggs* into their websites that will trigger image changes or other changes on a site when a mouse hovers over them or when someone clicks on certain hidden areas on a page.

Table 13-2	Properties of the Image Object
Property	**Description**
alt	Gets or sets the value of an image's alt attribute
complete	Is true when the browser is finished loading the image
height	Gets or sets the value of an image's height attribute
isMap	Gets or sets whether an image should be part of a server-side image-map
naturalHeight	Gets the image's original height
naturalWidth	Gets the image's original width
src	Gets or sets the value of an image's src attribute
useMap	Gets or sets the value of an image's usemap attribute
width	Gets or sets the value of an image's width attribute

You can create rollovers using CSS, but for more sophisticated rollovers or image swapping, JavaScript, or a combination of JavaScript and CSS, is required.

The example in Listing 13-5 shows how to create a simple image rollover effect in JavaScript.

Listing 13-5:   An Image Rollover Effect

```
<html>
<head>
  <title>Rollover image</title>
  <script>

    function swapImage(imgToSwap){
      imgToSwap.src = "button2.png";
      imgToSwap.alt = "you're mousing over my button!";
    }
    function swapBack(imgToSwap){
      imgToSwap.src = "button1.png";
      imgToSwap.alt = "mouse over me!";
    }
```

```
   </script>
</head>
<body>
  <img src="button1.png" id="myButton"
       onmouseover="swapImage(this);"
       onmouseout="swapBack(this);" alt="mouse over
       me!">
</body>
</html>
```

In order for the page in Listing 13-5 to work correctly, you'll need to have the images named `button1.png` and `button2.png` saved in the same directory as your HTML file. You can create your own or download ours from the books' website.

Grow images on mouseover

Another useful user interface trick to make your websites more user-friendly is to slightly increase the size of image buttons when a user hovers over them. This nice little trick subtly indicates that the target image is clickable and provides a little bit of interactivity as well.

Listing 13-6 modifies the code from Listing 13-5 to increase the image size by 5 percent on `mouseover` events.

Be careful with increasing image sizes too far above the image's natural size. If you increase it too much, the image quality will be noticeably degraded.

Listing 13-6:   Increasing Image Size on mouseover

```
<html>
<head>
  <title>Rollover image size</title>
  <script>

    function growImage(imgToGrow){
      imgToGrow.width += imgToGrow.width * .05;
      imgToGrow.height += imgToGrow.width * .05;
    }
    function restoreImage(imgToShrink){
      imgToShrink.width = imgToShrink.naturalWidth;
      imgToShrink.height = imgToShrink.naturalHeight;
    }
  </script>
</head>
```

(continued)

Listing 13-6 *(continued)*

```
<body>
  <img src="button1.png" id="myButton"
          onmouseover="growImage(this);" onmouseout="rest
          oreImage(this);" alt="mouse over me!">
</body>
</html>
```

You may have noticed that Listings 13-5 and 13-6 used the inline event method. While not ideal for actual web application development, inline events are frequently used for simple `mouseover` effects that are really interface-related rather than functionality-related.

Creating an image slideshow

Slideshows (also known as carousels) are a popular way to display multiple images in a single space on a site. Often used on the homepage of websites, they can really liven up your site.

Slideshows often feature transition effects to switch between multiple images. These transition effects are generally created using a library of JavaScript functions, such as jQuery. You can also create transition effects using just ordinary JavaScript, CSS, and the DOM. In the interest of simplicity, the slideshow in Listing 13-7 only switches between images and doesn't feature a transition of any sort.

Listing 13-7:   A Slideshow Built Using JavaScript and CSS

```
<html>
<head>
  <title>JavaScript slideshow</title>

  <style>
    #carousel {
      position: absolute;
      width: 800px;
      height: 400px;
      top: 100px;
      left: 100px;
      display: hidden;
    }

  </style>
  <script>
    var slides = [
```

```
        "<div id='slide1'>my first slide<br><img
            src='image1.jpg'></div>",
        "<div id='slide2'>my second slide<br><img
            src='image2.jpg'></div>",
        "<div id='slide3'>my third slide<br><img
            src='image3.jpg'></div>"];

    var currentSlide = 0;
    var numberOfSlides = slides.length-1;

    window.addEventListener("load",loader,false);

    function loader(){
      changeImage();
    }

    function changeImage(){
      console.log("changeImage function");
      if (currentSlide > numberOfSlides){
        currentSlide = 0;
      }

      document.getElementById("carousel").
          innerHTML=slides[currentSlide];

      console.log('displaying slide' + currentSlide +
          "of " + numberOfSlides);
      currentSlide++;

      setTimeout(changeImage,1000);
    }

  </script>
</head>
<body>
  <div id="carousel"></div>
</body>
</html>
```

Using the Style Object's Animation Properties

CSS3 and the DOM's Style object have properties for simplifying the task of animating elements. Used together, the animation properties can enable you to create some pretty cool animations with minimal effort. The Style object's animation properties are listed in Table 13-3.

Table 13-3	Animation-Related Properties of the Style Object
Property	*Description*
`animation`	Sets all the animation properties except the `animationPlayState` property simultaneously.
`animationDelay`	Gets or sets a delay to happen before the animation starts
`animationDirection`	Gets or sets whether the animation should play in reverse on some or all cycles
`animationDuaration`	Gets or sets the length of time an animation takes to complete one cycle
`animationFillMode`	Gets or sets what values are applied by the animation outside the time it's executing
`animationIterationCount`	Gets or sets the number of times an animation should be played
`animationName`	Gets or sets a list of animations, using keyframe at-rules
`animationTimingFunction`	Gets or sets the speed curve that describes how the animation should progress over time
`animationPlayState`	Gets or sets whether the animation is running or paused.

In Listing 13-8, a simple animation is created using CSS. The timing and keyframes of the animation are first configured with CSS, and then JavaScript is used to pause and resume the animation. With a little creativity, there are many possibilities for how you could control this animation using JavaScript.

CSS3 animation is still pretty new, and not all browsers support it in the same way. Because it's still considered an experimental technology, some browsers require a browser prefix before the name of the animation properties.

In Listing 13-8, both the standard and prefixed CSS styles are included.

Listing 13-8: Controlling CSS3 Animation Using JavaScript

```
<!DOCTYPE>
<html>
<head>
  <style>
    #words {
```

```
       position: relative;
       width: 300px;
       height: 200px;
       text-align: center;
       padding-top: 20px;
       font-family: Arial;
       border-radius: 6px;
       color: white;

       /* Chrome, Safari, Opera */
       -webkit-animation-name: movewords;
       -webkit-animation-duration: 6s;
       -webkit-animation-timing-function: linear;
       -webkit-animation-delay: 0s;
       -webkit-animation-iteration-count: infinite;
       -webkit-animation-direction: alternate;
       -webkit-animation-play-state: running;
       /* Standard syntax */
       animation-name: movewords;
       animation-duration: 6s;
       animation-timing-function: linear;
       animation-delay: 0s;
       animation-iteration-count: infinite;
       animation-direction: alternate;
       animation-play-state: running;
     }

   /* Chrome, Safari, Opera */
   @-webkit-keyframes movewords {
       0%   {background:red; left:100px; top:0px;}
       25%  {background:blue; left:200px; top:100px;}
       50%  {background:blue; left:300px; top:200px;}
       75%  {background:blue; left:200px; top:200px;}
       100% {background:red; left:100px; top:0px;}
   }

   /* Standard syntax */
   @keyframes movewords {
       0%   {background:red; left:100px; top:0px;}
       25%  {background:blue; left:200px; top:100px;}
       50%  {background:blue; left:300px; top:200px;}
       75%  {background:blue; left:200px; top:200px;}
       100% {background:red; left:100px; top:0px;}
   }
 </style>
 <script>

   window.addEventListener("load",registerEvents,false);

   function registerEvents(e){
     document.getElementById("stop").addEventListener("
         click",stopAni,false);
```

(continued)

Listing 13-8 *(continued)*

```
        document.getElementById("go").addEventListener("clic
            k",startAni,false);
    }
    function stopAni(){
      document.getElementById("words").style.
          webkitAnimationPlayState = "paused";
      document.getElementById("words").style.
          AnimationPlayState = "paused";
    }
    function startAni(){
      document.getElementById("words").style.
          webkitAnimationPlayState = "running";
      document.getElementById("words").style.
          AnimationPlayState = "running";
    }

  </script>
</head>
<body>

  <h1 id="words">Movin' Around</h1>

  <button type="button" id="stop">Pause</button>
  <button type="button" id="go">Run</button>

</body>
</html>
```

Part IV
Beyond the Basics

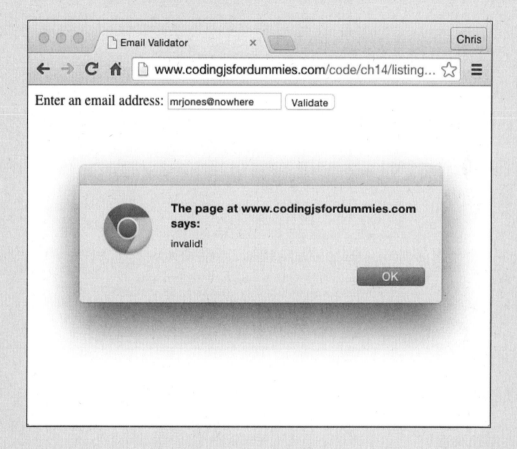

Find out how to force web browsers to run a restricted version of JavaScript in the article "JavaScript Strict Mode" online at www.dummies.com/extras/codingwithjavascript.

In this part . . .

✔ Find out how to search with regular expressions.

✔ Discover how to use callbacks and closures.

✔ Go above and beyond by embracing AJAX and JSON.

✔ Find out how to force web browsers to run a restricted version of JavaScript in the article "JavaScript Strict Mode" online at `www.dummies.com/extras/codingwithjavascript`.

Chapter 14

Searching with Regular Expressions

"Creating problems is easy. We do it all the time. Finding solutions, ones that last and produce good results, requires guts and care."

— Henry Rollins

Regular expressions are a powerful tool within many programming languages that help you find and change text within documents according to patterns within the text. The syntax for regular expressions can be intimidating at first, but once you get the hang of it, there will be nothing you can't do with text.

Finding It Out with Regular Expressions

Regular expressions are a way to look for patterns or character combinations in strings.

Example uses for regular expressions include

✔ Checking a user-entered email address to make sure that it's in the right format

✔ Finding and replacing all instances of a person's name in an article

✔ Locating capitalized words in the middle of sentences throughout
a book

✔ Finding strings of numbers that look like phone numbers inside a
document

Here's what a regular expression looks like:

```
^((\(\d{3}\) ?)|(\d{3}-))?\d{3}-\d{4}$
```

Looks pretty intimidating, right? Don't worry, you'll very soon have the tools
needed to decode this expression, and you'll discover that it's a regular
expression designed to match a common format for U.S. phone numbers:

(555)555-5555

Regular expressions can be much simpler than the preceding example,
however. Listing 14-1 shows a simple example use for a regular expression,
and Figure 14-1 shows what Listing 14-1 looks like when rendered in a browser.

Listing 14-1:   Does the String Include "JavaScript"?

```
<html>
<head>
  <title>Looking for JavaScript</title>
  <script>
    window.addEventListener("load",registerEvents,false);

    function registerEvents(e){
      document.getElementById("ask")
    .  addEventListener("click",findAnswer,false);
    }

    function findAnswer(){
      //get the user's question
      var question = document.
          getElementById("userQuestion").value;
      /* create a new regular expression object that
          will look for an exact match of the string
          "JavaScript". */
      var re = new RegExp("JavaScript");

      // if "JavaScript" is found in the user's question
      if (re.test(question)===true){

        //print out an answer.
        document.getElementById("answer").innerHTML =
          "JavaScript Question? Check out Coding with
          JavaScript For Dummies by Chris Minnick and Eva
          Holland";
```

```
            //and yell "JavaScript!" in the console.
            console.log("JavaScript!");
          }
        }
      }
    </script>
  </head>
  <body>
    <form id="userInput">
      <label>Enter your question:
      <textarea id="userQuestion"/>
      </label>
      <button id="ask" type="button">Get An Answer</button>
    </form>
    <div id="answer"/>
  </body>
</html>
```

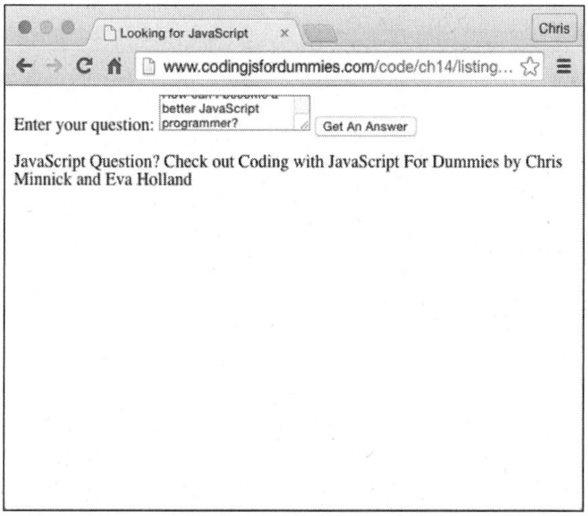

Figure 14-1:
The result
of running
Listing
14-1 in a
browser.

Writing Regular Expressions

Before you can make use of a regular expression, you need to create an object containing the expression. You can write regular expressions in one of two ways:

✓ By using a regular expression literal

✓ Through the constructor function of the RegExp object

Using the RegExp object

When you create a regular expression by calling the RegExp constructor function, the resulting object gets created at run time, rather than when the script is loaded. You should use the RegExp constructor function when you don't know the value of the regular expression when you're writing the script. For example, you may be asking the user to input a regular expression, or you may be getting the regular expression from an external source or calculating some part of the regular expression when the script runs.

The program in Listing 14-2 creates a regular expression using a random letter and then asks the user to type a sentence. When the user submits the form, the program calculates how many instances of the random letter were in the user-submitted text.

Listing 14-2: Creating Regular Expressions at Run Time with the RegExp object

```
<html>
<head>
  <title>Letter Counting Game</title>
  <script>
    window.addEventListener('load',loader,false);

    //get a random letter
    var letter = String.fromCharCode(97 + Math.floor(Math.
        random() * 26));

    /* Create a regular expression using the letter. Set
        the g option to find all occurrences. */
    var re = new RegExp(letter,'g');

    function loader(e){
      document.getElementById("getText").addEventListener(
        'submit',countLetter,false);
    }

    function countLetter(e){
      e.preventDefault();
      document.getElementById("results").innerHTML = "The
        secret letter was " + letter +".";
      var userText = document.getElementById("userWords").
        value;
      var matches = userText.match(re);
      if (matches){
        var count = matches.length;
      } else {
        var count = 0;
      }
```

```
      document.getElementById("results").innerHTML +=
         " You typed the secret letter " + count + "
         times.";
   }

  </script>
</head>
<body>
  <form id="getText">
    <p>I'm thinking of a letter! Type a sentence, and then
         I'll tell you how many times your sentence uses
         my secret letter!</p>
    <input type="text" name="userWords" id="userWords">
    <input type="submit" name="submit">
  </form>
  <div id="results"></div>
</body>
</html>
```

Figure 14-2 shows the result of running the preceding program in a web browser.

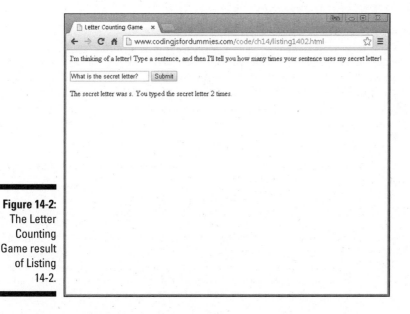

Figure 14-2:
The Letter
Counting
Game result
of Listing
14-2.

Regular expression literals

To create a regular expression literal, you enclose the value of the regular expression between slashes instead of quotes.

For example:

```
var myRegularExpression = /JavaScript/;
```

Regular expression literals are compiled by the browser when the script is loaded and remain constant through the life of the script. The result is that regular expression literals offer better performance for expressions that will be unchanging.

The preceding example uses a regular expression to look for an exact match of the string `"JavaScript"`. A regular expression containing a string of characters to be matched exactly is called a *simple pattern*.

In a real application or program, you'll want to account for users who use some variation on the correct spelling. For example, a user may input any of the following words and clearly mean JavaScript:

- ✔ javascript
- ✔ Javascript
- ✔ java script
- ✔ JS
- ✔ js

There may even be more exotic variations. One of the wonderful and frustrating things about dealing with input from real live people is that you never know for sure what they're going to do! In order to be able to detect variations in capitalization and spelling, you can use more sophisticated regular expressions to look for patterns or sets of characters, rather than just literal strings.

The following is a revised regular expression that will match `"JavaScript"` as well as `"Javascript"` or `"javascript"`:

```
var myRegularExpression = /[Jj]ava[Ss]cript/;
```

Things are starting to look a little foreign, but if you understand the meaning of the different characters, you'll see that this is actually still pretty simple. The square brackets in a regular expression define a character set and will match any one of the characters within that set. By writing `[Jj]`, what you're saying is that either a capital or lowercase j will match.

Testing regular expressions

Sometimes when you're writing regular expressions, it's helpful to have an easy way to test an expression to make sure that it's actually doing what you want. A number of websites and tools can help you test your regular expressions. One such site is `http://regex101.com`. To use regex101.com, type your regular expression in the box at the top of the screen and type some text in the box underneath it. The site checks the text against using your regular expression and highlights the matches that are found.

Figure 14-3 shows regex101.com using our example regular expression to test against a question about JavaScript.

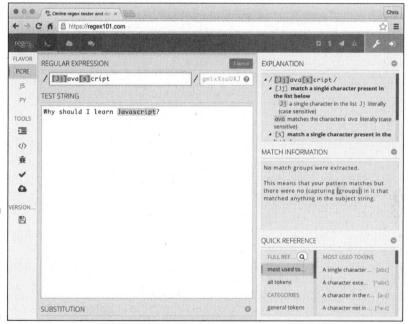

Figure 14-3:
Using regex101.com to test a regular expression.

Special characters in regular expressions

Regular expressions make it possible for you to look for numbers in strings, letters, groups of letters, repetitions of characters, and much more.

To create complex search patterns, you can use the regular expression special characters. The most commonly used special characters are listed in Table 14-1.

Table 14-1	Regular Expression Special Characters
Special Character	*Meaning*
\	Designates whether the next character should be treated as a special character or whether it should be treated as a literal character. If the following character is a special character, the \ designates that it should be treated literally.
^	Finds the beginning of the input.
$	Finds the end of the input.
*	Finds the preceding character 0 or more times.
+	Finds the preceding character 1 or more times.
?	Finds the preceding character 0 or 1 time.
.	Finds any single character except the newline character.
x|y	Finds either x or y.
{n}	Finds exactly n occurrences of the preceding character.
[xyz]	Finds any one of the characters in the brackets.
[^xyz]	Finds any characters other than the ones in the brackets.
[\b]	Finds a backspace.
\b	Finds a word boundary.
\B	Finds a nonword boundary.
\d	Finds a digit character.
\D	Finds any nondigit character.
\n	Finds a line feed.
\s	Finds a single white space character, including space, tab, form feed, and line feed.
\S	Finds a single nonwhite-space character.
\t	Finds a tab.
\w	Finds any alpha-numeric character, including an underscore.
\W	Finds any nonword character.

Using Modifiers

Modifiers can be used to modify several parameters of the search as a whole. To use modifiers, pass them as the second argument to the RegExp() constructor function when you're creating your regular expression object or put them after the ending / in a regular expression literal.

The three modifiers are

- ✔ g (global): Indicates that the entire string should be searched, rather than just searching until the first match is found.

- ✔ i (case insensitive): Indicates that the case (upper or lower) of the characters in the input should be ignored.

- ✔ m (multiline): Performs multiline matching. For example, when using ^ (start) and $ (end) special characters, treat each new line as a new start and end, rather than just considering the start and end of the input.

The following regular expression will match all the variations of the word JavaScript that we show earlier in this chapter throughout a document:

```
/javascript/ig
```

Coding with Regular Expressions

Regular expressions are used with the regular expression methods and with a subset of the string functions (see Chapter 3).

The regular expression methods are

- ✔ test: Tests for a match and returns true if a match is found and false if none is found.

- ✔ exec: Tests for a match and returns an array of information about the match.

If all you need to know is whether a string contains a match for the regular expression, you should use the test method. If you need to know where the match or matches are in a string, how many matches there are, and the text that was matched, you should use exec.

The string functions that can use regular expressions are shown in Table 14-2.

Email verification is a good, and surprisingly complex, use for regular expressions. Every valid email address has certain rules that it conforms to. The basic rules are

- ✔ Must contain one @ symbol

- ✔ Must contain characters before and after the @ symbol

- ✔ Must contain at least one separating groups of characters after the @ symbol

Table 14-2	String Functions That Use Regular Expressions
Function	**Use**
match	Looks for a match of for the regular expression in a string. It returns an array of information about the match or returns null if no match is found.
search	Tests for a match in a string. If one is found, it returns the index of the match. If no match is found it returns -1.
replace	Searches for a match in a string and replaces the match with a replacement string.
split	Breaks a string into an array of substrings, using a regular expression or fixed string.

There are other rules, but things get complicated pretty quickly when you start talking about details, such as the fact that spaces are allowed in email addresses in certain cases, as are international characters.

For someone who is asking users to input a valid email address, usually any sort of simple test of the email address before accepting the input will dramatically cut down on fake entries.

Listing 14-3 demonstrates an email validation script. After a user enters an email address and presses the validate button, the script tests the email address against the following regular expression literal:

```
/\b[A-Z0-9._%+-]+@[A-Z0-9.-]+\.[A-Z]{2,4}\b/i
```

This regular expression starts out with \b, the word boundary special character. A word boundary matches the start of a new word. After that, we have the following pattern:

```
[A-Z0-9._%+-]+
```

This matches one or more combination of letters or numbers, which may contain underscores, percent signs, or dashes.

```
@[A-Z0-9.-]+
```

This part requires the @ symbol, followed by one or more combinations of letters, numbers, or dashes.

```
\.[A-Z]{2,4}\b/i
```

The end of the regular expression looks for a two to four character-long string (the com or net or org parts of an email address) followed by the end of the word. At the very end of the regular expression, it uses the /i modifier to indicate that the regular expression will match upper or lowercase characters.

If a match occurs, then the data entered has passed the test, and a popup declaring the address 'valid!' appears.

Listing 14-3:   An Email Validation Script

```
<html>
<head>
  <title>Email Validator</title>
  <script>
    window.addEventListener('load',loader,false);
    function loader(e){
      e.preventDefault();
      document.getElementById('emailinput').addEventListen
          er('submit',validateEmail,false);
    }

    function validateEmail(e) {
      var re = /\b[A-Z0-9._%+-]+@[A-Z0-9.-]+\.[A-Z]
          {2,4}\b/i;
      if (re.test(e.target.yourEmail.value)) {
        alert("valid!");
      } else {
        alert("invalid!");
      }
    }

  </script>
</head>
<body>
  <form id="emailinput">
    <label>Enter an email address:
      <input type="text" id="yourEmail">
    </label>
    <input type="submit" value="Validate" id="validate">
  </form>
</body>
</html>
```

The result of running Listing 14-3 in a browser is shown in Figure 14-4.

Figure 14-4:
Using a
regular
expression
in an email
validation
script.

Chapter 15

Understanding Callbacks and Closures

. . . .

In This Chapter

▶ Understanding callback functions

▶ Using callbacks

▶ Creating closures

. . . .

"O, call back yesterday, bid time return."

— William Shakespeare

Callbacks and closures are two of the most useful and widely used techniques in JavaScript. In this chapter, you find out how and why to pass functions as parameters to other functions.

Don't forget to visit the website to check out the online exercises relevant to this chapter!

What Are Callbacks?

JavaScript functions are objects. This statement is the key to understanding many of the more advanced JavaScript topics, including callback functions.

Functions, like any other object, can be assigned to variables, be passed as arguments to other functions, and created within and returned from functions.

Passing functions as arguments

A *callback function* is a function that is passed as an argument to another function. Callback functions are a technique that's possible in JavaScript because of the fact that functions are objects.

Function objects contain a string with the code of the function. When you call a function by naming the function, followed by (), you're telling the function to execute its code. When you name a function or pass a function without the (), the function does not execute.

Chapter 11 has examples of callback functions where you can use the addEventListener method, such as

```
document.addEventListener('click',doSomething,false);
```

This method takes an event (click) and a Function object (doSomething) as arguments. The callback function doesn't execute right away. Instead, the addEventListener method executes the function when the event occurs.

Writing functions with callbacks

Here's a simple example function, doMath, that accepts a callback function as an argument:

```
function doMath(number1,number2,callback) {
  var result = callback(number1,number2);
  document.write ("The result is: ": + result);
}
```

This function is a generic function for returning the result of any math operation involving two operands. The callback function that you pass to it specifies what actual operations will be done.

To call our doMath function, pass two number arguments and then a function as the third argument:

```
doMath(5,2,function(number1,number2){
  var calculation = number1 * number2 / 6;
  return calculation;
});
```

Listing 15-1 is a complete web page that contains the doMath function and then invokes it several times with different callback functions.

Listing 15-1:   Calling a Function with Different Callback Functions

```
<html>
<head>
 <title>Introducing the doMath function</title>
 <script>
   function doMath(number1,number2,callback){

     var result = callback(number1,number2);
     document.getElementById("theResult").innerHTML +=
         ("The result is: " + result + "<br>");
   }

   document.addEventListener('DOMContentLoaded',
         function() {

     doMath(5,2,function(number1,number2){
      var calculation = number1 * number2;
      return calculation;
     });

     doMath(10,3,function(number1,number2){
      var calculation = number1 / number2;
      return calculation;
     });

     doMath(81,9,function(number1,number2){
      var calculation = number1 % number2;
      return calculation;
     });

   }, false);
  </script>
</head>
<body>
  <h1>Do the Math</h1>
  <div id="theResult"</div>
</body>
</html>
```

The result of running Listing 15-1 in a browser is shown in Figure 15-1.

Using named callback functions

In the examples in the preceding section, the callback functions were all written as anonymous functions. It's also possible to define named functions and then pass the name of the function as a callback function.

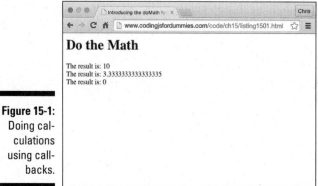

Do the Math

The result is: 10
The result is: 3.3333333333333335
The result is: 0

Figure 15-1:
Doing cal-
culations
using call-
backs.

Anonymous functions (see Chapter 7) are functions that you create without giving them names.

Using named functions as callbacks can reduce the visual code clutter that can come with using anonymous functions. Listing 15-2 shows an example of how to use a named function as a callback. This example also features the following two improvements over Listing 15-1:

- ✔ A test has been added to the doMath function to make sure that the callback argument is actually a function.

- ✔ It prints out the code of the callback function before it displays the result of running it.

Listing 15-2:   Using Named Functions as Callbacks

```html
<html>
<head>
  <title>doMath with Named Functions</title>
  <script>
    function doMath(number1,number2,callback){

      if (typeof callback === "function") {

      var result = callback(number1,number2);
      document.getElementById("theResult").innerHTML +=
          (callback.toString() + "<br><br>The result is:
          " + result + "<br><br>");

      }
    }

    function multiplyThem(number1,number2){
      var calculation = number1 * number2;
      return calculation;
    }
```

```
     function divideThem(number1,number2){
       var calculation = number1 / number2;
       return calculation;
     }
     function modThem(number1,number2){
       var calculation = number1 % number2;
       return calculation;
     }

     document.addEventListener('DOMContentLoaded',
           function() {

       doMath(5,2,multiplyThem);

       doMath(10,3,divideThem);

       doMath(81,9,modThem);

     }, false);
   </script>
</head>
<body>
   <h1>Do the Math</h1>
   <div id="theResult"></div>
</body>
</html>
```

The result of running Listing 15-2 in a browser is shown in Figure 15-2.

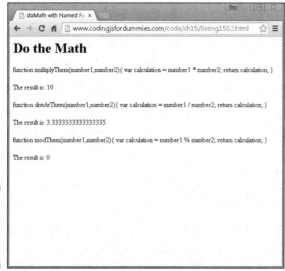

Figure 15-2:
Doing math
with named
callbacks.

Using named functions for callbacks has two advantages over using anonymous functions for callbacks:

- ✔ It makes your code easier to read.
- ✔ Named functions are multipurpose and can be used on their own or as callbacks.

Understanding Closures

A *closure* is the local variable for a function, kept alive after the function has returned.

Take a look at the example in Listing 15-3. In this example, an inner function is defined within an outer function. When the outer function returns a reference to the inner function, the returned reference can still access the local data from the outer function.

In Listing 15-3, the greetVisitor function returns a function that is created within it called sayWelcome. Notice that the return statement doesn't use () after sayWelcome. That's because you don't want to return the value of running the function, but rather the code of the actual function.

Listing 15-3:   Creating a Function Using A Function

```
function greetVisitor(phrase) {
  var welcome = phrase + ". Great to see you!"; // Local
        variable
  var sayWelcome = function() {
  alert(welcome);
  }
  return sayWelcome;
}

var personalGreeting = greetVisitor('Hola Amiga');
personalGreeting(); // alerts "Hola Amiga. Great to see
        you!"
```

The useful thing about Listing 15-3 is that it uses the greetVisitor function to create a new custom function called personalGreeting that can still access the variables from the original function.

Normally, when a function has finished executing, the local variables within it are inaccessible. By returning a function reference (sayWelcome), however, the greetVisitor function's internal data becomes accessible to the outside world.

The keys to understanding closures are to understand variable scope in JavaScript and to understand the difference between executing a function and a function reference. By assigning the return value of the `greetVisitor` function to the new `personalGreeting` function, the program stores the code of the `sayWelcome` function. You can test this by using the `toString()` method:

```
personalGreeting.toString()
```

If you add to Listing 15-3 an alert statement to output the `toString()` value of `personalGreeting`, you get the result shown in Figure 15-3.

In Figure 15-3, the variable `welcome` is a copy of the variable `welcome` from the original `greetVisitor` function at the time that the closure was created.

Figure 15-3:
A closure includes the code of the returned inner function.

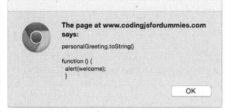

In Listing 15-4, a new closure is created using a different argument to the `greetVisitor` function. Even though calling `greetVisitor()` changes the value of the `welcome` variable, the result of calling the first function (`personalGreeting`) remains the same.

Listing 15-4: Closures Contain Secret References to Outer Function Variables

```
<html>
<head>
  <title>Using Closures</title>
  <script>
    function greetVisitor(phrase) {

      var welcome = phrase + ". Great to see
          you!<br><br>"; // Local variable
      var sayWelcome = function() {
      document.getElementById("greeting").innerHTML +=
          welcome;
      }
```

(continued)

Listing 15-4 *(continued)*

```
       return sayWelcome;
       }
       // wait until the document is loaded
       document.addEventListener('DOMContentLoaded',
              function() {

       // make a function
       var personalGreeting = greetVisitor("Hola Amiga");
       // make another function
       var anotherGreeting = greetVisitor("Howdy, Friend");

       // look at the code of the first function
       document.getElementById("greeting").innerHTML +=
       "personalGreeting.toString() <br>" + personalGreeting.
              toString() + "<br>";

       // run the first function
       personalGreeting(); // alerts "Hola Amiga. Great to
              see you!""

       // look at the code of the 2nd function
       document.getElementById("greeting").innerHTML +=
       "anotherGreeting.toString() <br>" +
              anotherGreeting.toString() + "<br>";

       // run the 2nd function
       anotherGreeting(); // alerts "Howdy, Friend. Great to
              see you!"

       // check the first function
       personalGreeting(); // alerts "Hola Amiga. Great to
              see you!""

       // finish the addEventListener method
       }, false);
   </script>
</head>
<body>
   <p id="greeting"</p>
</body>
</html>
```

The result of running Listing 15-4 in a web browser is shown in Figure 15-4.

Closures are not hard to understand after you know the underlying concepts and have a need for them. Don't worry if you don't feel totally comfortable with them just yet. It's fully possible to code in JavaScript without using closures, but once you do understand them, they can be quite useful and will make you a better programmer.

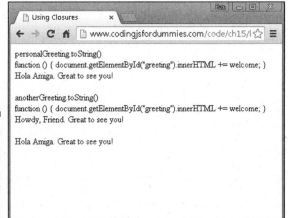

Figure 15-4:
Creating
customized
greetings
with
closures.

Using Closures

A closure is like keeping a copy of the local variables of a function as they were when the closure was created.

In web programming, closures are frequently used to eliminate the duplication of effort within a program or to hold values that need to be reused throughout a program so that the program doesn't need to recalculate the value each time it's used.

Another use for closures is to create customized versions of functions for specific uses.

In Listing 15-5, closures are used to create functions with error messages specific to different problems that may occur in the program. All the error messages get created using the same function.

When a function's purpose is to create other functions, it's known as a *function factory*.

Listing 15-5:   Using a Function to Create Functions

```
<html>
<head>
  <title>function factory</title>
  <script>
```

(continued)

Listing 15-5 *(continued)*

```
    function createMessageAlert(theMessage){
      return function() {
        alert (theMessage);
      }
    }

    var badEmailError = createMessageAlert("Unknown email
        address!");
    var wrongPasswordError = createMessageAlert("That's
        not your password!");

    window.addEventListener('load', loader, false);
    function loader(){
      document.login.yourEmail.addEventListener('change',
        badEmailError);
      document.login.yourPassword.addEventListener('change
        ',wrongPasswordError);
    }

  </script>
</head>
<body>
  <form name="login" id="loginform">
    <p>
      <label>Enter Your Email Address:
        <input type="text" name="yourEmail">
      </label>
    </p>
    <p>
      <label>Enter Your Password:
        <input type="text" name="yourPassword">
      </label>
    </p>
    <button>Submit</button>
</body>
</html>
```

The key to understanding Listing 15-5 is the factory function.

```
function createMessageAlert(theMessage){
    return function() {
      alert (theMessage);
    }
  }
```

To use this function factory, assign its return value to a variable, as in the following statement:

```
var badEmailError = createMessageAlert("Unknown email
        address!");
```

The preceding statement creates a closure that can be used elsewhere in the program just by running badEmailError as a function, as in the following event handler:

```
document.login.yourEmail.addEventListener('change',badEmai
        lError);
```

Chapter 16

Embracing AJAX and JSON

> *"The Web does not just connect machines, it connects people."*
>
> — Tim Berners-Lee

AJAX is a technique for making web pages more dynamic by sending and receiving data in the background while the user interacts with the pages. JSON has become the standard data format used by AJAX applications. In this chapter, you find out how to use AJAX techniques to make your site sparkle!

Working Behind the Scenes with AJAX

Asynchronous JavaScript + XML (AJAX) is a term that's used to describe a method of using JavaScript, the DOM, HTML, and the `XMLHttpRequest` object together to refresh parts of a web page with live data without needing to refresh the entire page. AJAX was first implemented on a large scale by Google's Gmail in 2004 and then was given its name by Jesse James Garret in 2005.

The HTML DOM changes the page dynamically. The important innovation that AJAX made was to use the `XMLHttpRequest` object to retrieve data from the server asynchronously (in the background) without blocking the execution of the rest of the JavaScript on the web page.

Although AJAX originally relied on data formatted as XML (hence the X in the name), it's much more common today for AJAX applications to use a data format called JavaScript Object Notation (JSON). Most people still call applications that get JSON data asynchronously from a server AJAX, but a more technically accurate (but less memorable) acronym would be AJAJ.

AJAX examples

When web developers first started to use AJAX, it became one of the hallmarks of what was labeled Web 2.0. The most common way for web pages to show dynamic data prior to AJAX was by downloading a new web page from the server. For example, consider `craigslist.org`, shown in Figure 16-1.

To navigate through the categories of listings or search results on Craigslist, you click links that cause the entire page to refresh and reveal the content of the page you requested.

While still very common, refreshing the entire page to display new data in just part of the page is unnecessarily slow and can provide a less smooth user experience.

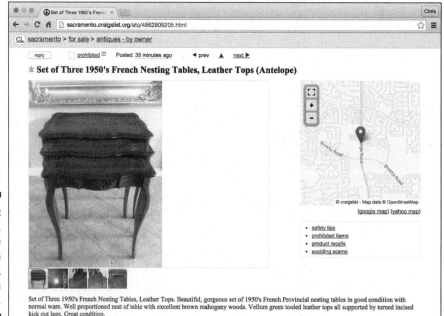

Figure 16-1: Craigslist.org is quite happy with Web 1.0, thank you very much.

Compare the craigslist-style navigation with the more application-like navigation of Google Plus, shown in Figure 16-2, which uses AJAX to load new content into part of the screen while the navigation bar remains static.

In addition to making web page navigation smoother, AJAX is also great for creating live data elements in a web page. Prior to AJAX, if you wanted to display live data, a chart, or an up-to-date view of an email inbox, you either needed to use a plug-in (such as Adobe Flash) or periodically cause the web page to automatically refresh.

With AJAX, it's possible to periodically refresh data through an asynchronous process that runs in the background and then update only the elements of the page that need to be modified.

See Chapter 10 to find out how to update the HTML and CSS of a web page using the HTML DOM's methods and properties. AJAX relies on these same techniques to display web pages with updated data.

Weather Underground's Wundermap, shown in Figure 16-3, shows a weather map with constantly changing and updating data overlays. The data for the map is retrieved from remote servers using AJAX.

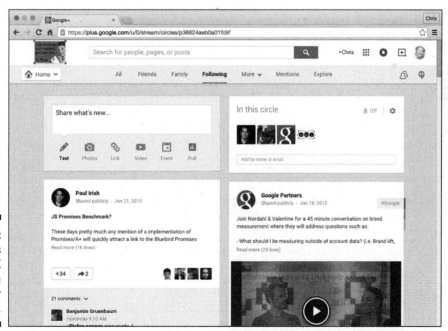

Figure 16-2: Google Plus uses AJAX to provide a modern user experience.

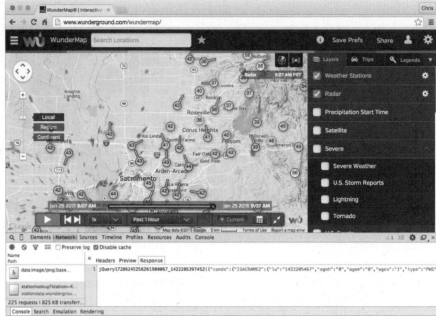

Figure 16-3:
Wundermap uses AJAX to display live weather data.

Viewing AJAX in action

In Figure 16-3, shown in the preceding section, the Chrome Developer Tools window is open to the Network tab. The Network tab shows all network activity involving the current web page. When a page is loading, this includes the requests and downloads of the page's HTML, CSS, JavaScript, and images. After the page is loaded, the Network tab also displays the asynchronous HTTP requests and responses that make AJAX possible.

Follow these steps to view AJAX requests and responses in Chrome:

1. **Open your Chrome web browser and navigate to**
   www.wunderground.com/wundermap.

2. **Open your Chrome Developer Tools by using the Chrome menu or by pressing Command+Option+I (on Mac) or Control+Shift+I (on Windows).**

3. **Open the Network tab.**

   Your Developer Tools window should now resemble Figure 16-4. You may want to drag the top border of the Developer Tools to make it larger at this point. Don't worry if this makes the content area of the

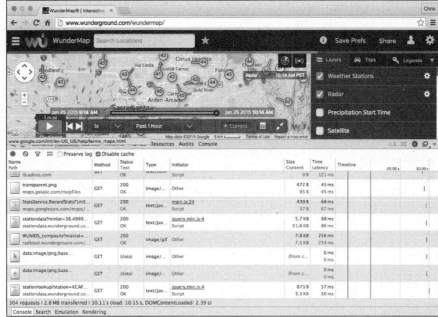

Figure 16-4:
The
Network
tab of the
Developer
Tools.

browser too small to use. What's going on in the Developer Tools is the important thing right now.

Notice that new items are periodically appearing in the Network tab. These are the AJAX requests and responses. Some of them are images returned from the server, and some are data for use by the client-side JavaScript.

4. **Click on one of the rows in the Name column of the Networks tab.**

Additional data will be displayed about that particular item, as shown in Figure 16-5.

5. **Click through the tabs (Headers, Preview, Response and so on) in the detailed data pane and examine the data.**

The first tab, Headers, displays the HTTP request that was sent to the remote server. Take a look in particular at the Request URL. This is a standard website address that passes data to a remote server.

6. **Select and copy the value of the Request URL from one of the items you inspected.**

7. **Open a new tab in your browser and paste the entire Request URL into the address bar.**

A page containing data or an image opens, as in Figure 16-6.

8. **Compare the results of opening the Request URL in a new tab with the results shown in the Response tab in the Developer Tools.**

   They should be similar, although they may not look identical because they weren't run at the same time.

As you can see, there's really no magic to AJAX. The JavaScript on the web page is simply requesting and receiving data from a server. Everything that happens behind the scenes is open to inspection through the Chrome Developer Tools (or the similar tools that are available with most other web browsers today).

Using the XMLHttpRequest *object*

The XMLHttpRequest object provides a way for web browsers to request data from a URL without having to refresh the page.

The XMLHttpRequest object was created and implemented first by Microsoft in its Internet Explorer browser and has since become a web standard that has been adopted by every modern web browser.

You can use the methods and properties of the XMLHttpRequest object to retrieve data from a remote server or your local server. Despite its name, the XMLHttpRequest object can get other types of data besides XML, and it can even use different protocols to get the data besides HTTP.

Listing 16-1 shows how you can use XMLHttpRequest to load the contents of an external text document containing HTML into the current HTML document.

Listing 16-1:   Using XMLHttpRequest to Load External Data

```html
<html>
<head>
 <title>Loading External Data</title>
 <script>
  window.addEventListener('load',init,false);
  function init(e){
   document.getElementById('myButton').
          addEventListener('click',documentLoader,false);
  }

  function reqListener () {
   console.log(this.responseText);
   document.getElementById('content').innerHTML = this.
          responseText;
  }
```

(continued)

Listing 16-1 *(continued)*

```
function documentLoader(){
  var oReq = new XMLHttpRequest();
  oReq.onload = reqListener;
  oReq.open("get", "loadme.txt", true);
  oReq.send();
}
</script>
</head>
<body>
 <form id="myForm">
  <button id="myButton" type="button">Click to
         Load</button>
 </form>
 <div id="content"></div>
</body>
</html>
```

The heart of this document is the documentLoader function:

```
function documentLoader(){
  var oReq = new XMLHttpRequest();
 oReq.onload = reqListener;
 oReq.open("get", "loadme.txt", true);
 oReq.send();
}
```

The first line of code inside the function creates the new XMLHttpRequest object and gives it the name of oReq:

```
var oReq = new XMLHttpRequest();
```

The methods and properties of the XMLHttpRequest object are accessible through the oReq object.

This second line assigns a function, reqListener, to the onload event of the oReq object. The purpose of this is to cause the reqListener function to be called when oReq loads a document:

```
oReq.onload = reqListener;
```

The third line uses the open method to create a request:

```
oReq.open("get", "loadme.txt", true);
```

In this case, the function uses the HTTP GET method to load the file called loadme.txt. The third parameter is the async argument. It specifies whether the request should be asynchronous. If it's set to false, the send method won't return until the request is complete. If it's set to true, notifications about the completion of the request will be provided through event listeners. Because the event listener is set to listen for the load event, an asynchronous request is what's desired.

It's unlikely that you'll run into a situation where you'll want to set the async argument to false. In fact, some browsers have begun to just ignore this argument if it's set to false and to treat it as if it's true either way because of the bad effect on the user experience that synchronous requests have.

The last line in the documentLoader function actually sends the requests that you created with the open method:

```
oReq.send();
```

The .open method will get the latest version of the requested file. So-called live-data applications often use loops to repeatedly request updated data from a server using AJAX.

Working with the same-origin policy

If you save the HTML document in Listing 16-1 to your computer and open it in a web browser, more than likely, you won't get the results that you'd expect. If you load the document from your computer and then open the Chrome Developer Tools JavaScript console, you will see a couple of error messages similar to the error in Figure 16-7.

Figure 16-7: Errors when trying to use XMLHttp Request on a local file.

The problem here is what's called the same-origin policy. In order to prevent web pages from causing users to unknowingly download code that may be malicious using XMLHttpRequest, browsers will return an error by default whenever a script tries to load a URL that doesn't have the same origin. If you load a web page from www.example.com and a script on that page tries to retrieve data from www.watzthis.com, the browser will prevent the request with a similar error to the one you see in Figure 16-7.

The same-origin policy also applies to files on your local computer. If it didn't, XMLHttpRequests could be used to compromise the security of your computer.

There's no reason to worry about the examples in this book negatively affecting your computer. However, in order for the examples in this chapter to work correctly on your computer, a way around the same-origin policy is needed.

The first way around the same-origin policy is to put the HTML file containing the documentLoader function and the text file together onto the same web server. You can see an example of this working by going to www.codingjsfordummies.com/code/ch16/listing16-1.html.

The other way around the same-origin policy is to start up your browser with the same-origin policy restrictions temporarily disabled.

These instructions are to allow you to test your own files on your local computer only. Do not surf the web with the same-origin policy disabled. You may expose your computer to malicious code.

To disable the same-origin policy on MACOS:

1. **Close your Chrome browser.**

2. **Open the Terminal app and launch Chrome using the following command:**

```
/Applications/Google\ Chrome.app/Contents/MacOS/
        Google\ Chrome --disable-web-security
```

To disable the same-origin policy in Windows:

1. **Close your Chrome browser.**

2. **Open the Command prompt and navigate to the folder where you installed Chrome.**

3. **Type the following command to launch the browser:**

```
Chrome.exe --disable-web-security
```

Once the browser starts up, you'll be able to run files containing AJAX requests locally until you close the browser. Once the browser is closed and reopened, the security restrictions will be re-enabled automatically.

Figure 16-8 shows the result of running Listing 16-1 in a browser without the same-origin policy errors.

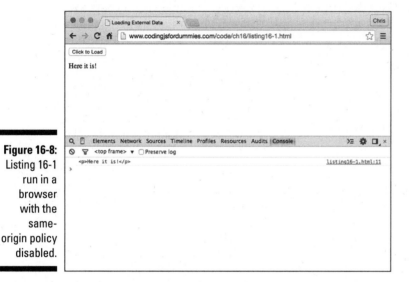

Figure 16-8:
Listing 16-1
run in a
browser
with the
same-
origin policy
disabled.

Using CORS, the silver bullet for AJAX requests

It's quite common for a web application to need to make requests to a different server in order to retrieve data. For example, Google provides map data for free to third-party applications.

In order for the transactions between servers to be secure, mechanisms have been created for browsers and servers to work out their differences and establish trust.

Currently, the best method for allowing and restricting access to resources between servers is the standard called *Cross-Origin Resource Sharing* (CORS).

To see CORS in action, take a look at the Network tab in the Chrome Developer Tools while browsing Weather Underground's Wundermap. Click on one of the requests starting with the following URL:
`http://stationdata.wunderground.com/cgi-bin/stationlookup`.

Click on the Headers tab, and you'll see the following text within the HTTP header:

```
Access-Control-Allow-Origin: *
```

This is the CORS response header that this particular server is configured to send. The asterisk value after the colon indicates that this server will accept requests from any origin. If the owners of wunderground.com wanted to restrict access to the data at this script to only specific servers or authenticated users, they could do so using CORS.

Putting Objects in Motion with JSON

In Listing 16-1, you use AJAX to open and display a text document containing a snippet of HTML. Another common use for AJAX is to request and receive data for processing by the browser.

For example, gasbuddy.com uses a map from Google along with data about gas prices, to present a simple and up-to-date view of gas prices in different locations, as shown in Figure 16-9.

Figure 16-9: gasbuddy.com uses AJAX to display gas prices on a map.

If you examine gasbuddy.com in the Network tab, you'll find that some requests have responses that look something like the code shown in Listing 16-2.

Listing 16-2:   Part of a Response to an AJAX Request on gasbuddy.com

```
([{id:"tuwtvtuvvvv",base:[351289344,822599680],zrange:[
      11,11],layer:"m@288429816",features:[{id:"172
      43857463485476481",a:[0,0],bb:[-8,-8,7,7,-47-
      ,7,48,22,-41,19,41,34],c:"{1:{title:\"Folsom
      Lake State Recreation Area\"},4:{type:1}}"}]},
      {id:"tuwtvtuvvvw",zrange:[11,11],layer:"m@2884
      29816"},{id:"tuwtvtuvvwv",base:[351506432,8242
      91328],zrange:[11,11],layer:"m@288429816",feat
      ures:[{id:"8748558518353272790",a:[0,0],bb:[-
      8,-8,7,7,-41,7,41,22],c:"{1:{title:\"Deer Creek
      Hills\"},4:{type:1}}"}]},{id:"tuwtvtuvvww",zran
      ge:[11,11],layer:"m@288429816"}])
```

If you take a small piece of data out of this block of code and reformat it, you get something like Listing 16-3, which should look more familiar to you.

Listing 16-3:   gasbuddy.com Response Data, Reformatted

```
{id:"tuwtvtuvvvv",
base:[351289344,822599680],
zrange:[11,11],
layer:"m@288429816",
features:[{
id:"17243857463485476481",
a:[0,0],
bb:[-8,-8,7,7,-47,7,48,22,-41,19,41,34],
c:"{
1:{title:\"Folsom Lake State Recreation Area\"},
4:{type:1}
}"}
]}
}
```

By looking at the format of the data, you can see that it looks suspiciously like the `name:value` format of a JavaScript object literal (see Chapter 8).

The main reason JSON is so easy to use is because it's already in a format that JavaScript can work with, so no conversion is necessary. For example, Listing 16-4 shows a JSON file containing information about this book.

Listing 16-4: JASON Data Describing Coding with JavaScript For Dummies

```
{ "book_title": "Coding with JavaScript For Dummies",
 "book_author": "Chris Minnick and Eva Holland",
 "summary": "Everything beginners need to know to start
         coding with JavaScript!",
 "isbn":"9781119056072"
}
```

Listing 16-5 shows how this data can be loaded into a web page using JavaScript and then used to display its data in HTML.

Listing 16-5: Displaying JSON data with JavaScript

```
<html>
<head>
 <title>Displaying JSON Data</title>
 <script>
 window.addEventListener('load',init,false);
 function init(e){
   document.getElementById('myButton').
         addEventListener('click',documentLoader,false);
 }

 function reqListener () {
  // convert the string from the file to an object with
         JSON.parse
  var obj = JSON.parse(this.responseText);

  // display the object's data like any object
  document.getElementById('book_title').innerHTML =
         obj.book_title;
  document.getElementById('book_author').innerHTML =
         obj.book_author;
  document.getElementById('summary').innerHTML =
         obj.summary;
 }

 function documentLoader(){
  var oReq = new XMLHttpRequest();
  oReq.onload = reqListener;
  oReq.open("get", "listing16-4.json", true);
  oReq.send();
 }
 </script>
</head>
```

```
<body>
 <form id="myForm">
  <button id="myButton" type="button">Click to
          Load</button>
 </form>
 <h1>Book Title</h1>
 <div id="book_title"></div>
 <h2>Authors</h2>
 <div id="book_author"></div>
 <h2>Summary</h2>
 <div id="summary"></div>
</body>
</html>
```

The key to displaying any JSON data that's brought into a JavaScript document from an external source is to convert it from a string to an object using the JSON.parse method. After you do that, you can access the values within the JSON file using dot notation or bracket notation as you would access the properties of any JavaScript object.

Figure 16-10 shows the results of running Listing 16-5 in a web browser and pressing the button to load the JSON data.

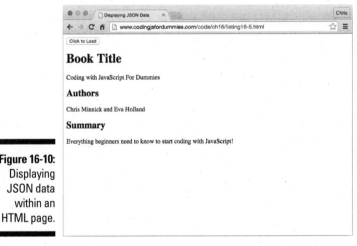

Figure 16-10:
Displaying
JSON data
within an
HTML page.

Part V
JavaScript and HTML5

Find out how to use polyfills to implement features in browsers that don't yet support them in the article "Using Polyfills" online at www.dummies.com/extras/codingwithjavascript.

In this part . . .

- ✔ Find out how to use HTML5's APIs to access a wide range of computer and mobile device functionality.

- ✔ Discover the basics of jQuery in order to speed up and simplify JavaScript development.

- ✔ Find out how to use polyfills to implement features in browsers that don't yet support them in the article "Using Polyfills" online at www.dummies.com/extras/codingwithjavascript.

Chapter 17

HTML5 APIs

"Language is a virus from outer space."

— William S. Burroughs

HTML5's APIs provide you with access to a wide range of computer and mobile device functionality. In this chapter, you discover how to use APIs, the standard methods and techniques used by APIs, and example code for working with some of the more exciting APIs.

Understanding How APIs Work

APIs, or Application Programming Interfaces, are sets of software routines and standards that give programmers access to the capabilities of a software application. APIs are the means by which one computer program gives another computer program the ability to interact with it. When a web browser allows a JavaScript program to interact with it, it does so by using APIs.

For example, the W3C's Battery Status APIs describes how browsers should report data about what's currently happening with the battery in a device (such as a smartphone or tablet). Other programs (for example, JavaScript programs within web pages) can access the Battery Status API to find out whether the device's battery is low, or charging, or how much battery time is left. You can then make use of this battery status information in your program.

The language in an API is highly precise and describes exactly how the API should be implemented by web browsers. Figure 17-1 shows a quote from the most recent version of the Battery Status API.

Figure 17-1:
An engaging excerpt from the Battery Status API.

The `charging` attribute MUST be set to false if the battery is discharging, and set to true, if the battery is charging, the implementation is unable to report the state, or there is no battery attached to the system, or otherwise. When the battery charging state is updated, the user agent MUST queue a task which sets the `charging` attribute's value and fires a simple event named `chargingchange` at the `BatteryManager` object.

The `chargingTime` attribute MUST be set to 0, if the battery is full or there is no battery attached to the system, and to the value positive Infinity if the battery is discharging, the implementation is unable to report the remaining charging time, or otherwise. When the battery charging time is updated, the user agent MUST queue a task which sets the `chargingTime` attribute's value and fires a simple event named `chargingtimechange` at the `BatteryManager` object.

The `dischargingTime` attribute MUST be set to the value positive Infinity, if the battery is charging, the implementation is unable to report the remaining discharging time, there is no battery attached to the system, or otherwise. When the battery discharging time is updated, the user agent MUST queue a task which sets the `dischargingTime` attribute's value and fires a simple event named `dischargingtimechange` at the `BatteryManager` object.

The `level` attribute MUST be set to 0 if the system's battery is depleted and the system is about to be suspended, and to 1.0 if the battery is full, the implementation is unable to report the battery's level, or there is no battery attached to the system. When the battery level is updated, the user agent MUST queue a task which sets the `level` attribute's value and fires a simple event named `levelchange` at the `BatteryManager` object.

Typically, an API is written up as a specification that tells what properties and methods are available to programmers, what arguments can be passed to the methods, and what sorts of values are returned by the properties.

In many cases with the APIs developed by standards bodies like the World Wide Web Consortium, the APIs are written to describe how programs should be able to interact with web browsers, rather than how they actually can. It's up to the browser makers to decide whether to actually implement an API standard.

An API tells programmers how they can interact with software and how the software should respond. When you're reading about APIs that describe ways to interact with web browsers, it's important to keep in mind that just because an API exists doesn't mean that programmers can actually use it. Many APIs have been proposed and written that haven't yet been implemented or that have only been partially implemented in web browsers.

Checking HTML5 API browser support

The best source for checking which web browsers support a particular standard or proposed standard is www.caniuse.com. CanIUse.com lists all of HTML5's elements and APIs and provides a table of browser support for each of them. Figure 17-2 shows the browser support, at the time of this writing, for the IndexedDB standard.

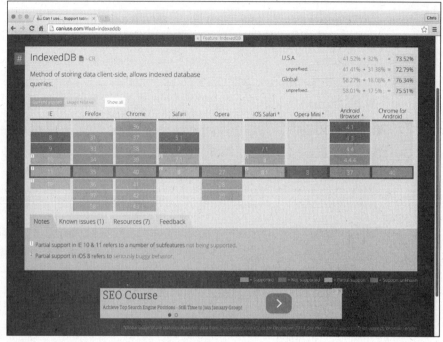

Figure 17-2:
Browser
support for
IndexedDB,
according
to caniuse.
com.

Getting to know HTML5's APIs

The HTML5 standard defines and documents a number of APIs that
JavaScript programmers can use to access the capabilities of web browsers
in a standardized way.

Many of the HTML5 APIs are still not finalized and implemented by every web
browser. The APIs that have been implemented are extremely useful and are
expanding the limits of what's possible in web apps.

The list of HTML5 APIs is constantly changing and growing. Table 17-1 lists
the most popular and well-supported APIs that are defined in HTML5 at
this time.

You can find a more exhaustive list of HTML5 APIs on the website for this
book at www.dummies.com/extras/codingwithjavascript.

Each HTML5 API is designed to precisely specify how programmers should
be able to interact with functionality of web browsers or computers. The process for these APIs to get from idea to reality, however, can be painfully long
and complex.

Table 17-1	HTML5 APIs
API	*Use*
Battery Status	Provides information about the battery status of the device
Clipboard	Provides access to the operating system's copy, cut and paste functionality
Drag and Drop	Supports dragging and dropping items within and between browser windows
File	Provides programs with secure access to the device's file system
Forms	Gives programs access to the new data types defined in HTML5
Geolocation	Provides web applications with access to geographical location data about the user's device
getUserMedia/Stream	Provides access to external device data (such as webcam video)
Indexed database	Creates a simple client-side database system in the web browser
Internationalization	Provides access to local-sensitive formatting and string comparison
Screen Orientation	Reads the screen orientation state (portrait or landscape) and gives programmers the ability to know when it changes and to lock it in place
Selection	Supports selecting elements in JavaScript using CSS-style selectors
Server-sent events	Allows the server to push data to the browser without the browser needing to request it
User Timing	Gives programmers access to high precision timestamps to measure the performance of applications
Vibration	Allows access to the vibration functionality of the device
Web Audio	Processes or synthesizes audio
Web Speech	Provides speech input and text-to-speech output features
Web storage	Allows the storage of key-value pairs in the browser
Web sockets	Opens an interactive communication session between the browser and server

API	Use
Web workers	Allows JavaScript to execute scripts in the background
XMLHTTPRequest 2	Improves XMLHttpRequest to eliminate the need to work around the same-origin Policy errors and to make XMLHttpRequest work with new features of HTML5

Several of the HTML5 APIs have passed through the gamut of test and review processes needed in order to become well supported standards. Foremost among these is the Geolocation API.

Using Geolocation

The Geolocation API gives programs access to the web browser's geolocation functionality, which can tell the program the device's location on Earth.

The Geolocation API is among the most well-supported HTML5 APIs and is implemented in about 90 percent of desktop and mobile browsers, including all of the big ones, except for Opera Mini.

What does geolocation do?

The Geolocation API describes how JavaScript can interact with the navigator.geolocation object in order to get data about a device's current position, including

- **Latitude:** The latitude in decimal degrees
- **Longitude:** The longitude in decimal degrees
- **Altitude:** The altitude in meters
- **Heading:** The direction the device is traveling
- **Speed:** The velocity of the device in meters per second
- **Accuracy:** The accuracy of the latitude and longitude, measured in meters

By obtaining some or all of this data, a JavaScript application running in a web browser can place a user on a map, query sources such as Google Maps for landmarks or restaurants local to the user, and much more.

How does geolocation work?

When JavaScript initiates a request for the devices position, through the `Geolocation` object, a number of steps take place, prior to the position information being returned.

The first thing to happen is that the browser needs to make sure that the user has given permission for the particular web app to access the device's geolocation information. Different browsers prompt the user for permission in different ways, but it's typically done through some sort of popup or notification.

The Chrome browser displays a geolocation icon and a message below the address bar when a website requests access to geolocation data, as shown in Figure 17-3.

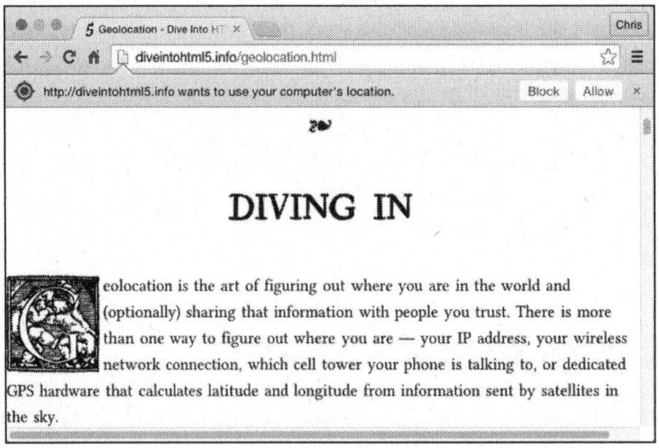

Figure 17-3: Chrome displays geolocation requests below the address bar.

After you give a website access to your geolocation data, the browser tries to find you. It does this through a number of different means, starting with the most accurate and proceeding through to less accurate ways.

If the program indicates that high accuracy is required, geolocation will spend a longer time trying to access highly accurate GPS information. Otherwise, the browser will attempt to balance speed with accuracy to obtain the most accurate results from any of the following sources, when available:

- GPS satellite positioning
- Your wireless network connection
- The cell tower your phone or mobile device is connected to
- The IP address of your device or computer

How do you use geolocation

The key to using geolocation is the `navigator.geolocation` object's `getCurrentPosition` method. The `getCurrentPosition` method can take three arguments:

- ✔ `success`: A callback function that's passed a `Position` object when geolocation is successful

- ✔ `error`: An optional callback function that's passed the `PositionError` object when geolocation fails

- ✔ `options`: An optional `PositionOptions` object that can be used to control several aspects of how the geolocation lookup is performed

The `Position` object that's returned by the `getCurrentPosition` method contains two properties:

- ✔ `Position.coords`: Contains a `Coordinates` object that describes the location

- ✔ `Position.timestamp`: The time when the location was retrieved

Listing 17-1 shows how you can use the `getCurrentPosition` method to get the `Position` object and loop through the return values in `Position.coords`.

Listing 17-1:   Getting Position Information and Displaying It in the Browser

```html
<html>
<head>
  <title>The Position object</title>
  <script>
    var gps = navigator.geolocation.getCurrentPosition(

    function (position) {
      for (key in position.coords) {
        document.write(key+': '+ position.coords[key]);
        document.write ('<br>');
      }
    });
  </script>
</head>
<body>

</body>
</html>
```

If the device you run this code on supports geolocation and the browser can determine your location, the results of running this script should resemble Figure 17-4.

Figure 17-4:
Printing the
return val-
ues of the
`Position`
object.

Notice in Figure 17-4, that several of the properties of the `Coordinates` object are all null. This is because it was run using a desktop computer that doesn't have the ability to get some of these coordinates. The result of running the same script in a mobile browser on a smartphone is shown in Figure 17-5.

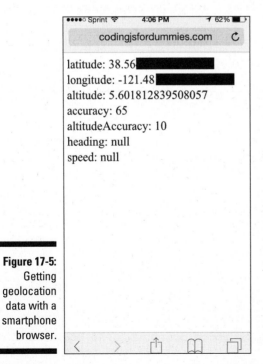

Figure 17-5:
Getting
geolocation
data with a
smartphone
browser.

Notice that the mobile browser displays figures for altitude, but heading and speed are still null because the device was stationary at the time when the page was loaded.

Combining geolocation with Google maps

One of the most common things that programmers need to do with geolocation data is to display a location on a map. In order to do this, you first need to get the latitude and longitude. You've got that now. But, how do you draw the map and figure out where on the map that latitude and longitude are? That, it seems, is the daunting task.

Fortunately, there are people who have done this before and who have created an API for interacting with their mapping software. Most famously, Google makes their mapping software available for free to anyone through the Google Maps API (even for commercial purposes, in most cases).

To use the Google Maps API, follow these steps:

1. **Go to the Google APIs console at `http://code.google.com/apis/console` and log in with your Google Account.**

2. **After you log in, you may be asked to agree to the terms of use; if so, click Accept.**

3. **Click the button labeled Enable an API.**

   Your screen now displays a list of APIs and a Browse APIs search box.

4. **In the Browse APIs search box, type Google Maps JavaScript API v3.**

   The link for this API appears.

5. **Click the button that says OFF under the status heading.**

   This step turns the API ON.

   After you activate the Google Maps JavaScript API, a green ON appears next to the API, as shown in Figure 17-6.

6. **Click the Credentials link on the left navigation bar.**

   You see the API Access Screen.

7. **Click the link labeled Create New Key.**

   The Create a New Key dialog box appears.

8. **Click Browser key in the Create New Key dialog box.**

   A dialog box containing a text input field labeled Accept requests from these HTTP Referrers opens.

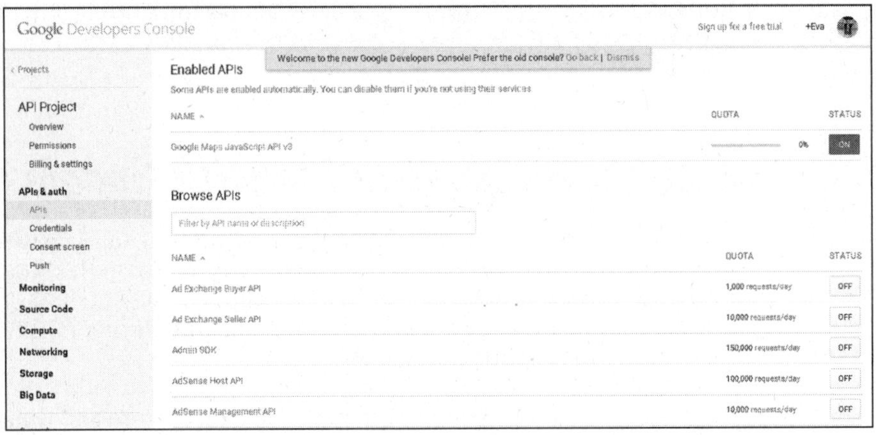

Figure 17-6:
Activating
the Google
Maps API.

9. **Leave the input box labeled Accept requests from these HTTP refer-rers blank and click Create.**

   The dialog box closes, and your API key will be created.

   In the Public API access section, you now find a long string of letters and numbers inside a box labeled Key for browser applications. This is your API key.

The API key is all you need to gain access to all the great functionality of the Google Maps API.

Now that you have access to the Google Maps JavaScript API, it's time to try it out. The web page in Listing 17-2 gets the location of your computer using the `navigator.geolocation` object and then passes it to Google Maps to get a map. Notice the highlighted area of the code, showing where to insert your API key.

Listing 17-2:   Mapping Your Location with the Geolocation API and the Google Maps API

```
<!DOCTYPE html>
<html>
<head>
  <title>Mapping your location</title>
  <style type="text/css">
    html, body, #map-canvas { height: 100%; margin: 0;
           padding: 0;}
  </style>
```

```
<script type="text/javascript"
    src="https://maps.googleapis.com/maps/api/js?key=YO
        UR_API_KEY">
</script>

<script>

// run the initialize function after the map loads
google.maps.event.addDomListener(window, 'load',
        initialize);

function initialize() {

  // get the Position object and send it to a callback
        function
  var gps = navigator.geolocation.getCurrentPosition(

  // the callback function
  function (position) {

    //set Google Map options, using latitude and
        longitude from position object
    var mapOptions = {
      center: { lat: position.coords.latitude, lng:
        position.coords.longitude},
      zoom: 8
    };

    // make the map and load it into the map-canvas div
        in the <body>
    var map = new google.maps.Map(document.
        getElementById('map-canvas'),
          mapOptions);
  }
  );
};
</script>

</head>
<body>
  <div id="map-canvas"></div>
</body>
</html>
```

In order for this script to run correctly, you have to replace the text YOUR_
API_KEY with the API key that you obtained from Google.

The results of running Listing 17-2 in a browser are shown in Figure 17-7.

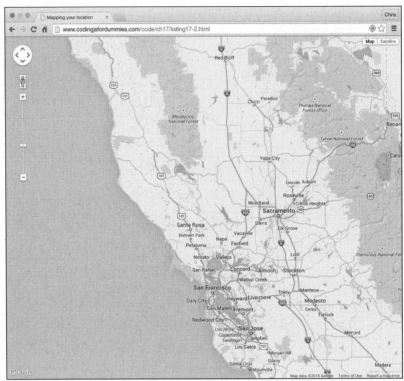

Figure 17-7:
Finding
yourself.

Accessing Audio and Video

Prior to HTML5, the only way for a web page to use a camera connected to a computer or built into a computer was through the use of plugins, such as Flash.

One of the major goals of HTML5 is to eliminate the need for plugins, with their constant updates and security issues. Since HTML5 was first proposed, there have been several attempts to define a standard for using input from cameras.

The latest and greatest API for enabling live video and audio communications through web browsers is called WebRTC (Web Real Time Communications).

At the heart of WebRTC is `navigator.getUserMedia()`, which does exactly what its name would imply: It gets media (audio and video) from the user (well, from the user's device, specifically).

TIP `getUserMedia` is currently supported in Chrome, Opera, and Firefox. If you want to use it in other browsers, such as Safari or Internet Explorer, you'll need to use a tool called a polyfill. Visit the book's website at `www.dummies.com/extras/codingwithjavascript` to learn about polyfills.

The first parameter of `getUserMedia` is an object with properties indicating what type of media you want to access. For example, if you want to access both video and audio, you would use the following object as the first parameter:

```
{video: true, audio: true}
```

The other parameters that `getUserMedia` takes are a success callback and an error callback. Listing 17-3 shows a sample use of `getUserMedia`.

Listing 17-3:   Getting and Displaying User Video and Audio

```
<!DOCTYPE html>
<html>
<head>
  <title>Get the Media</title>
  <style type="text/css">
    html, body, #map-canvas { height: 100%; margin: 0;
        padding: 0;}
  </style>
  <script>
  window.addEventListener('DOMContentLoaded', function()
        {
  var v = document.getElementById('v');
  navigator.getUserMedia = (navigator.getUserMedia ||
                    navigator.webkitGetUserMedia ||
                    navigator.mozGetUserMedia ||
                    navigator.msGetUserMedia);

      if (navigator.getUserMedia) {
        // Request access to video only
        navigator.getUserMedia(
          {
            video:true,
            audio:false
          },
          function(stream) {
            var url = window.URL || window.webkitURL;
            v.src = url ? url.createObjectURL(stream) :
             stream;
            v.play();
          },
```

(continued)

Listing 17-3 *(continued)*

```
        function(error) {
          alert('Something went wrong. (error code ' +
          error.code + ')');
          return;
        }
      );
    } else {
      alert('Sorry, the browser you are using doesn\'t
        support getUserMedia');
      return;
    };
  });
  </script>
</head>
<body>
  <video id = "v"/>
</body>
</html>
```

Examine Listing 17-3's key lines:

```
window.addEventListener('DOMContentLoaded', function() {
```

An event listener that waits until the DOM is loaded before running the rest of the code is

```
var v = document.getElementById('v');
```

The preceding line creates a new variable, called v, to hold a reference to the video element with an id ="v":

```
navigator.getUserMedia = (navigator.getUserMedia ||
          navigator.webkitGetUserMedia ||
          navigator.mozGetUserMedia ||
          navigator.msGetUserMedia);
```

getUserMedia is an experimental technology still not fully standardized. Because of this, web browsers have different implementations of it, which they indicate by using vendor prefixes. This statement sets the value of the standard navigator.getUserMedia object to the vendor prefixed version supported by the user's current browser. So, when you're using Firefox and call navigator.getUserMedia, you're actually calling navigator.mozGetUserMedia:

```
if (navigator.getUserMedia) {
```

which checks to see whether the user's browser supports getUserMedia:

```
navigator.getUserMedia(
```

Call the `getUserMedia` method:

```
{
  video:true,
  audio:false
}
```

The first parameter is an object telling which media you want to access:

```
function(stream) {
```

The success callback runs if the request to `getUserMedia` succeeds. It takes a single argument:

```
var url = window.URL || window.webkitURL;
v.src = url ? url.createObjectURL(stream) : stream;
```

The preceding two lines smooth out the differences between how different browsers handle the media stream object. The second line features our pal, the ternary operator! This statement sets the `src` property of the video element to either `url.createObjectUrl(stream)` or to `stream`, depending on which method is supported by the browser:

```
v.play();
```

Finally, the video is played. If your computer supports `getUserMedia` and you have a camera, you'll see video of yourself (or whatever the camera is pointing at) at this point:

```
function(error) {
  alert('Something went wrong. (error code ' + error.code
       + ')');
  return;
}
```

The preceding code is an error callback. If the browser does support `getUserMedia()`, but the user doesn't allow the browser to access the camera, this function will run and print out a specific error message:

```
else {
  alert('Sorry, the browser you are using doesn\'t support
        getUserMedia');
  return;
};
```

The preceding code is the `else` condition. If the user's browser doesn't support `getUserMedia()`, this alert will be displayed:

If the user's browser does support `getUserMedia`, the user has a camera, and they allow the app to access the camera, the app will display live video in the browser window, as shown in Figure 17-8.

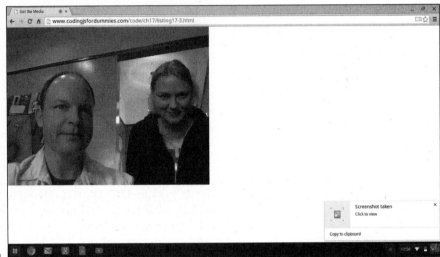

Figure 17-8:
Success!
The browser
is displaying
live video
without a
plugin.

Chapter 18

jQuery

. . . .

. . . .

"It's best to have your tools with you. If you don't, you're apt to find something you didn't expect and get discouraged."

— Stephen King

*j*Query is the most popular JavaScript framework around and is used by nearly every JavaScript programmer in order to speed up and simplify JavaScript development. In this chapter, you discover the basics of jQuery and see why it's so popular.

Don't forget to visit the website to check out the online exercises relevant to this chapter!

Writing More and Doing Less

jQuery is currently used by more than 61 percent of the top 100,000 websites. It's so widely used that many people see it as an essential tool for doing JavaScript coding.

jQuery smoothes out some of the rough spots in JavaScript, such as problems with browser compatibilities, and makes selecting and changing parts of an HTML document easier. jQuery also includes some tools that you can use to add animation and interactivity to your web pages.

The basics of jQuery are easy to learn once you know JavaScript.

Getting Started with jQuery

To get started with jQuery, you first need to include the jQuery library in your web pages. The easiest way to do this is to use a version hosted on a content delivery network (CDN). The other method for including jQuery is to download the library from the jQuery website and host it on your server. Listing 18-1 shows markup for a simple web page that includes jQuery.

Google has hosted versions of many different JavaScript libraries, and you can find links and include tags for them at `http://developers` `.google.com/speed/library`.

Once you've found a link for a CDN-hosted version, include it between your `<head>` and `</head>` tags in every page that will use jQuery functionality.

There are currently two branches of jQuery: the 1.x branch and the 2.xbranch. The difference between the latest versions of the 1.xbranch and the latest versions of the 2.xbranch is that the 1.xbranch works in Internet Explorer 6-8, while the 2.xbranch had eliminated support for these old and buggy browsers.

Listing 18-1:   Your First Web Page with jQuery

```
<html>
<head>
  <title>Hello JQuery</title>
  <style>
    #helloDiv {
      background: #333;
      color: #fff;
      font-size: 24px;
      text-align: center;
      border-radius: 3px;
      width: 200px;
      height: 200px;
      display: none;
    }
  </style>
  <script src="http://code.jquery.com/jquery-
          1.11.2.min.js"></script>
</head>
<body>
  <button id="clickme">Click me!</button>
  <div id="helloDiv">Hello, JQuery!</div>

  <script>
  $( "#clickme" ).click(function () {
    if ( $( "#helloDiv" ).is( ":hidden" ) ) {
```

```
      $( "#helloDiv" ).slideDown( "slow" );
    } else {
      $( "div" ).hide();
    }
  });
  </script>
</body>
</html>
```

The jQuery Object

All of jQuery's functionality is enabled by the `jQuery` object. The `jQuery` object can be referenced using two different methods: the `jQuery` keyword or the `$` alias. Both methods work exactly the same. The difference is that `$` is shorter, and so it's become programmers' preferred method for using jQuery.

The basic syntax for using jQuery is the following:

```
$("selector").method();
```

The first part (in parentheses) indicates what elements you want to affect, and the second part indicates what should be done to those elements.

In reality, jQuery statements often perform multiple actions on selected elements by using a technique called *chaining,* which just attaches more methods to the selector with additional periods. For example, in Listing 18-2, chaining is used to first select a single element (with the ID of `pageHeader`) and then to style it.

Listing 18-2:   Using Chaining

```
<html>
<head>
  <title>JQuery Chaining Example</title>
  <script src="http://code.jquery.com/jquery-
          1.11.2.min.js"></script>
</head>
<body>
  <div id="pageHeader"/>
  <script type="text/javascript">
    $("#pageHeader").text("Hello, world!").css("color",
          "red").css("font-size",
          "60px");
  </script>
</body>
</html>
```

Chained jQuery methods can get pretty long and confusing after you put just a couple of them together. However, keep in mind, JavaScript doesn't really care much about whitespace. It's possible to reformat the chained statement from Listing 18-2 into the following, much more readable, statement:

```
$("#pageHeader")
  .text("Hello, world!")
  .css("color", "red")
  .css("font-size", "60px");
```

Is Your Document Ready?

jQuery has its own way to indicate that everything is loaded and ready to go: the document ready event. To avoid errors caused by the DOM or jQuery not being loaded when the scripts run, it's important to use document ready, unless you put all your jQuery at the very bottom of your HTML document (as we do with Listing 18-1 and Listing 18-2.)

Here's the syntax for using document ready:

```
$(document).ready(function(){

  // jQuery methods go here. . .

});
```

Any jQuery that you want to be executed upon loading of the page needs to be inside of a document ready statement. Named functions can go outside of document ready, of course, because they don't run until they're called.

Using jQuery Selectors

Unlike the complicated, and limited, means that JavaScript provides for selecting elements, jQuery makes element selection simple. In jQuery, programmers can use the same techniques they use for selecting elements with CSS. Table 18-1 lists the most frequently used jQuery and CSS selectors.

In addition to these basic selectors, you canmodify a section or combine selections in many different ways. For example, to select the first p element in a document, you can use

```
$('p:first')
```

Table 18-1	The Common jQuery/CSS Selectors	
Selector	*HTML Example*	*jQuery Example*
`element`	`<p></p>`	`$('p').css ('font-size','12')`
`.class`	`<p class="redtext"> </p>`	`$('.redtext').css`
`#id`	`<p id="intro"> </p>`	`$('#intro'). fadeIn('slow')`
`[attribute]`	`<p data-role="content"> </p>`	`$('[data-role]'). show()`

To select the last p element, you can use

```
$('p:last')
```

To select the even numbered elements, you can use

```
$('li:even')
```

To select the odd numbered elements, you can use

```
$('li:odd')
```

To combine multiple selections, you can use commas. For example, the following selector selects all the p, h1, h2, and h3 elements in a document.

```
$('p,h1,h2,h3')
```

You can selecteelements in many more ways with jQuery than with plain JavaScript. To see a complete list, visit `www.dummies.com/extras/ codingwithjavascript`.

Changing Things with jQuery

After you make a selection, the next step is to start changing some things. The three main categories of things you can change with jQuery are attributes, CSS, and elements.

Getting and setting attributes

The `attr()` method gives you access to attribute values. All that you need in order to use `attr()` is the name of the attribute whose value you want to get or set. In the following code, the `attr()` method is used to change the value of the `href` attribute of an element with an id of `"homepage-link"`.

```
$('a#homepage-link').attr('href') =
          "http://www.codingjsfordummies.com/";
```

The result of running this statement is that the selected element's `href` attribute will be changed in the DOM to the new value. When a user clicks the modified link, the browser will open the web page at the specified address, rather than the one that was originally written in the `img` element.

Modifying an element using jQuery changes only the element's representation in the DOM (and therefore on the user' screen). jQuery doesn't modify the actual web page on the server, and if you view the source of the web page, you won't see any changes.

Changing CSS

Changing CSS using jQuery is very similar to the technique we describe in Chapter 13 for modifying the Style object's properties. jQuery makes modifying the style properties much easier than standard JavaScript, and the style properties are spelled exactly the same as in CSS.

Listing 18-3 combines live CSS style changes with form events to give the user control over how large the text is.

Listing 18-3:   Manipulating Styles with jQuery

```
<html>
<head>
  <title>JQuery CSS</title>
  <script src="http://code.jquery.com/jquery-
          1.11.2.min.js"></script>
  <script type="text/javascript">
    $(document).ready(function(){

    $('#sizer').change(function() {
      $('#theText').css('font-size',$('#sizer').val());
    });
    });
```

```
    </script>
  </head>
  <body>
    <div id="theText">Hello!</div>
    <form id="controller">
      <input type="range" id="sizer" min="10" max="100">
    </form>
  </body>
</html>
```

Figure 18-1 shows the results of running Listing 18-3 in a browser.

Figure 18-1:
Changing
CSS with
an input
element.

Manipulating elements in the DOM

jQuery features several methods for changing the content of element, moving
elements, adding element, removing elements, and much more. Table 18-2 lists
all the available methods for manipulating elements within the DOM.

Table 18-2   Manipulating Elements within the DOM

Method	Description	Example
text()	Gets the combined text content of the matched elements, or sets the text content of the matched elements	`$('p').text('hello!')`

(continued)

Table 18-2 *(continued)*

Method	Description	Example
html()	Get the value of the first matched element, or set the contents of every matched element	`$('div').html('<p>hi</p>')`
val()	Get the value of the first matched element, or set the value of every matched element	`$('select#choices').val()`
append()	Insert content to the end of the matched elements	`$('div #closing').append('<p>Thank You</p>')`
prepend()	Insert content at the beginning of the matched elements	`$('dive #introduction').prepend('<p>To whom it may concern:</p>')`
before()	Insert content before the matched elements	`$('#letter').before(header)`
after()	Insert content after the matched elements	`$('#letter').after(footer)`
remove()	Remove the matched elements	`$('.phonenumber').remove()`
empty()	Remove all of the child nodes of the matched elements	`$('.blackout').empty()`

Events

Chapter 11 discusses the different methods for registering event handlers in JavaScript, which are all still perfectly valid in jQuery. However, jQuery has its own syntax for registering event listeners and handling events.

jQuery's event method, on(), handles all of the complexity of ensuring that all browsers will handle events in the same way, and it also requires far less typing than the pure JavaScript solutions.

Using on () to attach events

The jQuery on() method works in much the same way as addEvent
Listener(). It takes an event and a function definition as arguments. When
the event happens on the selected element (or elements), the function is
executed. Listing 18-4 uses on() and a jQuery selector to change the color
of every other row in a table when a button is clicked.

Listing 18-4: Changing Table Colors with the Click of a Button

```
<html>
<head>
  <title>jQuery CSS</title>
  <style>
    td {
      border: 1px solid black;
    }
  </style>
  <script src="http://code.jquery.com/jquery-
          1.11.2.min.js"></script>
  <script type="text/javascript">
    $(document).ready(function(){

      $('#colorizer').on('click',function() {
        $('#things tr:even').css('background','yellow');
      });

    });

  </script>
</head>
<body>
  <table id="things">
    <tr>
      <td>item1</td>
      <td>item2</td>
      <td>item3</td>
    </tr>
    <tr>
      <td>apples</td>
      <td>oranges</td>
      <td>lemmons</td>
    </tr>
    <tr>
      <td>merlot</td>
      <td>malbec</td>
      <td>cabernet sauvignon</td>
    </tr>
```

(continued)

Listing 18-4 *(continued)*

```
    </table>
    <form id="tableControl">
        <button type="button" id="colorizer">Colorize</button>
    </form>
</body>
</html>
```

Figure 18-2 shows the alternating table colors after the button is clicked.

Figure 18-2:
Alternating
table colors.

 Do you notice something seemingly odd about the colorized rows in Figure 18-2? The first and third rows of the table are colorized, but we told jQuery to colorize the even numbered rows. The explanation is simple: The even and odd determinations are based on the index number of the `tr` elements, which always start with 0. So, the colorized ones are the first (index number 0) and the third (index number 2).

Detaching with off()

The `off()` method can be used to unregister a previously set event listener. For example, if you want to disable the button in Listing 18-4 (maybe until the user paid for the use of this feature), you use the following statement:

```
$('#colorizer').off('click');
```

Or, if you want to remove all event listeners on an element, you can do so by calling off with no arguments:

```
$('colorizer').off();
```

Binding to events that don't exist yet

With the dynamic nature of today's web, you sometimes need to register an event listener to an element that is created dynamically after the HTML loads.

To add event listeners to elements that are created dynamically, you can pass a selector that should be monitored for new elements to the `on()` method. For example, if you want to make sure that all rows, and all future rows, in the table are clickable, you can use the following statement:

```
$(document).on('click','tr',function(){
  alert("Thanks for clicking!");
}
```

Other event methods

Besides `on()`, jQuery also has a simplified shortcut syntax for attaching event listeners to selected elements. jQuery has methods with the same names as the events that you can just pass the event handler to. For example, both of these statements accomplish the same thing:

```
$('#myButton').on('click',function() {
 alert('Thanks!');
}
$('#myButton').click(function() {
 alert('Thanks!');
}
```

Other shortcut event methods include

- ✔ `change()`
- ✔ `click()`
- ✔ `dblclick()`
- ✔ `focus()`
- ✔ `hover()`
- ✔ `keypress()`
- ✔ `load()`

For a complete list of event methods, visit the jQuery website at `http://api.jquery.com/category/events`.

Effects

jQuery makes a JavaScript programmer's life much easier. It even makes simple animations and effects easier.

jQuery effects are so simple that they're often overused. Once you see what can be done and have played with each of the different variations, it would probably be a good idea to build one web app that uses them all every time any event happens. Then, delete this file and consider this urge to overuse effects to be out of your system.

Basic effects

jQuery's basic effects simply control whether selected elements are displayed or not. The basic effects are

- ✔ hide(): The hide method hides the matched elements.
- ✔ show(): The show method shows the matched elements
- ✔ toggle(): The toggle method toggles between hiding and showing the matched elements. If the matched element is hidden, toggle will cause it to be shown. If it's shown, toggle will cause it to be hidden.

Fading effects

You can transition selected elements between displaying and hiding by using a fade effect. The fading effects are

- ✔ fadeIn(): The fadeIn method causes the matched element to fade into view over a specified amount of time (become opaque).
- ✔ fadeOut(): The fadeout method causes the matched element to fade out over a specified amount of time (become transparent).
- ✔ fadeTo(): The fadeTo method can be used to adjust the opacity of elements to a specified level over a specified amount of time.
- ✔ fadeToggle(): The fadeToggle method fades matched elements in or out over a specified amount of time.

Sliding effects

The sliding effects transition selected elements between showing and hiding by using an animated slide effect. The sliding effects are

- ✔ slideDown(): The sildeDown method displays the matched elements with an upward sliding motion.

- ✔ slideUp(): The slideUp method hides the matched elements with an upward sliding motion.

- ✔ slideToggle(): The slideToggle method toggles between sliding up and sliding down.

Setting arguments for animation methods

Each of the jQuery animation methods has a set of optional arguments that control the details of how the animation takes places and when.

The arguments of the basic, sliding and fading methods are

- ✔ duration: Duration is a numeric value indicating how long (in milliseconds) the animation should take.

- ✔ easing: Easing is a string value telling what easing function should be used to do the animation. An easing function determines how the element animates. For example, it may start slow and speed up or start fast and slow down. jQuery has two easing functions built-in:

  - • swing (default): Progress slightly lower at the beginning and end than in the middle.

  - • linear: Progress at a constant rate through the animation.

- ✔ complete: The complete argument specifies a function to execute when the current animation is finished.

Custom effects with animate ()

The animate method performs a custom animation of CSS properties. To specify the animation, you pass a set of properties to the animate method. When it runs, the animation will move toward the values you set for each property. For example, to animate increasing with width and color of a `div`, you could use this statement:

```
('div #myDiv').animate(
{
 width: 800,
 color: 'blue'
}, 5000);
```

In addition to the required CSS properties argument, the `animate` method takes the same optional arguments as the other animation methods.

Playing with jQuery animations

Listing 18-5 implements several of the jQuery animation methods. Try changing values and experimenting with the different settings for each of these methods and see what you come up with!

Listing 18-5   Fun with jQuery Animations

```
<html>
<head>
  <title>JQuery CSS</title>
  <style>
    td {
      border: 1px solid black;
    }
  </style>
  <script src="http://code.jquery.com/jquery-
          1.11.2.min.js"></script>
  <script type="text/javascript">
    // wait for the DOM to be ready
    $(document).ready(function(){
    // when the animator button is clicked, start doing
          things
    $('#animator').on('click',function() {
      $('#items').fadeToggle(200);
      $('#fruits').slideUp(500);
      $('#wines').toggle(400,'swing',function(){
        $('#wines').toggle(400,'swing');
      });
      $('h1').hide();
      $('h1').slideDown(1000).animate({
        'color': 'red',
        'font-size': '100px'},1000),;
      });
    });
  </script>
```

```
</head>
<body>
  <h1>Here are a bunch of things!</h1>
  <table id="things">
    <tr id="items">
      <td>item1</td>
      <td>item2</td>
      <td>item3</td>
    </tr>
    <tr id="fruits">
      <td>apples</td>
      <td>oranges</td>
      <td>lemmons</td>
    </tr>
    <tr id="wines">
      <td>merlot</td>
      <td>malbec</td>
      <td>cabernet sauvignon</td>
    </tr>
  </table>
  <form id="tableControl">
    <button type="button" id="animator">Animate
           Stuff!</button>
  </form>
</body>
</html>
```

AJAX

One of the most useful things about jQuery is how it simplifies AJAX and makes working with external data easier.

Chapter 16, discusses AJAX, the technique of loading new data into a web page without refreshing the page. It also covers how to use JSON data in JavaScript.

Using the ajax() method

At the head of jQuery's AJAX capabilities lies the `ajax()` method. The `ajax()` method is the low-level way to send and retrieve data from an external file. At its most simple, the AJAX method can take just a filename or URL as an argument, and it will load the indicated file. Your script can then assign the content of that file to a variable.

You can also specify many different options about how the external URL should be called and loaded, and you can set functions that should run if the request succeeds or fails.

For a complete list of the optional arguments of the `ajax()` method, visit `http://api.jquery.com/jQuery.ajax`.

In Listing 18-6, the script opens a text file containing a paragraph of text and displays that text inside of a `div` element.

Listing 18-6:   Loading and Displaying an External File with jQuery and AJAX

```
<html>
<head>
  <title>Dynamic Introduction</title>
  <script src="http://code.jquery.com/jquery-
          1.11.2.min.js"></script>
  <script>
    // wait until everything is loaded
    $(document).ready(function(){
      // when the button is clicked
      $('#loadIt').on('click',function(){
        // get the value of the select and add .txt to it
        var fileToLoad = $('#intros').val() + '.txt';
        // open that file
        $.ajax({url:fileToLoad,success:function(result){
          // if successful with opening, display the file
            contents
          $('#introtext').html(result);
        }});
      });
    });
  </script>
</head>
<body>
  <h1>Select the type of introduction you would like:</h1>
  <form id="intro-select">
    <select id="intros">
      <option value="none">Please Select</option>
      <option value="formal">Formal</option>
      <option value="friendly">Friendly</option>
      <option value="piglatin">Piglatin</option>
    </select>
    <button id="loadIt" type="button">Load It!</button>
  </form>
  <div id="introtext"></div>
</body>
</html>
```

If you try to run Listing 18-6 on your local computer, you'll run into the browser security restriction called same-origin policy, which won't allow data to load via AJAX unless it's loading from the same domain (see Chapter 16). To try out this example, visit `http://www.codingjsfor dummies.com/extras/coding with javascript`, upload it to your own web server, or disable your browsers security restrictions.

Shorthand AJAX methods

jQuery also has several shorthand methods for handling AJAX. The syntax for these is simplified because they're designed for specific tasks. The shorthand AJAX methods are as follows:

- ✔ `.get()` loads data from a server using an HTTP GET request.
- ✔ `.getJSON()` loads JSON data from a server using an HTTP GET request.
- ✔ `.getScript()` loads a JavaScript file from a server using an HTTP GET request and then executes it.
- ✔ `.post()` loads data from a server and place the returned HTML into the matched element.

To use the shorthand methods, you can pass them a URL and, optionally, a success handler. For example, to get a file from a server using the `get()` method and then insert it into the page, you can do the following:

```
$.get( "getdata.html", function( data ) {
  $( ".result" ).html( data );
});
```

The preceding example is equivalent to the following full `.ajax()` statement:

```
$.ajax({
  url: getdata.html,
  success: function( data ) {
  $( ".result" ).html( data );
  }
});
```

The savings in effort isn't enormous in this example. With more complex AJAX requests, learning and using the shorthand AJAX can result in more understandable and concise code.

Part VI

The Part of Tens

Enjoy an additional Part of Tens chapter at www.dummies.com/extras/codingwithjavascript.

In this part . . .

- ✔ Figure out which ten JavaScript frameworks and libraries to learn next.

- ✔ Discover ten common JavaScript bugs and how to avoid them.

- ✔ Take advantage of ten online tools that help you write better JavaScript.

- ✔ Enjoy an additional Part of Tens chapter at www.dummies. com/extras/codingwithjavascript.

Chapter 19

Ten JavaScript Frameworks and Libraries to Learn Next

In This Chapter

▶ Discovering some popular JavaScript frameworks and libraries

▶ Seeing what sites are using what frameworks and libraries

"I am hitting my head against the walls, but the walls are giving way."

— Gustav Mahler

You've only just begun your JavaScript journey. The universe of tools, frameworks, and libraries built with JavaScript and that will help you write better JavaScript programs is vast and growing at a mind-boggling pace.

In this chapter, we list ten of our favorite JavaScript frameworks and libraries. You don't need to learn them all, but a familiarity with all of them and proficiency in a couple will help you tremendously in your JavaScript voyage.

Each of these tools has a loyal base of users, fans, and people who contribute to it. Under each tool, we list a few of the most well-known sites that use it.

Don't forget to visit the website to check out the online exercises relevant to this chapter!

Angular JS

Angular JS, commonly referred to as Angular, is an open source JavaScript application framework (see Figure 19-1). Often confused with a library because of its lightweight design, Angular JS is maintained by Google and the community of developers.

Figure 19-1:
http://
angularjs.
org.

The framework adapts and extends traditional HTML to serve dynamic content through two-way data-bindings that allow for the automatic synchronization of models (data) and views (web pages). As a result, AngularJS de-emphasizes DOM manipulation with the goal of improving testability and performance.

Angular's design goals are to

✔ Improve testability of the code by separating DOM manipulation from application logic.

✔ Emphasize the testing of code just as much as the writing of code.

✔ Create separation between the client-side of the application and the server side.

✔ Provide structure for the application building process, from designing to the UI through writing logic to testing.

Who uses it? YouTube.com, Lynda.com, Netflix.com, and freelancer.com.

Backbone.js

Backbone.js, shown in Figure 19-2, is an open source MVC JavaScript library designed for building single-page web apps. Developing web apps with Backbone gives your app structure and enforces the very good principle that communication with the server should be done through a RESTful API.

The result of using Backbone is that your code will be more modular, and you'll be able to build and keep track of very complicated web apps with minimal code and in an organized way.

Backbone only has one dependency (underscore.js) and adds very minimal load to your web app.

Who uses it? reddit.com, bitbucket.org, tumblr.com, pintrest.com, and linkedin.com.

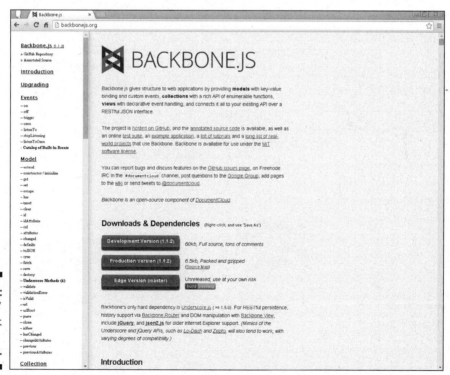

Figure 19-2:
http://
back
bonejs.
org.

Ember.js

Ember.js is one of the older MVC JavaScript frameworks, with roots going way back to 2007. Ember, shown in Figure 19-3, calls itself "a framework for creating ambitious web applications." Like many of the other frameworks described in this chapter, it's based on the MVC software architecture pattern. Like Backbone, it's designed for creating single-page web applications.

Ember has a reputation for having a steep learning curve. However, once you know it, the benefits of using Ember are many. Ember is designed to favor convention over configuration. What this means for Ember developers is that if they write code according to Ember's normal practices, Ember will infer much of the configuration of the app, rather than requiring the developer to specify everything about the app manually. This can be a great timesaver.

Who uses it? digitalocean.com, vine.co, nbcnews.com, twitch.tv, and mediabistro.com.

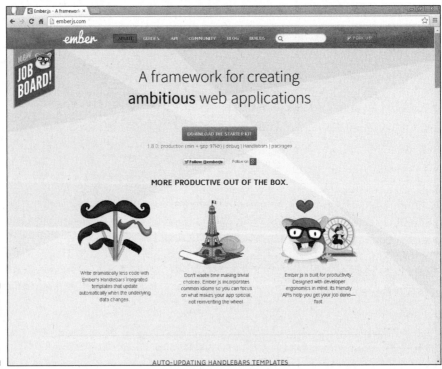

Figure 19-3:
http://
emberjs.
com.

Famo.us

Famo.us, shown in Figure 19-4, is an open source JavaScript framework for creating complex user interfaces for any screen. It has a 3D rendering engine built into it, which makes it possible for developers to write JavaScript code that can move objects around the browser in 3D and to create effects and interfaces that previously were only available in native software applications. The result is that web apps created with Famo.us can be much faster and work much more smoothly than web apps built using just HTML5, CSS3, and JavaScript.

Who uses it? InkaBinka.com, SuperStereo, Requested App, and Japan Today.

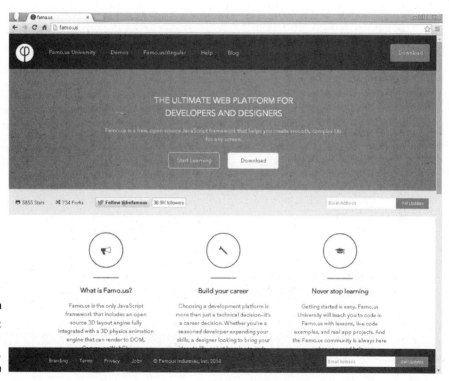

Figure 19-4:
http://
famo.us.

Knockout

Knockout, shown in Figure 19-5, is an open source JavaScript framework for simplifying dynamic JavaScript user interfaces. It uses the Model-View-View-Model pattern.

Knockout includes

- Declarative bindings
- Automatic User Interface Refresh (the UI updates automatically when data changes)
- Dependency tracking
- Templating

Who uses it? mlb.com, ancestry.com, Eventbrite.com, and ameritrade.com.

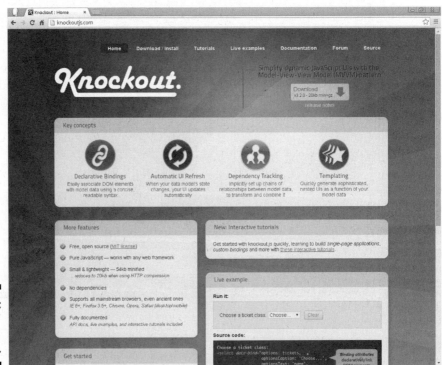

Figure 19-5:
http://
knockoutjs.
com.

QUnit

QUnit (see Figure 19-6) is a unit testing framework for JavaScript, which is used by many open source JavaScript projects, including jQuery. It can test any generic JavaScript code and is known for being powerful as well as easy to use.

Who uses it? jQuery, jQuery UI, jQuery Mobile, sitepoint.com, and many JavaScript developers.

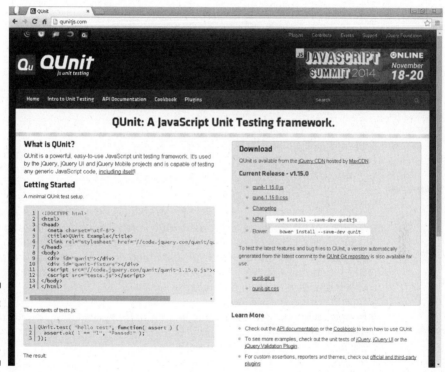

Figure 19-6:
http://
qunitjs.
com.

underscore.js

Underscore (see Figure 19-7) is a JavaScript library that provides many useful helper functions to programmers. Once you start using the features of Underscore, you'll wonder how you ever got by without them.

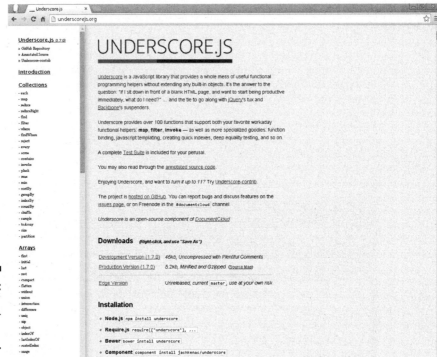

Figure 19-7:
`http://`
`under`
`scorejs.`
`com.`

Examples of Underscore helpers include sortBy (for sorting lists), groupBy (for grouping a collection into sets), contains (returns true if a list contains a specified value), shuffle (returns a shuffled copy of a list), and around 100 other functions — many of which should have been built into JavaScript from the beginning.

Who uses it? dropbox.com, lifehacker.com, theverge.com, att.com, and gawker.com.

Modernizr

Modernizr, shown in Figure 19-8, is a JavaScript library for detecting the features of a web browser in which it's running. It's most often used as a very simple and handy way to check whether a user's browser can run a particular bit of JavaScript or make use of an API prior to attempting to use that feature. Modernizr is often used in conjunction with tools called Polyfills, which provide alternative ways to accomplish cutting-edge features of modern browsers in less-capable devices and browsers.

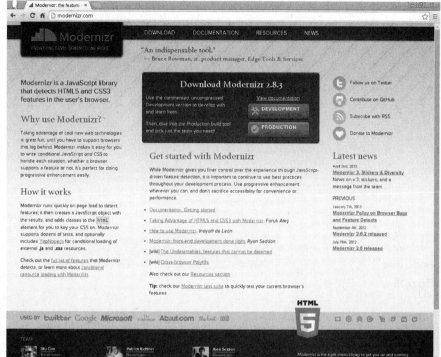

Figure 19-8:
http://
modernizr.
com.

Who uses it? go.com, about.com, hostgator.com, addthis.com, and usatoday.com.

Handlebars.js

Handlebars, shown in Figure 19-9, is a client-side JavaScript templating engine. It makes it possible for programmers to insert templates into HTML pages that will be parsed using live data that is passed to the Handlebars.js function.

Who uses it? meetup.com, mashable.com, flickr.com, wired.com, and overstock.com.

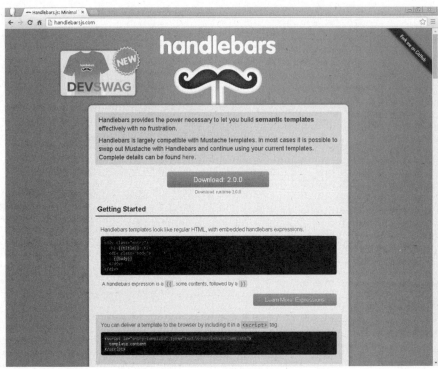

Figure 19-9:
http://
hand
lebarsjs.
com.

jQuery

JQuery (see Figure 19-10) is the "Write Less, Do More" JavaScript library. Used by over 60 percent of the most popular sites on the web, it has become an indispensable tool for most JavaScript programmers. Just a few of the things that jQuery makes easier include document manipulation, event handling, animation, and Ajax.

In addition, jQuery has a plug-in architecture that allows other developers to build upon the core jQuery functionality in order to create new libraries and frameworks.

Some of the most popular jQuery plugins include jQuery UI, jQuery Mobile, numerous effects, data pickers, image manipulation tools, and image sliders. You can find a complete list of available jQuery plugins at http://plugins.jquery.com.

Who uses it? WordPress.com, Pinterest, Amazon, Microsoft.com, Etsy, and many, many more.

Figure 19-10:
http://
jquery.
com

Chapter 20

Ten Common JavaScript Bugs and How to Avoid Them

In This Chapter

▶ Catching mismatched brackets

▶ Steering clear of incorrect punctuation

▶ Fixing errors

▶ Adjusting bad variable names

"Have no fear of perfection — you'll never reach it."

— Salvador Dali

Even the best JavaScript programmers make mistakes. Sometimes, these mistakes cause your program to not produce the results that you wanted, and sometimes they cause the program to not run at all. Any problem that causes a program not to run or not to run as expected is called a bug. Throughout this book, we give you tips and tools for finding and correcting bugs as they come up.

Part of becoming a better programmer is to be able to identify potential sources of bugs and stomp them out faster and earlier. Eventually, you'll start noticing that you make fewer and fewer mistakes and that beautiful bug-free code flows from your fingertips on a regular basis. When this happens, you're well on your way to becoming a JavaScript ninja.

In this chapter, we point out ten common mistakes that JavaScript programmers at all levels often make. We also give you pointers on how to prevent them.

Don't forget to visit the website to check out the online exercises relevant to this chapter!

Equality Confusion

Does *x* equal *y*? Is *x* true? The questions of equality are central to JavaScript and can seem quite confusing. They revolve around three areas in JavaScript: namely conditional statements and operators (if, &&, and so on), the equals operator (==), and the strict equals operator (===).

To complicate our lives even more, the assignment operator (=) looks suspiciously like what most of us call an equals sign. Don't be fooled! Here's a quick rundown, with examples, of when each of =, ==, and === are appropriate and useful.

Avoiding misuse of assignment

The assignment operator assigns the operand on the right to the operand on the left. For example:

```
var a = 3;
```

This statement gives the new variable, named a, the value of 3.

An *operand* is anything in a program. Think of it as similar to a noun in language, whereas operators (+, -, *, / and so on) are like verbs.

Assignment operators may also have expressions (sometimes quite complicated expressions) on the right side, which are evaluated and then assigned to the variable on the left.

A common mistake that beginners to the language make is to mistake assignment for comparison — for example:

```
if (a=4){.. .}
```

This code won't run as expected if what you expected is to compare the value of a to the number 4.

Dodging the equals pitfalls

The equals operator (==) and its evil twin the not equals operator (!=) can be quite flexible, but also quite dangerous. We recommend that you use it as little as possible, if at all. Here's why:

```
0 == '0'
```

Everyone who's spent any time programming knows that a number inside of quotes isn't really a number. But the == operator considers them to be the same, because it will make the two values the same type prior to comparing. This can lead to all sorts of problems that are difficult to track down.

If you do want to compare a string with a number and get a result of true if they appear the same, it's much safer to do this explicitly as follows:

```
parseInt(0) === parseInt("0")
```

This statement also evaluates to true, but there is no voodoo magic involved. This brings us to our friends, the strict equals (===) and the strict not equals (!==). These guys will do exactly what you would expect. What would you think would be the result of the following statement?

```
0 === '0'
```

Correct! The two operands are clearly different types, and the result is false.

Mismatched Brackets

As a program becomes more complicated, and especially when you're working with JavaScript objects, the brackets start to pile up. You start to see weird behaviors or cryptic errors in your JavaScript console.

Here's a JavaScript object with mismatched brackets:

```
{
    "status": "OK",
    "results": [{
        "id": 12,
        "title": "Coding JavaScript For Dummies",
        "author": "Chris Minnick and Eva Holland",
        "publication_date": "",
        "summary_short": "",
        "link": {
            "type": "review",
            "url": "",
            "link_text": "Read the New York Times Review
            of Coding JavaScript For Dummies"
        },
        "awards": [{
            "type": "Nobel Prize",
            "url": "",
        }]
}
```

Can you see the problems here? It may take some counting and matching, and if you don't find it, you have a serious bug! When this happens, a good code editor can be invaluable! Sublime Text has a feature that will show you a brackets match (or at least what Sublime Text believes to be the match) when you place your cursor next to either a starting or ending bracket, as shown in Figure 20-1.

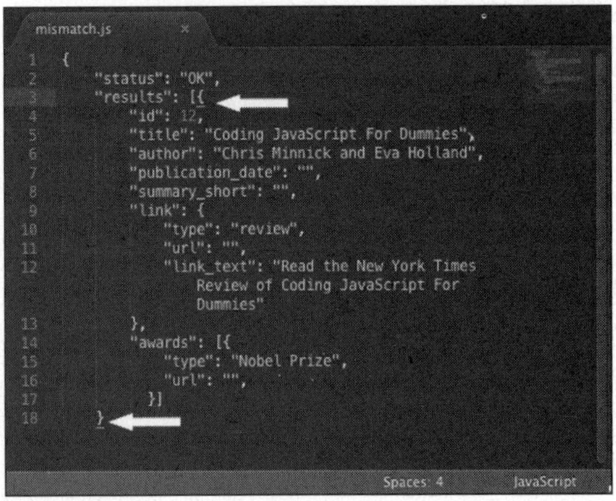

Figure 20-1:
Highlighting matching brackets in Sublime Text.

Mismatched Quotes

JavaScript allows you to use either single quotes or double quotes to define strings. However, JavaScript is not at all flexible with the rule that you must end your string with the same type of quote you started with. Also, look out for quotes and apostrophes in strings that are the same characters as the quotes surrounding the string! For example:

```
var movieName = "Popeye'; // error!
var welcomeMessage = 'Thank you, ' + firstName + ', let's
        learn JavaScript!' // error!
```

Missing Parentheses

This error most often crops up in conditional statements, especially those in which there are multiple conditions. Consider this example:

```
if (x > y) && (y < 1000) {
...
}
```

What we want to do here is check that both of the conditions are true. However, there are actually three conditions at work here, and they all need parentheses. What's missing in the preceding example is the parentheses around the big && condition, which says that both of the other conditions must be true in order to proceed with the code between the brackets.

In order to be correct, this statement should read as follows:

```
if ((x > y) && (y < 1000)) {
...
}
```

Missing Semicolon

JavaScript statements should always end with a semicolon. However, if you put each statement on its own line and leave off the semicolons, the code will still run as if the semicolons are there. Even though the code still runs, leaving off the semicolon can lead to problems when you rearrange code or when two statements end up on the same line somehow.

The best way to avoid this error is to always use a semi-colon at the end of a statement.

Capitalization Errors

JavaScript is case-sensitive. This means that the variables you create need to be capitalized exactly the same every time you use them. It also means that functions (including built-in JavaScript functions) need to be capitalized correctly in order to work.

One of the most common places to see this error happen is with the getElementById method of the Document object. You would think that it would be spelled getElementByID because that would make more grammatical sense, but it isn't correct!

Referencing Code Before It's Loaded

JavaScript code (that isn't functions) normally loads and runs in the order that it appears in a document. This can create problems if you reference HTML that's positioned later in the document from a script that's in the head of the document. For example, Listing 20-1 shows a script that the author intended to change the HTML between the start and end tags of an element within the HTML document, and Figure 20-2 shows how this script results in an error when previewed.

Listing 20-1: Watch Out for Referencing Code or Markup Before It's Loaded

```
\<html>
<head>
  <script>
  document.getElementById("myDiv").innerHTML = "This div
        is MY div";
  </script>
</head>
<body>
  <div id = "myDiv">This div is your div.</div>
</body>
</html>
```

This code will result in an error because at the time the JavaScript runs, the browser doesn't yet know about the `div` with the `id = "myDiv"` that comes later in the web page.

Figure 20-2:
Referencing
HTML
before it
is loaded
results in an
error.

In order to avoid this issue, you have a couple of options:

✔ Place your JavaScript at the bottom of your HTML file, right before `</body>`.

✔ Put your JavaScript code into a function. Then you can call the function using an `onload event` attribute in the starting `body` tag.

In Listing 20-2, we resolved the problem shown in Listing 20-1 using the second method. Figure 20-3 shows the result when previewed in a web browser.

Listing 20-2:   Waiting Until the Page Is Finished Loading Before Running the Script

```html
<html>
<head>
  <script>
  function nameMyDiv() {
    document.getElementById("myDiv").innerHTML = "This div
        is MY div";
  }
  </script>
</head>
<body onload = "nameMyDiv();">
  <div id = "myDiv">This div is your div</div>
</body>
</html>
```

Figure 20-3: Wait until the HTML is loaded before running the script.

Bad Variable Names

The rules of variable naming in JavaScript are covered in detail in Chapter 3. One particularly hard-to-track-down rule is the prohibition against using reserved words as variable names.

Interestingly, JavaScript has over 60 reserved words and many others that you just shouldn't use as variable names. Rather than memorizing all of the reserved words, the best way to avoid these types of naming errors is to simply come up with a more descriptive naming scheme that is highly unlikely to ever cross paths with a reserved word.

For example, the word `name` is one of JavaScript's reserved words. If you get into the habit of being specific with what you're naming, you'll name variables for storing things, such as `firstName`, `lastName`, `dogName`, and `nameOfTheWind`; thus totally avoiding conflicts with reserved words.

Scope Errors

JavaScript has function scope and global scope. If you declare a variable without using the `var` keyword, that variable will have global scope and will be usable anywhere in your program. As we demonstrate in Chapter 3, the results can be detrimental to your program. In order to avoid scope errors, make sure to always use the `var` keyword to create new variables.

Missing Parameters in Function Calls

Whenever you create a function, you declare the number of parameters that should be passed to that function when it's called. Calling the wrong number of functions won't always result in an error in JavaScript, but it can produce unexpected results if the code within the function requires parameters that aren't present.

Make sure to give your parameters descriptive names when you create a function and double-check every time that a function is called in order to make sure that the right number of parameters is passed.

Counting Errors: Forgetting That JavaScript Counts from 0

If you count to 10 in a JavaScript array, you'll actually have 11 items (see Figure 20-4). Never forget that the first item in an array has an index of 0.

```
var myArray = new Array();
myArray[10] = "List of 10 Common Mistakes";
myArray.length; // produces 11!
```

Figure 20-4: Forgetting that JavaScript counts from 0 can lead to unexpected results.

```
Q  🗋   Elements  Network  Sources  Timeline  Profiles  Resources  Audits  | Console |
⊘  ▽  <top frame>  ▼  ☐ Preserve log
>  var myArray = new Array();
<  undefined
>  myArray[10] = "List of 10 Common Mistakes";
<  "List of 10 Common Mistakes"
>  myArray.length;
<  11
>
```

Chapter 21

Ten Online Tools to Help You Write Better JavaScript

> *"Never underestimate the power of a simple tool."*
>
> — Craig Bruce

JavaScript has more libraries, resources, and helpful tools for working with it than for any other programming language. This chapter introduces ten of the best resources for helping you write more and better JavaScript.

Don't forget to visit the website to check out the online exercises relevant to this chapter!

JSLint

JSLint, created by JavaScript super-genius Douglas Crockford, is a code checker that is designed to tell you where your code has problems — and not just the kind of problems that would generate errors.

JSLint, shown in Figure 21-1, will tell you about things that thousands of JavaScript programmers do all the time, but that are problematic for one reason or another. If your code passes JSLint's tests, it's probably some pretty good code.

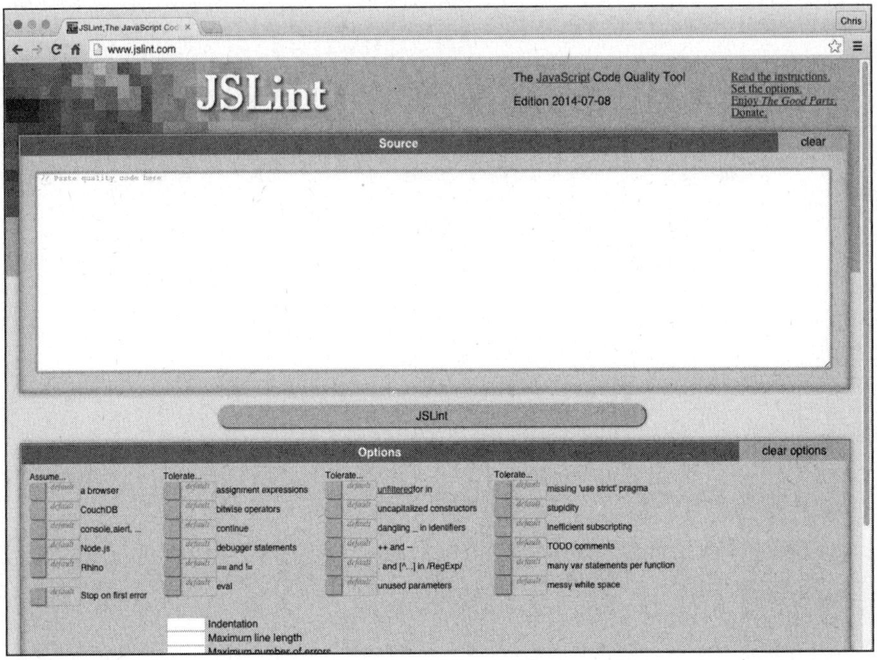

Figure 21-1:
JSLint
shows you
where your
code has
problems.

JSFiddle.net

JSFiddle, shown in Figure 21-2, is an online program for running web applications in a test environment. When you go to JSFiddle.net, the first thing you see is a grid with four panes:

- ✔ One for HTML
- ✔ One for CSS
- ✔ One for JavaScript
- ✔ One for Results

Enter the appropriate type of code into any of the first three boxes and press the Run button, and the results will be displayed in the Results pane.

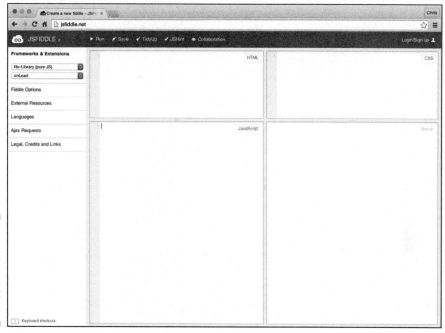

Figure 21-2:
JSFiddle.
net is a
complete
JavaScript
playground.

With JSFiddle, you can even save your fiddles and email the urls to other people to check out.

JSBin

JSBin (see Figure 21-3) is a code-sharing site that allows you to write code while other people watch you. Whether you have exhibitionist tendencies, you're teaching a junior developer, or you're collaborating with other programmers on a project, the functionality in JSBin can be very helpful for working out bugs, getting feedback, and sharing code.

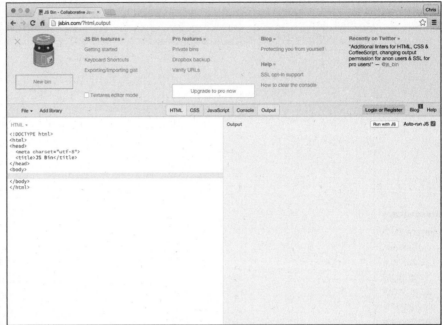

Figure 21-3:
Collaborate
with JSBin.

javascriptcompressor.com

The smaller your JavaScript files are, the faster they'll load. JavaScript
Compressor.com, shown in Figure 21-4, has a window where you can drop
your JavaScript. When you press Compress, a new version that's function-
ally the same as your original code, but compressed, shows up in the lower
window. Not only does the compressed code take up less disk space and
bandwidth, it's also obfuscated, to hide its inner secrets from prying eyes.

Figure 21-4:
javascript-
compressor.
com makes
files smaller.

jsbeautifier.org

JSBeautifier (see Figure 21-5) is an online tool that takes your sloppy
JavaScript and makes it pretty. Some of the techniques that it uses to
beautify code include

- ✔ Inserting new lines
- ✔ Breaking lines of chained code
- ✔ Inserting spaces before conditional statements
- ✔ Making indentations standard throughout the script

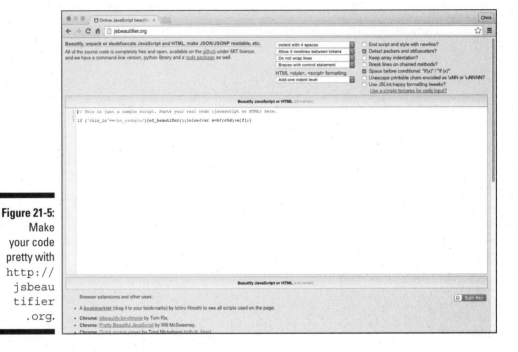

Figure 21-5:
Make
your code
pretty with
`http://`
`jsbeau`
`tifier`
`.org.`

JavaScript RegEx generator

JavaScript Lab's JavaScript RegEx Generator (`www.jslab.dk/tools.regex.php`), shown in Figure 21-6, is a user-friendly form for pointing and clicking your way to writing regular expressions. Simply click some buttons, enter text to match, set some options, and your regular expression shows up at the bottom.

Figure 21-6:
Point and
click regular
expressions.

JSONformatter

The JSON formatter and validator (`http://jsonformatter.curious concept.com`), shown in Figure 21-7, allows you to paste in unformatted JSON code, such as the code you would get from copying from the Chrome Developer Tools. It then makes the code pretty and makes sure that it's valid.

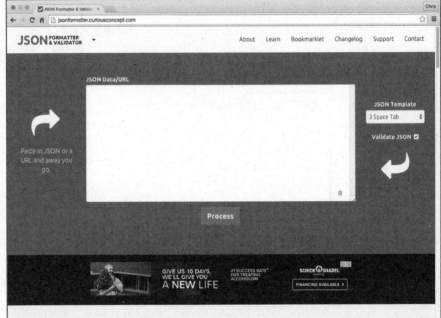

Figure 21-7:
The JSON formatter validates and arranges JSON data.

jshint.com

JShint (see Figure 21-8) is a tool that helps you detect errors and potential problems in your JavaScript. In addition, it will give you useful information about your JavaScript code as you write it.

Figure 21-8:
JShint
detects
problems
with your
code as you
write it.

Mozilla Developer Network

The Mozilla Developer Network's JavaScript section (https://developer.mozilla.org/en-US/docs/Web/JavaScript) is an essential resource for information about everything having to do with JavaScript. Its JavaScript resources, shown in Figure 21-9, include reference material, tutorials, articles, and demos for programmers at every level.

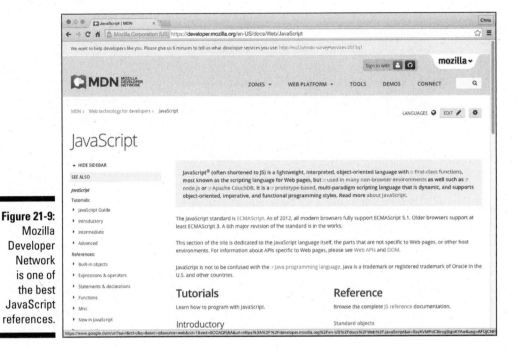

Figure 21-9:
Mozilla
Developer
Network
is one of
the best
JavaScript
references.

Douglas Crockford

Douglas Crockford is a hero to many JavaScript programmers. His website (`http://javascript.crockford.com`), shown in Figure 21-10, has a great collection of free videos on every aspect of JavaScript. These videos are essential to a programmer who is looking to move past beginner and into the more advanced levels of JavaScript expertise.

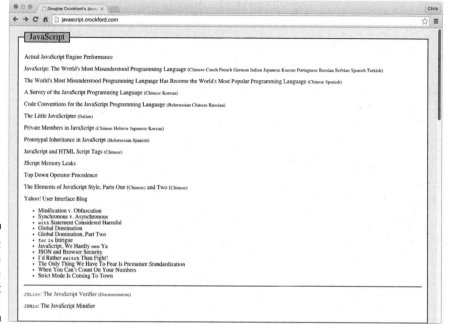

Figure 21-10:
Douglas
Crockford's
JavaScript
videos.

Index

About the Authors

Chris Minnick is an accomplished author, trainer, and web developer. Prior to cofounding WatzThis?, Chris was CEO of Minnick Web Services for 18 years, where he managed and worked on hundreds of web and mobile projects for customers ranging from small businesses to some of the world's largest companies.

Other books he's authored or coauthored include *Beginning HTML5 and CSS3 For Dummies, Webkit For Dummies, CIW eCommerce Certification Bible,* and *XHTML*. Since 2001, Chris has trained thousands of students in HTML, JavaScript, CSS, and mobile development.

Chris is an enthusiastic amateur winemaker, fiction writer, swimmer, and musician.

Eva Holland is an experienced writer, trainer, and cofounder of WatzThis?. She excels in presenting complicated subjects in easy-to-understand language for beginners of all levels.

Eva has written, designed, and taught online, in-person, and video courses. She has created curriculum for web development, mobile web development, and search engine optimization (SEO). Prior to founding WatzThis?, Eva served as COO of MWS, where she provided astute leadership, management, and vision that guided the company to its goals.

Eva is an outdoor enthusiast, songstress, tennis player, and lover of life.

Dedication

"A child of five would understand this. Send someone to fetch a child of five."

— Groucho Marx

Authors' Acknowledgments

Chris Minnick and Eva Holland:

This book was really fun to write. Throughout the writing process, we worked hard to think about topics from a beginner's perspective and to present the most modern and up-to-date introduction to JavaScript and web programming possible. We're proud of the result and would love to hear what you think of it and answer any questions you have.

This book is the result of a team effort, not only by your humble authors, but also by a talented crew of editors and other publishing professionals who are credited on the next page and who we'd like to personally thank for their great efforts.

Thank you to everyone at Wiley, including executive editor Steve Hayes, our project editor Kelly Ewing, and our technical editor Todd Shelton.

Thank you also to our agent, Carole Jelen.

Eva Holland: Thank you to my coauthor, business partner and friend, Chris Minnick, for the opportunity to work on this book and for his continued support and his inspiring expanse of vision.

Chris Minnick: Thanks to my coauthor, esteemed colleague, and friend Eva Holland for simplicity, clarity, and inspired addition by subtraction.

Publisher's Acknowledgments

Executive Editor: Steve Hayes

Project Editor: Kelly Ewing

Copy Editor: Kelly Ewing

Editorial Assistant: Claire Brock

Sr. Editorial Assistant: Cherie Case

Production Editor: Siddique Shaik

Cover Image: ©Getty Images/Alwyn Cooper